THE INSANITY DEFENSE

THE INSANITY DEFENSE

by Abraham S. Goldstein

New Haven and London, Yale University Press, 1967

For Ruth, Bill, and Marianne

Preface

This book was first undertaken at the suggestion of David L. Bazelon, Chief Judge of the United States Court of Appeals for the District of Columbia Circuit, who has done more than anyone else in our time to shape reconsideration of the insanity defense. His wise counsel through the years, even when he found himself opposed to my views, is gratefully acknowledged.

Financial support for most of the research was provided by the Foundations' Fund for Research in Psychiatry. This was supplemented by the Yale Law School, under a grant from the National Institute of Mental Health, and at the closing stages by a Guggenheim Fellowship. Much of the writing was done during a sabbatical year, 1964–65, which I spent as Visiting Fellow of the Institute of Criminology and Fellow of Christ's College at Cambridge University. My gratitude for the hospitality extended to me by the Director of the Institute, Professor Leon Radzinowicz, and the staff and by the Master and Fellows of Christ's College cannot adequately be expressed.

Throughout the period of research and writing, I enjoyed the generous intellectual support of my colleagues and students at the Yale Law School. I should like, however, to express my special appreciation for the aid of a series of extraordinarily able research assistants: Charles L. Battles, Mrs. Edith Fine, Jonathan Freedman, Ira Grudberg, John Koskinen, Mrs. Margaret Leavy, and Robert Weinberg. My wife, Ruth Goldstein, read the manuscript, made useful comments, read proof, and gave invaluable sustenance. A final word of appreciation is due to my secretary, Mrs. Gertrude Facciuto, and to the staff of the Yale Law Library, who worked loyally and conscientiously to bring the venture to a close.

Contents

PART I

The Setting

CHAPTER ONE

Introductory

For well over a century, the insanity defense has attracted more attention than any other issue in criminal law. It has engaged the minds and emotions of lawyers and psychiatrists, philosophers and laymen, to an extent entirely unrelated to the numerical importance of the problem. Some of the interest undoubtedly traces to the repellent fascination of the crime ostensibly committed by a madman. But more of it is probably due to the challenge, and the difficulty, of setting limits on man's responsibility to his fellow man. In the highly charged context of a criminal trial, often involving sensational crimes, the insanity defense calls upon a jury to decide whether the person accused of crime is to be condemned as a criminal or regarded compassionately as insane. Though it will soon become apparent that the consequences of condemnation and compassion may not be so very different, the trial of the defense is treated as if it were a contemporary morality play revolving around the issues of sickness and guilt.

The reason for such intense involvement is not difficult to find. However much men have tried to shield themselves from notions of personal responsibility and guilt, however much people are said to be less accountable for what they are than the institutions which surround them, the idea of responsibility remains an essential part of already frail defenses against aggressive impulses. The man who asserts he is not responsible threatens to weaken those defenses further and, by doing so, brings home how passionately we feel about being blamed and about blaming others. This feeling takes hold almost from the

moment humans emerge from the womb, as they are subjected to control after control, to rewards and to punishments,
designed to make them feel obligations to themselves, their
families, and their communities. The trial of the insanity defense captures these universal themes and brings them to bear
in a dramatic setting of extraordinary complexity.

The product of this preoccupation with the insanity defense
has been a voluminous literature, beginning in the nineteenth
century and reaching near-torrential proportions in the twentieth. In it we find a great many currents. Free will is arrayed
against determinism, retribution against rehabilitation, a new
psychology against an archaic law. The "law" is indicted for
its punitive cast, "psychiatry" and "do-gooders" are accused of
undermining the social order, age-old traditions are challenged, and motives are impugned. Even the advent of an
"Age of Psychology" has not changed the course of the debate.
Instead, as it becomes apparent that no clear line divides the
sane from the insane, that "we" and "they" are more alike
than we had suspected, the question of identifying those who
are not to be held responsible has nagged all the more.

Despite the age and the intensity of the debate, the literature of the insanity defense has not been at all satisfactory.
Again and again, in appellate opinions and in commentary,
it has tended to identify the defense with the entire problem of mental disorder and the criminal law, and to treat
the *M'Naghten* rules as if they represented the whole of the
insanity defense. Variations of the *M'Naghten* formula have
been ignored, other rules like "irresistible impulse" have been
misconstrued. The result has been a remarkable degree of
consensus among commentators that the existing rules are
patently inadequate, that a new rule is urgently needed, and
that such a rule will serve in some fundamental way to re-
shape the criminal law.

Unfortunately, the literature has been so polemical that it
has not provided the raw materials for appraisal of claim and

counterclaim. Assertions seemingly drawn from experience prove, on closer examination, to be based on textual analysis of the formula used to define insanity for the jury or on fragmentary and half-understood contacts with the trial. Very little effort has been made to place the words of the defense in the context of a process which includes not only the judge's charge to the jury but all the other material presented to the jury—as well as all that comes before and after the trial which is relevant to the insanity issue.

The words of the insanity test are the merest beginning of a set of inquiries which moves from difficult problems of trial practice to fundamental questions about crime and responsibility. At its narrowest, the defense can be appraised sensibly only if we know not only what its words signify but also what effect they have upon the evidence presented and the arguments made. There is little or nothing, for example, to tell us whether one rule is, or need be, more restrictive of the admissibility of evidence than another; or whether one of them requires more evidence to carry the defense to a jury; or how lawyer and expert fare under each of the rules; or how jurors respond to each of them; or how often the defense might be pleaded but is not; or the differential consequences of conviction, on the one hand, and acquittal by reason of insanity on the other. Even then, jurors are not blank slates—to be written on by witnesses and counsel and then moved inevitably in one direction or the other by the words of the judge's charge on the insanity issue. Jurors' decisions will be affected by the manner of men they are, the attitudes toward crime and insanity which they bring with them from the popular culture, the extent to which they know the consequences for the defendant and for society of a verdict of not guilty by reason of insanity.

In what follows, I shall try to rescue the insanity defense from the acrimony and the abstraction which have too long surrounded it. After a brief examination of the concept of insanity and its relation to the general body of criminal law, I shall appraise the words of the defense in operational terms, as they affect critical points in the trial process. I shall then consider the consequences of an acquittal by reason of insanity —whether it means release or wholly indeterminate commitment—and the impact of those consequences upon other processes competing with the insanity defense. Among these are a variety of civil commitment procedures, other defenses made available by the criminal law, and criminal conviction itself, particularly through the plea of guilty. Finally, I shall consider some of the problems involved in making an effective presentation of the defense.

As the rule of law is examined in the context of the society from which it comes, the people it affects, and the institutions through which it is applied, it will become necessary to treat the defense in dynamic terms. At each point where it interacts with a policeman or a prosecutor, a defense counsel or an expert, attention will be directed to the lines along which the defense can and should develop. Ultimately, I shall have to face the question whether words and institutions should be shaped in ways likely to class more or fewer offenders as criminals, more or fewer as patients. And that, in turn, will force consideration of whether the insanity defense makes very much difference, either to the offender or to society. My raw materials will be the cases, specimen trial transcripts, and relevant literature in psychiatry and sociology—used more as aids to analysis than as a means of presenting a comprehensive portrait.

There is ample justification for charting a course for the insanity defense at this particular point in time. Though thousands of pages have already been addressed to the problem, the bulk of them either predate World War II or have their intellectual foundations in the period before the war. Since that time there have been a number of developments of great importance. The British Royal Commission on Capital Pun-

ishment has made its report, the *Durham* rule has emerged, and the American Law Institute has made its proposals.*
These have excited spirited controversy and a swelling body of case law, but within a framework which had been set in the literature long before. In the writing which has ensued, with few exceptions, the old rules are taken as fixed, the new rules are disputed along conventional lines, and little effort is made to test anew the assumptions underlying old or new. Even more seriously, the debate has taken only glancingly into account several broader currents. For one thing, the institutions of criminal justice are being subjected to new and searching scrutiny. Gross omissions of the past, particularly in the area of effective representation, are being repaired and old hopes about the potential of an adversary process are being revived. For another, at the very time when it looks as if efforts will at last be made to implement a newly recast defense, the critics of *M'Naghten* are losing their confidence that a new rule will solve very many problems—in considerable part because voices are beginning to be heard among psychiatrists expressing concern about their ability to fulfill the promises of an earlier day. Finally, there is under way what might be regarded as a flight from criminal law. Increasing reluctance to impose the stigma of a conviction has made for pressure upon police and prosecutor to divert offenders from the criminal process toward agencies dedicated entirely to "helping" the deviant. At the same time, the idea of regarding offending behavior as sick rather than criminal has led to the development of a wide variety of civil commitment procedures, which involve placing offenders in institutions as part of a civil process. The statutes dealing with sexual psychopaths, defective delinquents, and narcotics addicts typify the trend, as do some of the more general procedures for committing the mentally ill. It is long past time to draw all these elements

*See the discussion in Ch. 6.

into consideration and to strike some balance among them, as a prelude to assessing the current state of the insanity defense.

In Part I, I shall paint in the background in fairly impressionistic fashion, describing first the objectives of the criminal law and the relation they bear to the insanity defense; then touching on the conflict between social control and a subjective theory of criminal liability; and finally presenting a picture of the sorts of people who are likely to figure large in the trial of the insanity defense, their mental disorders, and how they come to be known to the trial process. In Part II, the substantive law of insanity will be explored, both textually and as it plays a part in the trial of the insanity issue. This will be followed by a consideration of the major problems involved in administering the defense at trial—problems of expert testimony, of pleading and proof, and of assuring adequate litigating resources so that the defense may be tried properly. Part III will take up the problems which surround the insanity defense—the consequences it has for the defendant when he succeeds in it, the pressures upon him and upon others to avoid the defense, and the procedures and substantive rules through which such avoidance takes place. In Part IV, I shall offer some reflections by way of summary and conclusion.

CHAPTER TWO

Insanity and the Criminal Law

The insanity defense refers to that branch of the concept of insanity which defines the extent to which men accused of crime may be relieved of criminal responsibility by virtue of mental disease.* Its precise terms are to be found in the instructions presented by the trial judge to the jury at the close of a case. In almost two thirds of the states, these are cast in the language of the *M'Naghten* rule which asks, in substance, whether the defendant knew what he was doing when he committed the crime. In about one third of the states, the so-called "irresistible impulse" rule, emphasizing inability to exercise self-control, is presented in addition to *M'Naghten*. In the District of Columbia, Maine, and the Virgin Islands, the newer *Durham* rule is used. And several jurisdictions have adopted the rule of the Model Penal Code, which blends and refines the earlier ones.** These rules are sometimes specified in statutes, but more often they appear in cases interpreting statutory or common law establishing a defense of insanity. In either event, if a jury acquits a defendant by reason of insanity, it is ordinarily required to record that fact in its verdict.[1]

The formulations come to us as part of a tradition which makes the notion of "desert" or "blame" central to criminal responsibility and which tries to define a class of persons who

---

*The concept of insanity is sometimes used to refer to other types of mental incompetence—e.g. to contract or to make a will or to stand trial or to warrant civil commitment. See generally Lindman and McIntyre, *The Mentally Disabled and the Law*, Chs. 7 to 9 (1961).

**The cases are collected and discussed in Chs. 4, 5, and 6 infra.

fall outside the boundaries of blame. Though the tradition is an old one and is shared by most legal systems, it has not brought with it a consistently clear idea of how it should be applied. In its beginnings, for example, it meant little more than a search for the person who had caused an injury and concerned itself hardly at all with his mental state. As man moved to the center of the historical stage, the concept of purpose became the touchstone of criminal liability. Only the evil man, the one who intended to cause the injury, deserved to be condemned and punished.

From the moment the offender's mental state entered into consideration, it became necessary to account for those who could not think like other men and who could not, therefore, be blamed. These were the insane. As early as the thirteenth century, Bracton described "an insane person ... [as] one who does not know what he is doing, and is lacking in mind and reason." In the seventeenth century, Coke included among the insane the idiot, the lunatic, and the person who "by sicknesse, griefe, or other accident, wholly loseth his memorie and understanding" and the "lunatique that hath sometime his understanding and sometimes not." The view that certain men should not be "blamed" did not, however, always bring more compassionate treatment with it. Indeed, well into the eighteenth century, it was widely believed that the insane were possessed by the devil who could be driven out only by the harshest of measures. Many who did not accept the "devil theory" saw the insane as marked by God for misfortune. As a result, the mad were as likely as the bad to be beaten, exorcised, or burned.

By the end of the eighteenth century, the insane were viewed by the criminal law much as they are today. The formula then prevalent described them as persons who lacked the capacity to choose between good and evil. And the medical profession of the period brought within the group principally those who were obviously irrational or subject to delusions and hallucinations. There was even the beginning of awareness that there might be "moral" or emotional derangements as well as intellectual ones and that insanity might encompass them both.[2] At the time of the Constitution, the insanity defense had become firmly established. In some form or other, it has remained a fundamental part of the criminal law ever since. Only twice have deliberate efforts been made to eliminate the defense and on both occasions the statutes in question were declared unconstitutional.[3]

The basic outline of the defense is one which excludes from the ranks of criminals all persons who are mentally diseased and who cannot reasonably be used to serve the purposes of the criminal law. Unfortunately, we are at a point in history when it is not at all clear what those purposes are and, therefore, what the function of the insanity defense is or should be. The great age of the defense has meant that it has had to be as variable in purpose as the concept of crime itself. It took its meaning first from a body of criminal law which was primarily retributive in nature, then from one which tried to put retribution aside in favor of deterrence and, more recently, in favor of rehabilitation. Whatever the dominant function of the criminal law at any given time, it has had its corollary in the insanity defense. And today, when we are less confident than ever before of the utility of single-function theories, the insanity defense has been rationalized in ways designed to satisfy all the prevalent theories. In this chapter, I shall sound the major themes by way of background for the more detailed consideration which will follow.

I

At the present time, the objectives of the criminal law are ordinarily said to be retribution, deterrence, and rehabilitation —with the emphasis presumably shifting over time from crime to crime and from one to the other function.[4] The retributive function, building on the widely held feeling that the criminal owes the community a measure of suffering comparable to that which he has inflicted, was probably the first to be served. The criminal trial early became an instrument of the King's Peace, designed to channel the anger of victims (and of their friends) lest they seek personal revenge. But to do so, it was necessary to make a criminal conviction sufficiently consequential to satisfy those who were inclined to feel retributive. This was done not only by using the sanction of death or imprisonment but also by having the judgment of condemnation come from a jury speaking as surrogate for the community and the victim. A corollary of this, however, was the feeling that so serious a sanction ought not to be imposed in situations in which the initial impulse to anger was likely to give way, even among victims, to feelings of compassion. These were situations in which the offender seemed so obviously different from most men that he could not be blamed for what he had done. Even under a retributive theory, therefore, an insanity defense was needed to trace in outline those who could not be regarded as blameworthy.

Retribution remains, of course, one of the functions which must be taken into account by an effective criminal law. In recent times, however, there has been a conspicuous reluctance to base a theory of the insanity defense upon it. Instead, courts and commentators have based their discussions almost entirely upon the deterrence and rehabilitation functions.

Under the deterrent theory—which is probably the dominant one—the primary function of criminal law is to move men to conform to social norms, particularly those which cannot be left entirely to informal processes of social control or to those of the civil law. This is accomplished by announcing in a criminal code what conduct is prohibited and how much of a sanction of imprisonment or fine will be visited upon those who ignore the prohibition. Such a system can be effective only with men who can understand the signals directed at them by the code, who can respond to the warnings, and who can feel the significance of the sanctions imposed upon violators. When such a man commits a crime, the criminal sanction visits upon him exactly what he "deserves." At the same time, it uses his trial and conviction as an educative instrument, imposing sanctions in order to build and reinforce the general sense of self-discipline and personal responsibility. If a man cannot make the calculations or muster the feelings demanded of him by the theory, he is classed as insane. He lacks the requisite degree of intelligence, reasoning power, and foresight of consequence. If he were held criminally responsible, he would be made to suffer harsh sanctions without serving the purpose of individual deterrence.

It would still be possible, however, to conceive that such a man might serve the ends of general deterrence. Though he might himself be incapable of responding, he might be used as an example to others of what would happen if they did not comply with the law's directives. Fortunately, there has been very little inclination to adopt this line of argument. For one thing, there is some suspicion that the threats and the examples are likely to deter only if the person who is *not* involved in the criminal process regards the lessons as applicable to him. He is likely to do so only if he identifies with the offender and with the offending situation. This feat of identification is difficult enough to achieve under ordinary circumstances, with men so much given to shielding from themselves their inclinations to behave badly. It is probably hopeless if the deterrent example is so different from most men that the crime can be attributed to the difference. Yet it is difficult to avoid the suspicion that the "public" is not watching all that closely whose punishment is held up to it by way of example and that talk of "identification" masks a fundamental limit upon how far one may use law as an instrument of terror. It would be widely regarded as incalculably cruel and unjust to incarcerate men who are not personally responsible in order to serve social functions. The notion of "desert"

or culpability is too deeply rooted. Under the deterrent theory, therefore, the insanity defense describes the man who is sufficiently different from the rest of us that he cannot be used as an effective example and who, in quite personal terms, cannot be expected to approach events mindful of the warnings sent to him by the criminal code.

The third view of the insanity defense reflects widespread skepticism about the desirability of using the criminal law to feed retributive inclinations, or of describing with precision persons who can or cannot respond, who can or cannot "identify." Putting aside most such concerns, or assuming they will be adequately served by any body of criminal law, this view sees the defense almost entirely as a path to treatment in a mental hospital. Long regarded as the "liberal" position, it tends to view deviant behavior as psychological maladjustment, the product of forces beyond the individual's control; he is less to be blamed than to be helped to restore the balance between him and his background or his environment. The tacit assumption is that a paternal state can put him right by psychotherapy or by judicious social planning, if only the "helping" professions are provided with the resources to do the job.

This "mental health" image has unquestionably captured the imagination of the reformers and has been propagated almost as a faith. It has won the support of generations of psychiatrists (and a goodly number of lawyers) who wanted to "do something" about the criminal law. Their badge has been the elimination of the *M'Naghten* rule, the introduction of impartial experts, a distaste for the adversary process, the development of treatment tribunals and wholly indeterminate sentences and a general hostility to law and legal institutions.[5] Impatient with the demands of the criminal law for a "guilty" man, they saw the insanity defense as a way of saving people from a harsh and punitive criminal process. By broadening the defense, they hoped to withdraw as many offenders as possible from the criminal law and give them over to hospitals rather than prisons, to treatment rather than punishment, to doctors rather than guards. Their writings left the impression that insanity was a transitional concept which would leave to the criminal process only those who could not yet be classed as "sick"—in part because the medical profession was not yet willing to do so but more importantly because there were effective limits on how far the public would allow compassion to be carried.

Discussions of the insanity defense draw upon all of the currents I have described, sometimes emphasizing one of them, sometimes another. In this respect, they reflect the fact that ours is a pragmatic age, impatient with large generalizations and single explanations of crime or mental illness or both. No one is willing to assert that any one of the themes underlying the criminal law and the defense is entirely invalid. Ideological differences manifest themselves in degrees of emphasis, in the choice of one form of words over another, one set of practices over another. Yet underlying all, as the single constant element, is the concept of blame. Because it is widely assumed that "blame" plays a critical role in maintaining individual responsibility and social order, the insanity defense continues to be regarded as exceptional. It becomes the occasional device through which an offender is found to be inappropriate for the social purposes served by the criminal law. He is too much unlike the man in the street to permit his example to be useful for the purposes of deterrence. He is too far removed from normality to make us angry with him. But because he is sick rather than evil, society is cast as specially responsible for him and obligated to make him better.

II

Both the criminal law and the insanity defense are deceptive. The first speaks principally in accents of personal guilt and uses the concept of *mens rea* to assure that only blameworthy individuals are subject to criminal sanctions. The second speaks of acquittal and carries the sound of freedom with it. Yet the criminal law is not as much concerned with individual guilt, and the insanity defense with genuine acquittal, as is generally supposed. Each of the theories underlying the criminal law describes functions which can or should be carried out only with men capable of responding in accordance with the tenets of the theory. Each depends upon men who are capable of choosing how they will behave. And each expresses concern about imposing the "criminal" designation upon one who is not personally responsible. It would be reasonable to expect, therefore, that the criminal trial would concentrate very carefully upon the mind of the particular defendant. This proves not to be the case.

The criminal law generally shields from view the extent to which a given individual was really capable of responding to situations of stress in the ways demanded by the underlying theory. It does this by using a psychological model of "criminal man," much as the economists work with "economic man," endowing it with the characteristics believed necessary to serve the purpose of social control and seeing to it that guilt in a particular case is made to depend upon whether the model man could properly be regarded as guilty.[6] This theory of objective liability (which is to be contrasted with a subjective theory) is a blunt instrument for assessing criminal responsibility but the bluntness is largely concealed from public view by the extent to which the criminal law uses words like "intent" and "malice." The objective theory is probably used because there is no psychology that can tell with precision which men have the characteristics required by the theory and which do not; and because there is a deeply rooted feeling, which many hesitate to articulate, that it is more important to do the job of social control efficiently than sensitively.

The objective theory is enforced through rules regarding presumptions and the admissibility of evidence. The law assumes for most situations that all men have the necessary qualities to make the expected responses, until it is demonstrated otherwise. This assumption is reflected in the presumption that all men are sane and that they intend the natural and probable consequences of their acts. If, therefore, an individual's *acts* mark him as a criminal, it is ordinarily inferred that he intended to commit crime or was insufficiently attentive to the objective circumstances and therefore either reckless or grossly negligent. If, for example, the prosecution established that the defendant struck the head of another with a bat and that death ensued, it would have proved not only the criminal act but the criminal intent. This inference of intent would attach by virtue of the assumption which follows from the presumption of sanity—that the defendant knew the consequences which would follow from his physical movements.

These presumptions may endow the defendant with characteristics which are not his at all. They posit as the normal man a "reasonable man," who responds within predictable limits to the situations served up by his environment. He is permitted to strike back just enough to repel the aggressor but no more. When his property is invaded, he must use reason rather than force if the circumstances allow him to do so. He may even be required to retreat. But he need not retreat too far; certainly he need not leave his real property to the aggressor, though he may be required to leave his personal property behind as he goes in search of the police. This "normal" man may find himself obligated to sacrifice his honor rather than kill another but not his life. If he finds himself in a situation which provokes him beyond the limits of endurance and he kills, his killing will be completely "justified" or "excused" only if it fits within the range of what reasonable men would have done. Even partial excuse, as when provocation reduces the grade of a crime from murder to manslaughter, will depend upon the accused having been provoked no more than a reasonable man would have been.

In short, a large part of the criminal law, and particularly that part which figures in the insanity defense, holds defendants to a standard of liability which is objective in nature while at the same time speaking subjective-sounding words to juries. The objective standard is administered by rejecting evidence that a given defendant was more fearful than most, more moved to anger than most, more suggestible than most. The courts thus make it appear to juries that the fates of reasonable men are being weighed when, in fact, they may be dealing with quite unreasonable ones. It is, of course, true that the jurors may render their verdict on subjective grounds but they will do so in sub rosa fashion. It is also true that there are offenses, requiring a "specific intent," which call for a subjective standard. But these are almost always aggravated offenses which sit at the top of a series of graduated sanctions, leaving other offenses which apply the objective standard.

The insanity defense marks the transition from the adequate man the law demands to the inadequate man he may be. If the accused asserts the insanity defense in any of its forms, he can have the benefit of detailed concentration on him. He can then prove he is not like most men, that he comes to the tension-producing situations of his environment ill-equipped to weigh nicely the values of life and property, blow and counterblow. He can urge that it is unfair to infer intention or recklessness from his acts.

In all jurisdictions, however, he must first show he suffered from a "mental disease or defect" at the time of the crime and that the disease or defect was of a sort which kept him from meeting the demands of a criminal code. By introducing this issue, the defendant is in effect conceding that he cannot prove his innocence in the conventional way. While making this concession—that he was indeed behaving like a murderer or a rapist or a burglar or a robber—he tries to shift the responsibility from himself to something called

THE INSANITY DEFENSE

he way of material success and status, to believe
possible to achieve these rapidly, and to feel
d angry when they find there is a considerable gap
ideal and reality. Increasingly, this frustration is
d in groups which feel themselves shut out from
aths of upward movement and which seek targets
nity, even if they involve delinquency, to solve their

a time, it is asking a good deal to expect that either
nal law or the insanity defense—and the ideal of
responsibility they represent—will or should play
a role in strengthening the social order, or in bolster-
character structures of very many persons considering
is for these reasons, however, that the debate about
nity defense is conducted so passionately. Because the
calling criminal responsibility into question are so
those who look to the criminal law to shore up
ed social supports see the insanity defense as a call to

"mental disease," which kept him from being what he appeared to be, a man committing crime with a full measure of
culpability. In the course of these efforts, the inquiry becomes
more subjective in nature. Where before he was limited in the
degree to which he could show that he did not intend the
"natural and probable consequences of his acts," now his
mental life is wide open. His life history can be presented in
elaborate detail—his school problems, his prior aberrational
behavior, his experience with psychiatric clinics and mental
hospitals. The search becomes one for information regarding
what the accused was *really* thinking when he committed the
crime, how he was *really* functioning, rather than for inferences drawn from his acts at the time of the crime.

The insanity defense has not threatened the general scheme,
which made "blame" and social control the pervasive response
to crime, because it was built upon the concept of mental
disease. That concept has long been regarded as a restrictive
one, extending only to those who had obviously lost touch
with reality.* Though the concept has broadened considerably
in recent years, two other factors have held the defense in
check. The fact that it could ordinarily be raised only by one
who was competent to stand trial (and who seemed, therefore,
to be quite rational) made it extremely unlikely that a jury
would be persuaded that he was seriously disordered only a
short time before. And, most important of all, insanity has
become a defense in name alone. In virtually every state, a
successful insanity defense does not bring freedom with it.
Instead, it has become the occasion for either mandatory
commitment to a mental hospital or for an exercise of discretion by the court regarding the advisability of such commitment. And because the commitment is for treatment, it continues until such time as the hospital authorities conclude the
patient is ready for release.** The defense has become, there-

*See the fuller discussion infra, pp. 25–36.
**See Ch. 10 infra.

fore, a way of avoiding one species of state control and of substituting another for it. It fuses criminal law with a species of administrative law, shifting the defendant from a criminal process to a civil-medical one which explicitly incorporates elements of preventive detention. In substance, defendant may make out his defense only if he authorizes the court to protect the community from him.

The man who is insane, therefore, may not fare very differently from the man who is sane and guilty, except in capital cases when the insanity defense may save his life. For the rest, the advantage he enjoys is that he suffers no formal judgment of condemnation. He can tell himself he was not responsible for what he did and that "society" agrees. And the institution to which he is sent is ostensibly dedicated to the ideal of treating his illness and making him better. But he must weigh those advantages against the fact that his detention is for an entirely indeterminate period; that he may be kept in a hospital as long as or longer than he would have remained in prison; and that being regarded as mentally ill may bring him as much stigma, economic deprivation, family dislocation, and often as little treatment or physical comfort as being a criminal.

III

The insanity defense is caught up in some of the most controversial ideological currents of our time. The direction it takes depends, essentially, upon the place in social control one assigns to the criminal law as it competes with other methods of regulation by the state, to each of the themes underlying the criminal law, to the confidence one has that the mentally ill offender can be identified and treated, and the importance one attaches to the idea of blame. However difficult it has been in the past to find one's way among considerations of this sort, events are conspiring to make the problem even more complex. At the very time when the "mental

health" message is
psychiatrists and oth
the faith which had
defense. The professio
lest the possibilities of
ment of the mentally il
alone because the techr
economic. Even if such p
main true that too many
relative handful of menta
of the offender must compe
the mentally ill for already
crisis of conscience of sorts. T
tinues to be propagated from p
know full well that the messag
Yet they fear retreat, now tha
ceptance, because they feel they
capacity of society somehow to p
resources.

This combination of popular fai
comes at a time when the crime pr
than in the past. However much w
of criminal statistics, there seems to b
violence and disrespect for law. Two
planations have been offered of why
The first sees society as increasingly ato
the village, and the family less and le
individual with a constructive value
existential crisis of our time and fed by th
urbanization, and prosperity of the Am
duces more individuals who lack characte
resist the increasing temptations to crim
planation is, in a sense, the other side of tl
inadequate character structure in part built
out to meet, a society which conditions peop

and more in
it is entirely
frustrated ar
between the
concentrate
the usual p
of opportu
problems.
In such
the crimir
personal
much of
ing the c
crime. I
the insa
current
strong,
weake
battle.

CHAPTER THREE

The Defendant

Though the insanity defense has long dominated discussions about criminal law, it arises too rarely to deserve a place at the center of the stage. The statistics tell the tale with remarkable clarity. Of the total number of criminal acts committed, a relatively small proportion are detected; an even smaller proportion of offenders are formally charged with crime. Of those charged, some ninety per cent plead guilty; only a small number of the ten per cent who stand trial plead the insanity defense.*

That number is by no means the entire group which could plead the defense if it were so minded. The size of the group is affected, in the first instance, by the discretion residing in police and prosecutor to direct offenders to a wide variety of medical and welfare agencies or to civil commitment processes. Indeed, from the moment deviant acts are called to public notice, there begins a process which forces choices upon law enforcement officials. They must decide whether to treat the offending event as a crime or as a symptom of mental illness or to ignore it entirely. The more elastic the concept of mental illness becomes and the greater the faith of the public in the medical approach to deviant behavior, the more likely it will be that the group from which the insanity defense is drawn will be reduced.

---

*It has been estimated that about 70 per cent of acquittals by reason of insanity in the District of Columbia are uncontested acquittals by the court, sitting without a jury. Acheson, "McDonald v. United States: The Durham Rule Redefined," 51 *Geo. L. J.* 580, 589 (1963).[1]

The size of the group is reduced even more by the fact that most of those who are left in the criminal process and who could assert the insanity defense choose not to do so. The law permits the defendants to make the choice because they are "competent to stand trial." The reasons why they choose to forgo the defense are well known. For one thing, a verdict of insanity is still regarded as more stigmatizing than a verdict of criminality. For another, a finding of insanity may bring not freedom but indeterminate commitment to a mental hospital. For a third, the facilities for treatment and cure may be no better in the mental hospital system than in the correctional system to which the convicted offender is sent. As a result, insanity has become something to be asserted only when a death sentence or very long imprisonment is in the offing. Given the nature of our penal codes, this means the defendant asserting the insanity defense will most often be involved in a very serious charge such as murder or armed robbery or arson or rape.[2]

The fact that only serious offenders tend to assert the defense places a heavy burden upon them to prove they were very ill if they are to persuade the jury to "acquit" them. For jurors, like their fellow men, are likely to be particularly vengeful in just the cases which make defendants most anxious to avoid the law's penalties.[3] As a result, the natural protagonist of the insanity defense is the man whose illness is likely to have been most apparent. This is usually the psychotic. More than any other subgroup within the class of mentally ill, the psychotic may be able to present symptoms sufficiently bizarre to enable the jury to give up its retributive impulses and to make it willing to spare him the role of deterrent symbol. He comes closest to the lay conception of serious mental disorder and finds the jury more prepared to set him off from the "reasonable" men with whom the law is principally concerned. Yet those who are most persistently and obviously psychotic have probably been withdrawn from the general population by civil commitment processes or by findings that they are incompetent to stand trial. Left for the insanity defense, therefore, are those who do not at present seem mentally disordered but who feel they can demonstrate a serious disorder at the time of the crime.

In the next section, I shall describe briefly the nature of psychoses and other serious mental disorders in order to provide a background for the more detailed discussion of the insanity defense that will follow.

I

Some psychoses are the result of organic or physiological defects but the greatest number, at least in the present state of knowledge, are functional psychoses. These are known as illnesses only by their effect on functioning, though it is widely assumed that a physiological base will someday be found. Schizophrenia is the most common among them, with the manic-depressive psychosis ranking second, but very far behind. Whatever the form or origin of the psychosis, it is usually described by the symptoms manifested in the acute phase—breakdown of intellect, serious loss of self-control, loss of a sense of reality. These symptoms may appear in the form of delusions, hallucinations, disorientation, assaultive behavior, or extreme withdrawal.[4] However, the defendant alleging insanity will be displaying none or few of these symptoms to the jury which must pass on the defense. He will act and sound quite rational and will exhibit no bizarre behavior. His defense will be addressed to the time of the crime and to the assertion that he was then psychotic, not to the time of trial.

The principal thrust of the trial therefore is to recapture somehow the mental condition of the defendant at the earlier time, to ascertain whether he was as rational and in control then as he appears to be now. The prosecution will contend he was; the defendant that he was not. If the issues are developed at all adequately, testimony will be presented by both parties as to the defendant's mental condition at the time of the crime, before the crime, and after the crime. Lay witnesses, testifying for the prosecution, will report that the defendant "looked normal" to them. Policemen and prison guards will report responsiveness to discipline. Employers will describe satisfactory work records. Acquaintances will speak of adequate performance in day-to-day living. The defendant will, in turn, try to demonstrate that, however normal he may have appeared on those occasions, he was very different at the time of the crime. Alternatively, the defendant or his attorney may urge that the appearance of normality is a deceptive thing and that he has not been normal at all. He will try to make this point by producing lay witnesses who will report on the times when he acted badly, or strangely, lost control of himself, flew into a rage, thought he was being poisoned, etc. The impression will soon be abroad that someone is lying, that no one filling out the portrait painted by the prosecution can also have behaved the way the defendant's witnesses describe him.

It is at this juncture that the jury may turn to the expert testimony to explain away the discrepancy. The expert, usually a psychiatrist, will have to take the jury deep into the nature of mental illness if it is to understand in a meaningful way that men who look and act like us may really be seriously diseased. If the educative job is done well, jurors will learn that the psychotic is much less "crazy" than the general public imagines him to be. The degree to which he misperceives reality, or misunderstands or misinterprets it, is a variable thing. He may have delusions and hallucinations or he may not. He may have them sometimes or most of the time and with varying degrees of intensity. But it is only in an acute episode that he will resemble the popular conception of the lunatic who rants and raves, rushes about excitedly, shouts nonsense, acts violent, and seems to have no understanding of where he is or what he is doing. Particularly with the advent of tranquilizers, episodes of this sort are infrequent, brief, and rarely so extreme. Indeed, ever larger numbers of psychotics are being treated on an out-patient basis.[5]

Even when the acute psychotic seems out of touch with reality, the break may appear more pervasive than is really the case. As Harry Stack Sullivan pointed out regarding schizophrenia, "It is impossible to find a person who is utterly schizophrenic."[6] The sickest mental patient may act intelligently on many matters. This is most apparent in the case of chronic psychotics who are often able to function quite adequately in the hospital environment. They understand the rules of the ward. They obey orders. They are fairly well oriented in space and time and they can take care of their own personal needs.

These conclusions have been documented in a fairly detailed way in the research literature. Schizophrenics, for example, can memorize lists of words, solve problems, and form concepts. They react to anxiety and to the threat of failure. Moreover, they are perceived by those who work with them as capable of functioning in a wide variety of situations. They are given complicated intelligence, personality, and concept formation tests and are expected to understand instructions even though their performance on the tests themselves is likely to be abnormal. They, and psychotics generally, help maintain the hospital by doing work on the grounds, in the wards, and in the kitchens. They publish hospital newspapers and engage in athletics. Where there is a patient government, they take part in it. They react to sanctions and to threats of sanction. Belknap describes in great detail the use of punishment in the day-to-day administration of a mental hospital. Suspension of privileges, ridicule, corporal punishment, isolation, electro-shock treatment, assignment to bad wards or unpleasant jobs all served as effective punishments. Good jobs, better rooms and beds, coffee, privacy, grounds privileges, companionship, access to professional personnel, and kindness all served as rewards. Threats of punishment and promises of reward were also effective. "For most patients the threat of being put on the shock list had an instant effect in bringing their conduct into line." In short, patients realize the consequences of misbehaving and of disobeying the attendants. They behave in the hospital situation much as normal persons would.[7]

Although the psychotic is less "crazy" than he is usually thought to be, he is a good deal crazier than will be apparent to the casual or short-term observer. Except for psychoses due to traumatic brain damage or toxic substances, "mental disease is practically never acutely precipitated. . . . There is almost always . . . a varying period of time during which it is present, although incubating and not openly manifest."[8] Yet it is the casual observer who will sit on a jury and decide whether the seemingly normal person before him could have been insane when he committed the crime some time in the past. The juror will have to be persuaded of things which are commonplace to the psychiatrist: that a forbidden act may be committed for reasons which seem so overwhelmingly important as to obscure the threat of punishment; or because the threat suddenly lost its meaning; or because the threat took on some very special meaning. He may know the rules and the sanctions in a formal sense, but at any given moment he may misinterpret them or their application to him. For example, a rule against smoking may be viewed as an effort at castration which can only be avoided by continuing to smoke. A threat of corporal punishment may be construed as a homosexual approach which the patient unconsciously desires. The act of soiling may be more important than the threat of shock treatment because only by soiling can the patient demonstrate or deny his love for his mother. Though these phenomena are not confined exclusively to the psychotic, they are a more conspicuous part of his life. His thinking and behavior are disproportionately influenced by irrational beliefs, percep-

And some tend to be cyclical. For example, psychoses such as cerebral arteriosclerosis, senile psychoses, brain tumors, and traumatic brain injury are associated with permanent damage to the brain which makes it probable that they will be progressive or at least irreversible. Even a patient released from the hospital might continue to suffer from the disease and manifest it in his behavior. He might, for example, behave in a paranoid manner which would make him unduly suspicious and hostile and might lead to crime. Similarly, a person with traumatic brain injury might become aggressive, and even homicidal, to cover up confusion and loss of memory.[10] It could be said of such persons with a fair degree of certainty that they were suffering from the previous illnesses at the time their crimes were committed. And an examination at or near the time of trial would probably confirm the original diagnoses.[11] Comparable patterns may prevail in cases of psychoses caused by toxic substances.[12]

Epileptic states (including the most common, the grand mal and petit mal seizures) do not often lead to criminal behavior. There are occasions, however, when the so-called clouded states, epileptic furors and affect epilepsy, lead to sudden changes of mood which may last from a few minutes to a few hours and which may lead to antisocial behavior. In these instances, the task of estimating probabilities will be made easier because most epileptics will have a history of seizures going back many years.[13]

The organically based conditions are less often involved in the insanity defense than are the functional psychoses. The absence of a known organic cause for these diseases makes it much more difficult to assess whether the condition exists, how long it has continued, etc. Nevertheless, some probability statements are possible. For example, involutional melancholia is a depressive reaction which occurs in persons who are going through menopause or the male equivalent. Although the chief danger in such conditions is suicide, such

a person will occasionally kill members of his family in order
to save them from some other imagined fate. The condition
tends to last no more than eighteen months, although there
are many people who do not recover. When there is recovery,
it is usually gradual. It is quite possible, therefore, for a person
to be released as cured and then to have a relapse during which
a crime is committed. Since the onset of the disease is likely to
be both gradual and noticeable, it should be possible to determine fairly accurately whether or not a person was suffering
from it at the time of the crime.[14]

Manic-depressive psychosis is quite similar to melancholia.
During a manic state, a person might become violent and
aggressive. Recovery may be quick or gradual, complete or
partial, and may be preceded by a stuporous period. Since these
attacks are often cyclical or at least recurrent, it is possible for
a person to have been released from a hospital as "cured."
Thus, there may be no warning through obvious symptoms in
the period preceding the attack.[15] Nevertheless, as in all
functional mental illness, it is very likely that there were preceding and precipitating factors which can be used as a basis
for diagnosis.

In schizophrenia, diagnosis should be easier since the disease
tends to be associated with hallucinations, delusions, and a
relatively severe break with reality. Yet the large number of
schizophrenics released from mental hospitals—an increasing
proportion each year—and the almost equally large number
readmitted testifies to the fact that schizophrenia may present
itself in very different guises from time to time.[16] In general,
however, the appearance of the disease is gradual and follows
a long history of increasing disturbance which suddenly comes
to notice. It may be precipitated by some especially difficult
situation such as a love affair, marriage, sickness, or bereave-
ment. Thus, a person who had never appeared to be very different from others may suddenly have an acute schizophrenic
attack, commit a criminal act, and then seem to recover

completely.[17] In short, the factors that make the diagnosis of schizophrenia more or less likely will turn upon the individual and his history. If, for example, he is a paranoid schizophrenic and committed a crime which he justifies as self-defense, the probability that he was insane increases because his behavior fits the profile of the particular illness. If, on the other hand, he was an acute hebephrenic, has acted normally for some time, and then commits a carefully planned robbery, the probability of insanity decreases.

The essential point is that different mental diseases have different characteristics and different probabilities of occurring under various conditions. All the factors in a particular case must be evaluated in terms of the type of illness which the defendant is said to be suffering from. Taken out of this context, the other information has little significance. In context, fairly meaningful and reliable statements of probabilities can be made.

II

Mental illnesses other than psychoses have not often been proffered as bases for the insanity defense. The reasons will be considered in subsequent chapters. For the present, it suffices to note that the situation is changing and that conditions like psychopathy, narcotics addiction, and alcoholism may be involved in the insanity defense more often than in the past. Psychopathy is unquestionably the most important of these because it is most likely to be associated with serious crime and, therefore, with the insanity defense. The psychopath is commonly regarded as having either an antisocial character or no character at all. Though his cognitive faculties are likely to be intact, he is unable to defer his gratifications; he does as he pleases, often in a way which seems unmotivated by conventional standards, and feels neither anxiety nor guilt if he hurts others in the process. This is because he forms no lasting or close relationships. Far more than the psychotic, he is likely to find himself in violation of the criminal law. But because he will seem very much like the "normal" man in most respects, he will be less able to persuade a jury that he should be "acquitted."

The expert testifying on his behalf will confront the extraordinarily difficult task of showing how deep is the lack of feeling, its origins in the family situation and in the society, and the extent to which the defendant is unable to defer his gratifications or to weigh adequately the consequences of his actions, either to himself or to others. The difficulty is compounded by the fact that the offender may conceal the softer feelings which would mark him as someone who is not a psychopath at all. Even when he shows the signs, the psychiatrist may not be able to read them because there is a common failure of communication between upper-class psychiatrists and lower-class offenders. This situation is made even more complex because there is no common theoretical base for the clinical diagnoses. Some think psychopathy is a genetic or constitutional condition, others that it is the result of a weak super-ego, yet others that it is really a deeply concealed psychosis.[18]

Determining whether a person is a psychotic or a psychopath is not a simple matter. The person who seems to be a psychotic may really be a psychopath or a neurotic or he may be mentally retarded; or the converse may be true of each; or all may be malingerers. Diagnosis is an incredibly complex matter and can be understood in detail only by steeping oneself in the relevant body of literature. Even then, the diagnosis in any given case is a highly individual application of a variety of diagnostic instruments—the intelligence and personality tests of the clinical psychologist, the social history of the social worker, the neurological tests and the psychiatric observation and interview.

Diagnosis is made even more problematic because there is a great deal of disagreement about the diagnostic categories themselves. An extensive literature traces the problems in-

volved in definitions of mental health, mental illness, psychosis, psychopathy, and neurosis.[19] Very little can be said
with certainty except that there is no sharp line dividing the
normal from the abnormal, or the psychotic from the psychopath or neurotic. Mental disease tends to represent an
impairment of function by exaggeration or constriction of
forces which exist in all of us. These forces may be set onto
an abnormal course by a virtually infinite variety of pressures
and situations, each interacting in relatively invisible fashion
with elements in the life history of the individual. The result
is diagnostic problems of unbelievable complexity. For example, when does the person who "daydreams" a great deal
become "schizoid"? At what point does the "schizoid" become
a schizophrenic? And what is the difference between a day-
dream and a hallucination, between the John Birch Society
and paranoia? These problems are difficult enough for the
therapist groping for a criterion of mental illness as a guide
to diagnosis and treatment. Their utility is even more questionable when they are invoked in the courtroom as an instrument for dividing the responsible from the irresponsible.

The heart of the diagnostic problem, of course, is that most
mental diseases do not have the confirmatory physical evidence
which one expects of physical disease. There is no redness of
throat, hoarseness of voice, swelling of ankle. Especially with
functional psychoses, entire reliance must be placed upon the
patient's reports of his acts and thoughts and the reports of
others as to his acts, as they fit into a body of scientific knowledge and experience. The medical man thus becomes a judge
of the credibility of his sources and a classifier of the abnormal
quality of the acts and thoughts described. He can turn to no
physical phenomena which are psychologically neutral.

Because most of the concepts of mental illness involve
theoretical constructs based upon clues provided by the behavior and the words of the patient rather than upon some
identifiable organic pattern, they come to depend far too

much upon how the behavior and the words are perceived by the community, by the person making the diagnosis, and upon the purposes for which the diagnosis is being made. Behavior which is socially deviant or nonconforming may make a man seem mentally ill to communities or psychiatrists who are inexperienced or unsophisticated or simply intolerant. The felt need for some form of institutionalization may lead to diagnosis which will attain a desired result.

III

There is a great distance to be traveled between the facts of a particular defendant's mental life and the trial of the insanity defense. How does "the law" come to know those facts? In the beginning, there is only the disturbing event which brings the defendant to the attention of the public authorities—the act of violence, the theft, or the sexual misconduct. But it may occur in a context which marks the defendant as someone who is less like other men than most persons who commit crimes. To a public and police increasingly sensitive to such matters, the event may be translated into symptoms of mental illness and a psychiatric examination may be sought. The police may seek the examination when he is first apprehended, in order to determine whether he should be charged with crime at all or whether he should be directed instead into a medical process. The prosecutor may seek it because he too may think the offender should be moved into a medical process or because he thinks the defendant may not be competent to stand trial or because he anticipates the insanity defense may ultimately be raised.[20]

If the examination is conducted as part of the civil or medical process, the prosecutor will probably have a report of its results. But if there has been no examination, he will have to arrange for one. In most cases, the defendant will consent fairly readily because he is often unrepresented by counsel and is not entirely mindful of his rights. If the defendant will not consent, the clearest procedure for requiring him to submit to an examination is that provided to determine competency to stand trial. In all the states, the prosecutor may move for a psychiatric examination on that question, setting out in his motion papers his reason for believing the examination to be necessary. This motion is routinely granted, in part because the stated grounds are likely to be persuasive, in part because the defendant will not oppose it, again because he is often not represented by counsel. The informality surrounding the motion makes it quite easy for the prosecutor to use it not only when he suspects incompetency, which is permissible, but also when he thinks the defendant may assert the insanity defense at trial, which is not.[21] The motion may, of course, also be made by defense counsel and is likely to be as routinely granted. In his case, however, he may ask for an examination to aid him on either the competency or the insanity issue.

The examination will usually take place at a city or state mental hospital. In an unexpectedly large number of instances, it will disclose not only that the offender is suffering from some form of mental illness but also that he has an extensive history of aberrational behavior. He will have been in and out of clinics, juvenile institutions, prisons, and mental hospitals. He may have had a psychiatric history during a period of military service. Probation and parole officers' files may contain a great deal of information about him, his problems with the law, and his employment history. Members of his family will report on the wildness of his looks, his bizarre behavior, his fits of dejection, his bouts of weeping, his acts of violence, a record of truancy during the school years, a spotty employment record. Others may report on a broken home or on serious conflicts within the home situation. His educational background is likely to be poor and he may show telltale signs in the psychological tests administered to him.

All will point toward serious emotional problems in the past and at present.

If those problems render the defendant incompetent—that is, unable to understand the proceedings against him or to assist in his defense—he will be sent to a mental hospital until his competence is restored. This will ordinarily occur if he is currently psychotic in a way that keeps him from meeting moral responsibilities. The man who has auditory or visual hallucinations, or is in a catatonic state, for example, is not likely to participate effectively in his defense. If he never regains his competence, he will spend the rest of his days in confinement and his insanity defense will be lost.[22] But if he does return for trial, he will have added substantially to the raw materials of a defense. There will now be hospital reports containing statements of psychiatrists, social workers, nurses, ward attendants, all painting a picture of his mental condition shortly after the time of the crime.

For the defendant who is competent to stand trial (or who has no counsel to assert he is not, or who chooses not to raise the point), the case will move on toward trial. But before the trial actually takes place, a good deal of time may have elapsed —sometimes as much as several months. During that period, he will probably have remained in custody because he could not raise the monetary bond set as a condition of his release, or because he committed a crime which falls outside the newer pre-trial release programs.[23] Indeed, the fact that he has committed a serious crime (and that he shows signs of mental illness) will often result in the bond deliberately being set too high for him to meet it. As a result, by the time of trial, he will have been under continuous observation by prison officials and fellow inmates who will be able to testify in considerable detail as to his mental condition.

If the prosecution anticipates an insanity defense and wishes to add even more to its picture of the defendant and his mental condition, it may do so through the grand jury. For that body

has the subpoena power, which enables it to summon witnesses and documents relevant to the defendant and his case,
with the exception of the defendant himself.[24] The defendant
participates in this stage hardly at all. He will simply learn
one day that an indictment has been returned against him.

Not until the defendant is arraigned to plead to the indictment (or information) will he have to decide whether he
wishes to assert the insanity defense, or to forgo it and either
pursue some other defense or plead guilty. He will now not
only be advised of his right to retain counsel but, if he should
be indigent, the court will appoint one on his behalf. Too
often, however, appointed counsel will be young, inexperienced, and unpaid. His contacts with his client will be too
brief to permit detailed exploration of either the facts of the
case or the defendant's preferences among the alternatives
outlined to him. As a result, the defendant may plead guilty
on the basis of half-knowledge and the insanity defense will
simply disappear from view. In the relatively rare case when
the defendant pleads not guilty, or his counsel requests a
continuance while he considers how to advise his client, the
defendant's case may be carefully investigated for the first
time.

In the case of the affluent defendant, the investigative
process may have begun earlier. He may have been represented from the very beginning of his contacts with police
and prosecutor, and his lawyer may early have suspected his
client was mentally ill. If he had, a psychiatrist would have
been retained, an examination would have been made, and
additional investigation carried out. A decision would have
been made as to whether the defendant's competency to stand
trial should be contested or whether the insanity defense
should be raised at trial. After arraignment, trial preparation
would have begun in earnest. As much detail as possible
would have been accumulated about the defendant's life in
an effort to show the evolution of mental disease. Defense

counsel may have learned of a course of aberrational or
troublesome behavior beginning in school and continuing
through a variety of contacts with social agencies, psychiatric
clinics, juvenile institutions, prisons, or mental hospitals. He
may have had a clinical psychologist administer a variety of
tests from which an assessment could be made of the defendant's educational attainments and emotional development. A neurologist might have conducted an examination
for organic disorders. And the whole would have been appraised by a psychiatrist and by defense counsel, who would
then be able to fashion an insanity defense if defendant should
choose to assert it. In making that decision, the consequences
of an acquittal by reason of insanity would be measured
against those of conviction, the stigma and indeterminate
commitment of insanity compared with the stigma and relatively determinate sentence of crime.

In the case of the indigent defendant whose counsel first
enters on the scene at arraignment or who enters earlier but
lacks the resources to do very much, all of the foregoing will
have to be accelerated. He will have to make up somehow for
the time and the opportunities lost prior to arraignment. His
first step, after looking into the facts of the case and of defendant's background will be to petition the court for a
psychiatric examination. If the petition is granted, the defendant will probably be examined at the same public institution which played a part in determining his competence
to stand trial. Virtually never, however, will the defendant
be authorized to retain his own psychiatrist at state expense.
As a result, he and his counsel will ordinarily have quite
limited contacts with a psychiatrist before trial. Moreover, he
is likely to have very little control or influence over the investigative preparation for the psychiatric examination, or
on the decision whether psychological and neurological tests
should be administered.

The probability is, of course, that neither of the models I

have described will hold true for all cases. What I have referred to as the "affluent" defense represents an ideal of preparation which is not often realized. The defense tends to unfold almost as badly for those who are affluent as for those who are indigent. Rarely will enough investigative work have been done. Rarely will the psychiatric examination have been meticulously made, or neurological and psychological tests even administered. The more usual pattern has the defense coming to trial on the basis of fairly casual preparation— either because lawyer and psychiatrist assume the other will take control of the case and contribute more than he actually does, or because the resources and the will are lacking in either to develop the case properly.

In most cases, bits and pieces of lay and expert evidence are awkwardly presented in an effort to build a pattern of a diseased personality and to fit that pattern somehow to the time of the crime. Most of the testimony will be cast in the broadest of conclusionary terms, following the language of the applicable test of insanity and offering little or no personal history, little or no symptomatology, little or no explanation of what the defendant is and how he got that way. Distinctions between examinations conducted to ascertain competency to stand trial and insanity at the time of the crime will often be ignored. Words and phrases like "insane," "psychotic," "schizophrenic," and "knew right from wrong," will tend to dominate the scene, even when there exist lengthy psychiatric reports which are potentially able to tell a great deal about the defendant if anyone had the wit to draw upon them. Each side's witnesses will quite expectedly contradict the other's because the trial will so often represent an effort to recapture the acute stage of the psychosis of a defendant who now looks quite normal. Prosecution and defense counsel will challenge the qualifications of the expert witnesses, the bases for their conclusions, and the scientific credentials of psychiatry. The prosecutor will try to demonstrate that insanity can be feigned, that the psychiatrist must rely almost entirely upon what the defendant tells him. He may insinuate that acquittal by reason of insanity will mean that a dangerous offender will be released to prey upon the community. And he will emphasize the defendant's normal behavior—e.g. that he fled or picked a secluded spot for the crime or that he lied to the police or that he had an understandable motive—while the defense will emphasize the abnormal elements in the situation.[25]

In the midst of all this, the words of the insanity defense, of burden of proof and presumptions, will be uttered by judge to jury and the ultimate decision will depend not only upon the facts of mental illness, but upon how the jury approaches those facts, and how it feels about mental disease and crime. Here the dominant fact is, unquestionably, that laymen are remarkably unwilling to recognize mental illness. For the most part, behavior is not regarded by the public as reflecting serious mental disorder unless it fulfills three interrelated conditions which are reminiscent of the major characteristics of psychosis: breakdown of intellect, serious loss of self-control, and markedly inappropriate behavior. The public tends to regard such individuals not only as ill but as dangerous, not so much because of their past overt acts but because "you never know what they are going to do."[26]

Curiously, however, jurors are ordinarily told little or nothing about the consequences of an acquittal by reason of insanity. If they are told anything at all, it is that the disposition of the defendant—upon a finding of guilt or insanity—is no concern of theirs. Only in the District of Columbia must the trial judge inform the jury that such an acquittal will bring commitment to a mental hospital. Yet the issue has a way of intruding itself, not only because it is very much in the minds of jurors but because it may slip in as counsel question witnesses and as they argue to the jury.*

*See discussion infra, pp. 143–44.

PART II

The Defense and Its Administration

CHAPTER FOUR

M'Naghten: The Stereotype Challenged

The *M'Naghten* rule is the sole formula used by the courts of thirty states (and of Great Britain) to define insanity for the jury. In most of the remaining states, it is the first half of a two-part rule which includes the so-called "irresistible impulse" test.* The language of *M'Naghten* is fairly simple. It tells jurors

> that every man is to be presumed to be sane, and . . . that to establish a defence on the ground of insanity, it must be clearly proved that, at the time of the committing of the act, the party accused was labouring under such a defect of reason, from disease of the mind, as not to know the nature and quality of the act he was doing; or if he did know it, that he did not know he was doing what was wrong.[1]

The general thrust seems clear. It emphasizes knowledge of the sanctions threatened by the criminal code while ignoring self-control. The tacit assumption is that powers of self-control are strengthened by knowledge of sanctions; and that any injustices which might result—to those who were neverthe-

---

*The jurisdictions following some form of the so-called "irresistible impulse" (or "control") rule, in addition to *M'Naghten,* are set out in Ch. 5, note 1 infra. They include 17 states and the federal system. This last tabulation includes jurisdictions which have adopted the ALI rule, or a variant thereof, Ch. 6, note 23 infra. Jurisdictions following some other rule are set out in Ch. 6, notes 1, 10 infra. They include New Hampshire, the District of Columbia, Maine, and the Virgin Islands. The remaining states use some form of the *M'Naghten* rule.

less unable to control their conduct—are less important than exerting the maximum possible pressure toward conformity with law.[2] The rule also seems to assume that the community at large, acting through the jury, would be willing to "exempt" offenders from the criminal law only if they obviously did not know what they were about. Nevertheless, important questions of interpretation arise. What illnesses are to qualify as "diseases" of the mind? Is "know" to include emotional appreciation of the impact of an act upon both offender and victim or is it to be limited to abstract awareness? Does "wrong" refer to legal or moral wrong? Given the age of *M'Naghten,* it would be reasonable to assume that every one of these questions, and countless others, had been construed again and again in judicial opinions or settled by statute. The fact is that there has been surprisingly little construction of the words in the hundred-odd years since they were first formulated.

Despite this lack of authoritative interpretation, *M'Naghten* has long been a focal point of controversy. The rule has been condemned as retributive in nature, making scapegoats of offenders who could not possibly have done otherwise; and lauded as uniquely suited to serve the deterrent function of the criminal law. Until recently, the critics have been far more vocal than the defenders, at least in the learned journals, and it is the critics' *M'Naghten* which tends to dominate the debate. The picture they present is that of a restrictive rule which reflects an outmoded faculty psychology. It sees thought processes as separated into cognitive, emotional, and control components and classes a man as insane, as having a "defect of reason," only if he suffers from serious cognitive or intellectual impairment. This, the critics argue, is at odds with the "new psychology" which sees man's personality as dynamically integrated and his mental condition as necessarily unsound if any part of its functioning is disordered. The principal consequence of *M'Naghten* is said to be that it denies to the jury the "insights of modern psychology" because it restricts the flow of expert testimony. As a direct result, the insanity defense is said to be barred to the great majority of those who suffer from serious mental illness—because so few psychotics suffer from major cognitive impairment and most who do are so deteriorated that they will not be competent to stand trial. *M'Naghten* thus becomes an immoral instrument for condemning persons who may be psychotic and consigning them to prison where they will be punished, not treated; it keeps from the jury the "true" facts regarding the mental condition of the accused, so that the law can do its punitive worst.[3]

I

This interpretation of *M'Naghten* has been dinned into the professional literature for so long that it is generally assumed there can be no other. As a result, the elimination of *M'Naghten* and willingness to adopt one of the newer rules, has been treated as a test of liberal faith. It is not at all certain, however, that this picture is an accurate one. If an adequate assessment is to be made, *M'Naghten* must be seen as it is presented to the jury and as the jury is likely to understand it. An examination must be made of its effect upon counsel contemplating whether to assert the insanity defense, upon the evidence admitted to prove and disprove the defense, and upon the expert testimony offered by the parties. But first, the words themselves must be examined as they have fared in the courts, to see what limits they set to the inquiry.

"Disease of the Mind"

There has been almost no judicial definition of mental disease in cases concerned with the *M'Naghten* rule. The reason commonly advanced is that the more detailed part of the rule—dealing with knowledge—makes it plain that only a limited number of psychoses and the most extreme forms of mental defect can qualify.[4] In any event, the words are usually presented, without explanation, as part of the charge to the jury. What little law on the subject does exist is found in cases which reject efforts to assert insanity by persons whose mental conditions are clearly marginal. In this group are cases involving intoxication due to the use of alcohol, narcotics withdrawal, temporary insanity, and borderline mental defects.

The intoxication cases tell us that it is ordinarily not enough for the defendant to show that, at the time of the crime, his thought processes were seriously distorted by alcohol or narcotics.[5] And the "temporary insanity" cases tell us that it is not enough that the defendant acted during an "emotional frenzy." In others, the defense is said to be unavailable to "a person of weak intellect or one whose moral perceptions were blunted or ill developed."[6] In all these cases, the focus is not so much on whether the defendant entertained the requisite mental state at the time of the crime as it is upon whether he had, in addition, a disease—preferably one of "a fixed or prolonged nature."[7] The cases are relatively silent, however, on which diseases would qualify. The question is not treated as one of law at all, but rather as if the necessary link can be provided by the testimony of expert witnesses. If they are willing to affirm that the frenzy, or the distortion, was attributable to a mental disease and are willing to name and describe the disease, then the issue will ordinarily be passed to the jury.[8] The disease named most often is some form of psychosis, on the assumption that psychopathy and other nonpsychotic illnesses cannot qualify.[9]

The only other cases touching directly on the definition of "mental disease" are those dealing with the question whether a mental "defect," such as a low I.Q. or some other form of mental retardation, can qualify. While discussions of the question are often unclear and while there are some cases to the contrary, the rule generally seems to be that such defects qualify as mental diseases. However, to exculpate the defendant, the defects must be so severe as to deprive him of the "knowledge" specified by *M'Naghten*.[10]

"KNOW"

The word "know" has been at the center of the controversy surrounding *M'Naghten*. The bulk of the critics read it as referring to formal cognition or intellectual awareness alone. They distinguish this, the "law's" meaning, from what they describe as the "psychiatric" meaning—which they take to connote a fuller, deeper knowledge, involving emotional as well as intellectual awareness. This fuller knowledge can exist only when the accused is able to evaluate his conduct in terms of its actual impact upon himself and others and when he is able to appreciate the total setting in which he is acting. According to the critics, the law's type of knowledge is to be found even in the most serious psychoses. Indeed, to borrow from a well-known comment, it is absent only in the "totally deteriorated, drooling, hopeless psychotics of long-standing, and congenital idiots."[11] The consequence, the argument continues, is that *M'Naghten* directs jurors to hold responsible a great many persons who are seriously disturbed and makes successful assertion of the insanity defense virtually impossible. Moreover, since only a handful of psychotics can meet the requirements of "know," efforts to expand the concept of "disease" to include those who are not psychotic are doomed to fail. Indeed, there seems little point in trying—hence the lack of judicial definition of "mental disease."

The assertion that "know" is narrowly defined has been made so often and so insistently that it comes as a surprise to find that very few appellate courts have imposed the restrictive interpretation.[12] Indeed, most of the courts which have addressed themselves to the question have favored a rather broad construction. In eleven states, the jury is told that an accused "knows" only if he "understands" enough to enable him to judge of "the nature, character and consequence of the act charged against him," or if he has the "capacity to appreciate the character and to comprehend the probable or possible consequences of his act." The California court noted recently, for example, that "our trial courts place a commendably broad interpretation upon the M'Naghten 'knowledge' test."[13] Commenting on the Canadian practice which uses the broader wording, the Canadian Royal Commission on Insanity concluded that "the act must necessarily involve more than mere knowledge that the act is being committed; there must be an appreciation of the factors involved in the act and a mental capacity to measure and foresee the consequences of the violent conduct." In this view, the word "appreciate" draws most psychoses under the *M'Naghten* rules, because it addresses itself to the defendant's awareness of "the true significance of his conduct."[14] Even in the first *Durham* trial, the trial judge said it was necessary to determine whether the defendant "knew the difference between right and wrong in connection with governing his own actions," not as an abstract matter.[15]

In the remaining jurisdictions, some nineteen in number, the jury is simply given the words of the rule, without explanation, and left to find the "common sense" meaning from their own backgrounds or from the materials presented to them at trial. Nowhere, however, are they told they must adopt a restrictive interpretation.

"NATURE AND QUALITY OF THE ACT"

The phrase "nature and quality of the act" is sometimes omitted completely from the charge to the jury. More often, it is either stated to the jury without explanation or treated as adding nothing to the requirement that the accused know his act was wrong.[16] The underlying theory is that if the accused did not know the nature and quality of his act, he would have been incapable of knowing it was wrong. There have been a few efforts to treat the phrase as if it added something to the rule. In England, for example, it was suggested that "nature" meant the act's physical nature, while "quality" referred to its moral aspect. The court rejected the suggestion, holding that "nature and quality" refers solely to the physical character of the act.[17] In the United States, the rule seems to be similar,[18] though the Wisconsin court has held that "nature and quality" gives "important emphasis" to the realization of the wrongfulness of an act. It marks the distinction between "vaguely . . . [realizing] that particular conduct is forbidden" and "real insight into the conduct."[19] This construction illustrates the close connection between the definition of "know" and that of "nature and quality." The broader reading of "nature and quality" carries with it the broader construction of "know" and vice versa. To know the quality of an act, with all its social and emotional implications, requires more than an abstract, purely intellectual knowledge. Likewise, to talk of appreciating the full significance of an act means that "nature and quality" must be understood as including more than the physical nature of the act.

"WRONG"

In those situations where the accused does not know the nature and quality of his act, in the broad sense, he will not know that it was wrong, no matter what construction "wrong" is given. But assuming both "know" and "nature and quality" are read narrowly and the defendant knows the physical nature of his act, does "wrong" mean moral or legal wrong? The *M'Naghten* judges said a person is punishable "if he knew at the time of committing such crime that he was acting contrary to law; by which expression we . . . mean the law of the land." The matter was somewhat confused by a second passage in the opinion:

> If the question were to be put as to the knowledge of the accused solely and exclusively with reference to the law

of the land, it might tend to confound the jury by induc-
ing them to believe that an actual knowledge of the law
of the land was essential in order to lead to a conviction;
whereas the law is administered on the principle that
every one must be taken conclusively to know it, without
proof that he does know it. If the accused was conscious
that the act was one which he ought not to do, and if that
act was at the same time contrary to the law of the land,
he is punishable.[20]

The English courts have sought to remove the ambiguity by
holding that the accused must be aware that the act was legally wrong.[21]

In the United States, the issue has seldom been raised. The
word is generally given to the jury without explanation.[22]
Where it has been considered, the courts have split. One
group holds that an offender is classed as sane if he knew
the act was prohibited by law.[23] A second group takes the
position that "wrong" means moral wrong "according to
generally accepted standards" and offers, as an illustration of
insanity, the defendant who thought it morally right that he
kill (e.g. because he was ordered to do so by God) but knew
it was legally wrong.[24] The opponents of M'Naghten have
urged the adoption of this second view because of its seemingly liberalizing tendency. They are often unclear, however,
whether "moral wrong" is to be judged by the personal
standards of the accused or by his awareness that society views
the act as wrong. The latter, which is probably the one meant
by the courts, adds very little. This is because most cases involving the insanity defense will involve crimes sufficiently
serious to make society's moral judgment identical with the
legal standard. It might even be argued that in such cases
society's moral condemnation will be more apparent to the
accused than the fact that he violated the law, so that the use
of a standard of "moral" wrong would narrow the defense—

e.g. a man may think he has the defense of self-defense or superior order and yet feel it is immoral for him to kill. If the attempt to draw the distinction between moral and legal wrong adds little or nothing to the defense, the only reason for urging it must be that some writers see it as a way to broaden an otherwise narrow definition of "know." The apparent hope is to bring to the jury's attention the moral, and emotional, perspective of the defendant.[25]

II

The most pressing questions about *M'Naghten* have as yet been left unanswered; the key words remain undefined or only partially defined. Portraying the rule as rigid and narrow and condemning it wholesale would seem, therefore, to be unjustified. It may be, however, that the rule's impact is felt not when the jury is instructed on the law, which is all we have considered thus far, but at other stages of the process—as when evidence of mental illness is offered, or when experts seek to explain the facts of mental disease. Certainly, the criticism most frequently made of *M'Naghten* is that it "keeps out evidence of the defendant's mental life," denying the jury "the true picture of the defendant's mental condition" and the "insights of modern psychology."[26] This is presumably done by the trial judge who interprets the rule narrowly and admits only such evidence as satisfies its terms. But the critics seldom cite cases and leave unclear not only the kinds of evidence that will be barred but also the precise objections that would be leveled. For example, will the court exclude lay evidence of aberrational behavior by the accused at various times in his life? Will it exclude evidence of his teachers, or of psychiatrists, psychologists, or social workers who had contact with him in the past? Will it prevent a psychiatrist who examined him for purposes of trial from testifying in full regarding his examination?

There is virtually no support in law for the view that

M'Naghten is responsible for inhibiting the flow of testimony on the insanity issue. Wigmore states the rule to be that when insanity is in issue, "any and all conduct of the person is admissible in evidence." And the cases support Wigmore's view. The almost unvarying policy of the courts has been to admit *any* evidence of aberrational behavior so long as it is probative of the defendant's mental condition, without regard to the supposed restrictions of the test used to define insanity for the jury.[27] For example, where the defendant's father testified "that defendant was a pale, delicate boy from birth and disposed to be melancholic," the court held the testimony to be relevant to the condition of the defendant's mind.[28] Indeed, virtually never does one see any attempt to restrict the sort of lay evidence which is a staple of the insanity defense —that the defendant wept, or that he was given to violent rages, or that he threatened to throw his child out the window.

Even when the evidence offered seems to fly in the very face of *M'Naghten*, it has been admitted. *State v. Carlson* is an excellent illustration because it involved evidence of lack of self-control, the principal area allegedly removed from consideration by *M'Naghten*. A medical witness was called to testify that an electroencephalograph test showed the defendant could not control his behavior. This testimony had been rejected by the trial judge because

> it appeared that . . . [the doctor] would attribute any misconduct to irresistible impulse, rather than lack of ability to distinguish between right and wrong, and only the latter is the test of insanity under Wisconsin law.

The Supreme Court of Wisconsin held that the trial court had erred:

> We are of the opinion . . . that if the offered testimony, together with other expert testimony, had sufficiently tended to prove that at the time of the offense, defendant was subject to a compulsion or irresistible impulse by

reason of the abnormality of his brain, the testimony should have been admitted. *Even under the right-wrong test, no evidence should be excluded which reasonably tends to show the mental condition of the defendant at the time of the offense* [emphasis supplied].

The reason, said the court in a later opinion, is that a defendant who can show lack of the power to control his actions may generate a reasonable doubt in the minds even of jurors applying the *M'Naghten* standard.[29] Another example of the breadth of inquiry possible under *M'Naghten* is *State v. Wolak*.[30] There the defendant had offered his criminal record into evidence as part of an effort to prove he was a "constitutional psychopath." The trial judge admitted the evidence but then charged the jury that such evidence could be considered "for the sole purpose of determining his credibility as a witness." This was reversed on appeal because a history of crime was an "essential link in the proof" of psychopathy which was, in turn, probative of the insanity defense. Yet another illustration is *State v. Foster,* in which a psychiatrist testified that the defendant showed evidence of a "psychoneurotic reaction" and "some dissociative trends"; that "even in minor disorders, one may have conditions that do render the person incapable of discriminating right from wrong and weighing a situation accurately and coming up with an accurate judgment."[31] These cases are not exceptions to the rule. The American Law Institute has reported that it found

no American case . . . where a trial court excluded evidence or refused to charge on a defense of insanity merely because the evidence in support of the defense related to neurosis or psychopathic personality or other mental disturbance rather than a psychosis.[32]

In fact, judicial statements on the matter are sometimes so sweeping as to suggest that there is no restriction on the admissibility of evidence of a defendant's behavior when "insanity" is in issue, and that "every act of the . . . [defendant's] life is relevant to the issue and admissible in evidence."[33]

There is another facet to the argument of those who claim that *M'Naghten* limits the evidence to be presented. This is the complaint that the rule places the psychiatrist in a "straitjacket"; he is allegedly required to testify in terms of a definition of "know" which is limited to formal cognition and excludes any emotional appreciation of the act and its consequences. Here again there is no such general rule.[34] Indeed, an analysis of numerous transcripts shows that the psychiatrist is regularly permitted to explain his interpretation of the words of the rule.

In *People v. Roche,* for example, Dr. Brody, a psychiatrist for the defense, testified that the dictionary defines "to know" as meaning "to perceive with full clarity." To a psychiatrist, he continued,

> mere memory of details, or recitation of what has gone on, does not necessarily imply the knowledge, the full knowledge, the ethical consequences, or the moral consequences, or full understanding of what the man is doing. . . . A child, a reasonably bright child, or a schizophrenic, may say he hit someone with a club and bled from the scalp, or even that they die, and might go so far as to say that it is wrong to do so, but unless there is a certain amount of integration of the personality, and an ability to realize with full emotional clarity the consequences of his act, psychiatrists do not feel that such rote recitation of memory implies knowing, in the full sense.

He did not "see how a schizophrenic [like Roche] can perceive with full clarity." His conclusion, therefore, was that Roche did not know right from wrong at the time of the crime.[35]

For the prosecution, Dr. Herman defined "know" as referring to "an intellectual level," "a collection of information which is reasonably pertinent to . . . average individuals."[36] In his view, Roche did know right from wrong at the time of the crime. The trial judge adopted neither construction of the critical word. Instead, he told the jury to use the "commonly accepted" meaning of "know," thereby passing to it the choice between the broad and the narrow views.[37]

Cases like *Roche* are quite common. They present to the jury both testimony that the accused "verbalizes" that it is wrong to kidnap and also that he does not know right from wrong in the "broad sense";[38] that he was "intellectually aware of the nature and social consequences of his deed" and yet lacking in "a normal emotional awareness of the impact this act might have on his own life or [that of his victim]";[39] that, in one sense, he knew what he was doing but, in another, he did not because of the "shallowness of [his] understanding . . . [and] insight";[40] or because "his judgment was blunted by the emotions and he would not bother about thinking about the effects of his acts on right or wrong."[41] The choice among the conflicting interpretations is then made by the jury, which is aided in the matter by its common sense, by counsel in their closing arguments, and by its appraisal of the experts and of the entire case.

In short, *M'Naghten* does not preclude a presentation to the jury of "the true picture of the defendant's mental condition." The source of this line of criticism, and it is a recurring one, seems to be a misunderstanding of certain aspects of the trial process. Occurrences which should be passed off as rulings on procedure are seized upon as illustrations of the baleful influence of *M'Naghten*. This becomes quite evident if we look closely at the much-discussed case of *People v. Horton.*[42] On direct examination, the defense presented several psychiatrists who were allowed to testify in the most detailed terms about the nature of defendant's mental illness—that he was schizophrenic, that his behavior was delusional, that he was "incapable of distinguishing a right from wrong." They were also permitted to explain fully their understanding of the meaning of the words of the *M'Naghten* rule. Among them was Dr. Brancale. He testified that the defendant could not be said to "know" what he was doing unless he was emotionally aware of the significance of his actions. On cross-examination the prosecutor tried to obtain affirmative answers to questions which would show the defendant to be following a "normal behavior pattern" and to be aware of the physical nature of his acts. Again and again, Brancale, anticipating the implications of his answers and assuming that they would point to the sanity of the defendant, tried to qualify his answer by referring back to his definition of the word "know." The trial judge informed him that he should confine himself to specific answers to the questions; and that any elaboration could be brought out by the defense on redirect examination. From then on, the trial judge struck portions of Brancale's answers as going beyond the scope of the questions asked. This action was affirmed by the New York Court of Appeals which pointed out that ample opportunity for exploring the full meaning of the word "know" had been provided on direct. They did not add, as they might well have done, that the defense made no effort to go into the matter once again on redirect examination.

Horton illustrates not so much the failings of *M'Naghten* as it does the abrasive effect of the adversary process, particularly when its assumptions and procedures are not clearly understood. Certainly, it cannot be used to support the view that the meaning of "know" is the narrow one, or that psychiatrists will not be permitted to explain what they understand the word to mean. The case holds no more than that the evidence must be presented in the manner dictated by existing procedural rules, which would be applicable under any test of insanity.

III

This study of the effect of *M'Naghten* on various stages of the trial process has made it apparent that the case law is hardly well developed. Nevertheless, it can safely be said that existing rules of law do not force a narrow view upon the participants at trial. Generally, trial judges do not vary the *M'Naghten* formula and the trial judge imposes no restrictive interpretation when he charges the jury. But if all this is true, the question remains: what is it about *M'Naghten* which impedes the trial of the insanity defense? If the rule had not been the center of controversy for so long, it would be tempting to answer either with an emphatic "nothing at all" or "very little." However, the attacks on *M'Naghten* have been so persistent and have come from such substantial sources that a deeper explanation must be sought.

A first clue comes from the fact that there are forces in addition to the case law which define the scope of the insanity defense. The question of responsibility is, after all, presented through an adversary process which leaves the principal initiative to the parties. Judges will not ordinarily ask for evidence which is not presented to them. They will not rule on objections which are not made. They will not tell counsel and expert how to present their positions. However confident we may be that rules of law do not deny the insanity defense to anyone suffering from serious mental illness, it hardly follows that the defense will be asserted by everyone who can qualify for it. The preconceptions of the participants may be as important as the rules of law in determining the effective scope of the defense.

The most important of these preconceptions is the operative assumption of psychiatrists and lawyers that the law regards insanity and psychosis as identical. Certainly, the trial of the insanity defense tends to revolve around the issue of psychosis.[43] In their testimony, psychiatrists often define insanity as a "psychotic reaction" and psychosis as "the medical term for insanity." A man who does not have the symptoms of psychosis (e.g. "delusional beliefs" or "hallucinations") is "for that reason . . . considered to be sane." If he is "in contact with reality," then he is "sane in our sense."[44] Even as experienced a witness as Dr. Guttmacher testified that insanity required "delusions and hallucinations" or a "melancholic illness" or a suicidal "depression."[45] As the trial takes shape, the defense tries to bring its evidence within the framework of a psychosis, the prosecution outside it. For example, in *State v. Lucas,* defense psychiatrists characterized the defendant as suffering from "basic mental retardation which is congenital and a mental disease known as schizophrenia." The prosecution's experts described him as being of "low average mentality, . . . a psychopathic personality, . . . a sex deviate and a pyromaniac."[46] In *Mullin v. State,* the defense psychiatrist found the accused to be "schizophrenic, . . . psychotic, . . . suffering from delusions and hallucinations." The state's psychiatrist testified that the accused was a "psychopathic personality."[47]

Equating insanity with psychosis has two contradictory consequences. It confirms the earlier assertion that *M'Naghten* does not limit the defense to a small group of "totally deteriorated" psychotics. At the same time, it perpetuates the view that the "lesser" mental illnesses cannot qualify. The roots of the equation are to be found in the widespread assumption among lawyers that insanity describes medical entities, and among psychiatrists that psychosis is the only such entity which satisfies the law's requirements. The misunderstanding was facilitated by the tenets of pre-Freudian psychology which tended to see mental life as divided into discrete parts. And it reflected what is still the practice in civil commitment, which is the area of law most familiar to psychiatrists.[48]

It would be misleading, however, to leave the impression that the continuing emphasis on psychosis is entirely a matter of drift. Underlying it is a more purposive element—the quite widespread feeling among psychiatrists that all psychotics *should* be regarded as insane and that *M'Naghten* restricts the defense to a small number of psychoses. Psychiatrists holding these views tend to regard the equation of insanity and psychosis as accomplishing ends which may be contrary to law but which are justified by a higher moral obligation. Adopting the equation as a private definition, they communicate the definition to no one and answer "no" to the *M'Naghten* questions even when they believe a "yes" is required. The dilemma, and the method of resolving it, is described by the Group for the Advancement of Psychiatry (GAP): The psychiatrist called upon to answer the *M'Naghten* questions finds himself compelled to sacrifice his "honesty" if "psychiatric truth" is to carry the day. He must, therefore, answer in accordance with a "tacitly understood convention" and aver that the mentally ill defendant did not know right from wrong, even when he did. The psychiatric witness, GAP continues, has little alternative:

> For suppose he answers "no"—the defendant did not know the difference between "right and wrong." Now he has given the "legal" answer which conveys the psychiatric truth; the defendant is mentally ill. Next comes the cross-examination and the psychiatrist finds that he cannot relate any vital information about the defendant without contradicting himself . . . [T]he psychiatrist learns too late that the existence of psychosis as such at the time of the offense does not automatically exempt the offender from punishment. He knows that the psychosis about which he is testifying involves a very distinct appreciation of society's judgments of "right and wrong" but finds too late that in affirming this he has answered so as to convict the defendant.[49]

The most curious feature of the GAP statement is its assumption that the psychiatrist must testify falsely in order to provide "the psychiatric truth." The fact is, as we have seen, that there is nothing in the form of the *M'Naghten* questions, or in the directions of court or counsel, which prevents the psychiatrist from answering in accordance with *his* understanding of what the questions mean. If he is asked whether a psychotic "knows" right from wrong, he may properly construe "know" as he understands the word—as including emotional as well as intellectual components, deep as well as formal comprehension. Cross-examination would then not involve him in "contradicting himself" at all but only in explaining the assumptions underlying his testimony and in matching those assumptions with others presented by the cross-examiner in his questions.

The process described by GAP tends to perpetuate the *M'Naghten* stereotype in several ways: first, it gives seemingly authoritative support to the narrow view, while at the same time calling for its rejection; second, by adopting private definitions, psychiatrists deny the courts the opportunity to provide authoritative interpretations; third, those who feel they must manipulate the process in order to participate in it tend to come away with a feeling of distaste for the insanity issue and a reluctance to become involved with it, thus reducing the pool of psychiatrists likely to testify in ways which might produce broadening interpretations.

Another source of the misunderstanding about *M'Naghten,* perhaps the most important of all, is the tendency of psychiatrists to treat *jury* rejection of the insanity defense as if it represented "the law's" affirmation of the narrow interpretation. If, for example, the jury finds a defendant guilty when there was ample evidence that he was psychotic, even that his cognition was seriously impaired, the critics have held *M'Naghten* responsible. This overlooks, of course, the fact that the jury has the *power* to decide cases for reasons which have nothing to do with the instruction on the law. Indeed, the phenomenon of jury disregard of law, sometimes amounting to nullification, is well known. The risk of such disregard is particularly great when the crime charged is a serious one, exciting a full measure of retributive and deterrent feeling. Moreover, the criticism ignores the extent to which the jury decision may be based on appraisals of the credibility of witnesses, lay and expert, who testify on opposite sides of the same issue. Finally, it does not take adequately into account the inherent difficulty of recapturing, at the time of trial, the state of mind of the accused at the time of the crime.

Even if such considerations could be eliminated or held constant, the defense would probably be rejected quite often. Jurors find it difficult to accept the idea of serious mental disorder unless it is accompanied by visible and gross psychotic symptoms—either a breakdown in intellect or the loss of self-control. In this respect, they share the reluctance of most people to concede that persons who seem very much like themselves may be seriously ill. Under such circumstances, defense counsel is understandably reluctant to assert the defense unless his client is reasonably likely to be able to persuade the jury he is insane. The problem here is that public attitudes regarding crime and mental illness limit the practical utility of the insanity defense, in whatever form it may be cast and however freely evidence may be admitted.

Two additional reasons why the case law has not challenged the stereotype of *M'Naghten* are to be found in the hard facts of trial and appellate procedure. First, if a defendant does press for an expanded definition at trial and is acquitted, the prosecution will be unable to appeal because of established doctrines of double jeopardy. The expanded interpretation will not, therefore, be brought to the attention of an appellate court and will not be recorded in an appellate opinion. Second, if the trial judge does allow considerable freedom in presenting the defense and the accused is convicted, he will have no ground for appeal.

History, psychiatric convention, public attitudes, and procedure combine to sustain a narrow view of *M'Naghten* and, in a sense, to deny the legal process the opportunity to take a broader view. The stereotyped view is so firmly established in the popular culture of the insanity defense that it has been acted upon regularly by lawyers and psychiatrists. It has been said so often that "the law" refuses to accept the "insights of modern psychology"—that the only psychotic who can qualify is one so deteriorated that he could not muster the resources to commit a serious crime—that counsel rarely see any purpose in pursuing the issue. The result has been either premature abandonment of the defense or a token presentation, supported by little or no testimony describing in detail the life history of the accused, the parts of that history which demonstrate how his responses differ from the "normal," the extent to which he has developed control, etc.

The critics of *M'Naghten* may be correct in their allegation that many defendants who are seriously ill are arbitrarily excluded from the insanity defense. But the fault lies less with the formulation of the defense than with its presentation. The responsible parties are counsel and psychiatrist who have contributed to a failure of the adversary process, allowing an unwarranted assumption of what the rule "must" mean to govern their conception of the defense.

IV

The nagging questions about *M'Naghten* will be answered only if lawyers begin to play a more aggressive role than they have in the past. Only if evidence of insanity is offered whenever defense counsel thinks his client suffered from a mental illness at the time of the crime, and then forces prosecutors to object to such evidence and trial judges to rule it admissible or inadmissible, will we know whether the rule is restrictive at the trial level. Only if a convicted defendant urges on appeal that his evidence has been improperly excluded, or that his insanity defense should have been submitted to the jury, will we know whether appellate courts approve a narrow construction. Only if lawyers proffer constructions of "mental disease" or "know" or "nature and quality"—through request for instructions, through their experts, or through their arguments to the jury—will we know authoritatively what courts intend these words to mean. It may be that when all these failures are repaired, *M'Naghten* will be a narrow rule. At present, the law does not make it one and defense counsel should make the most of the opportunities available to them to keep it from becoming one. They should present the defendant's life history in full biographical and clinical detail and have experts explain carefully not only their diagnoses but the relation of those diagnoses to the words of the rule, as they believe they should be construed. If this course is successful and is ultimately approved by the appellate courts, it would, of course, leave us a *M'Naghten* which is little more than a legal standard applied to "any" evidence of mental condition, monitored only by fairly liberal rules regarding burden of proof. But that is the *M'Naghten* we now have whenever defense counsel chooses to make it so.

On analysis, the heart of the criticism may well be *not* that the words need have a narrow construction, either as a matter of law or as a matter of psychiatry, but that they will be given such a construction; that laymen are so given to associating serious mental disease with cognitive impairment that unless they are told, explicitly and emphatically, that they are to treat the matter more broadly, they will vote their preconceptions. It would, of course, take but a word from the judge to bring home to the jury that they are required to construe "know" to include emotional as well as cognitive impairment. That word should be spoken. There is already ample authority for the courts to construe *M'Naghten* broadly—as requiring of the defendant that he have enough grasp of a total situation to appreciate the full consequences of action. Yet it would be a mistake to assume that the words of *M'Naghten* are infinitely expansible. Even the broadest of constructions is not likely to communicate sufficiently the idea that impaired control should lead to acquittal by reason of insanity.

CHAPTER FIVE

The Misnamed "Irresistible Impulse" Rule

In eighteen states and in the federal system, juries considering the insanity defense are charged first in the words of *M'Naghten* and then in the words of a test which is generally described as the "irresistible impulse" rule.[1] This rule, broadly stated, tells jurors to acquit by reason of insanity if they find the defendant had a mental disease which kept him from controlling his conduct. They are to do so even if they conclude he knew what he was doing and that it was wrong. The lineage of this rule is at least as old as that of *M'Naghten,* with which it has often in the past competed for acceptance.[2] In more recent times, however, it has been regarded as a supplement to *M'Naghten* and has rested on four assumptions: first, that there are mental diseases which impair volition or self-control, even while cognition remains relatively unimpaired; second, that the use of *M'Naghten* alone results in findings that persons suffering from such diseases are not insane; third, that the law should make the insanity defense available to persons who are unable to control their actions, just as it does to those who fit *M'Naghten;* fourth, no matter how broadly *M'Naghten* is construed, there will remain areas of serious disorder which it will not reach.

The rule enjoyed a considerable renaissance during the 1920s when psychoanalytic psychology turned to criminal law and found *M'Naghten* far too rationalistic. Emphasis on loss of control seemed much more sensible, not only because it was more "correct" psychologically but also because it comported better with the other objectives of the insanity defense. It described persons who could not respond to the threat of sanction and who would readily be perceived by others as incapable of responding, thus intruding hardly at all upon the deterrent or retributive functions of criminal law. And it marked for hospital and treatment persons who were clearly diseased, thereby serving a useful diagnostic function. The "irresistible impulse" rule was widely heralded by many lawyers and psychiatrists as the way to remedy all that was wrong with *M'Naghten*. More recently, however, in a remarkable reversal of position, the rule has been dismissed summarily by most commentators on the theory either that it adds little to *M'Naghten* ("merely a gloss"), or that it expands the insanity defense far too much, or that it is impossible to apply, or that it is without scientific basis.[3]

I

The most influential of the early cases adding the "irresistible impulse" rule to *M'Naghten* was *Parsons v. State*. After referring to the requirement that the defendant have a "disease of the mind," the court put the following questions:

> Did he know right from wrong, as applied to the particular act in question? ... If he did have such knowledge, he may nevertheless not be legally responsible if the two following conditions concur: (1) If, by reason of the duress of such mental disease, he had so far lost the *power to choose* between the right and wrong, and to avoid doing the act in question, as that his free agency was at the time destroyed; (2) and if, at the same time, the alleged crime was so connected with such mental disease, in the relation of cause and effect, as to have been the product of it *solely*.[4]

Stated more simply, insanity could be posited upon a finding that the accused either lacked the "(1) capacity of intellectual discrimination . . . [or] (2) freedom of will." Evidence was invited which might aid the jury in deciding "as matter of fact, that the disease of insanity can . . . so affect the mind as to subvert the freedom of the will, and thereby destroy the power of the victim *to choose* between the right and wrong, although he perceive it."[5] The *Parsons* doctrine became the federal rule in *Davis v. United States,* albeit in somewhat altered form.[6]

Parsons and *Davis* soon became the leading authorities in the effort to broaden *M'Naghten.* But a wide variety of formulations was used to express the central idea of loss of control. Some emphasized that the defendant's disease must have "taken his acts beyond his control," or rendered him "incapable of choosing the right and refraining from doing the wrong," or made him unable to "resist doing the wrong."[7] Others, smaller in number, introduced the word "impulse," asking whether the defendant's mind was so diseased "that his reason, conscience, and judgment" were "overwhelmed," rendering him incapable of resisting and controlling an impulse which leads to the commission of a crime; or whether "his mind and will were governed by an uncontrollable and irresistible impulse produced and growing out of mental disease."[8] Yet others profess to follow the *Parsons-Davis* rule but discuss it as if the word "impulse" were an essential part of it; or abandon entirely the effort to select from among the competing formulations, directing the jury to acquit if the defendant was "unable to control his actions *or* [his] impulses," leaving the clear impression that any one of the formulae will suffice.[9]

These variations in construction have been presented in order to demonstrate that there is no monolith called the "irresistible impulse" test. Most of the cases do not even use the phrase. It is much more accurate to describe the rules as concerned with lack of control and to use the shorthand designation "control" test (as I shall do hereafter). The phrase "irresistible impulse" is in considerable part a text-writer's caption which has gained currency through the years as it has been uncritically used to describe all the "control" tests rather than a subgroup among them. Yet, more than any other factor, the phrase has become the focus of criticism of the rule and the principal reason for finding the test inadequate. If the criticisms of the "control" rules are to be discussed sensibly, it will be necessary to separate those which assume there must be an "impulse" from the ones directed at "control" tests generally.

II

The importance of the word "impulse" lies in the fact that it is the instrument through which commentators claim a restrictive interpretation must be attached to the "control" rules. The process resembles that which has occurred under *M'Naghten* with regard to the word "know." It has been widely assumed, first, that the "control" rules require acts which are the product of an "impulse," second, that the act must be both sudden and unplanned, and third, that evidence of mental conditions which do not meet these criteria is inadmissible. The British Royal Commission on Capital Punishment has played a leading role in propagating this view. In discussing the insanity defense, the Commission rejected the "irresistible impulse" test as a substitute for *M'Naghten* because the word "impulse" carried with it "an unfortunate and misleading implication." In its view, the word suggested to the jury that the insanity defense applied only to those crimes which "have been suddenly and impulsively committed after a sharp internal conflict." The Commission noted that "in many cases, such as those of melancholia, this is not true at all . . . The criminal act in such cases may be the reverse of impulsive" and yet be the product of insanity.[10] The *Durham* court enlarged upon this position. It converted the "implication" into the flat assertion that the irresistible impulse test gave "no recognition to mental illness characterized by brooding and reflection [e.g. melancholia] and so relegates acts caused by such illness to the application of the inadequate right-wrong test."[11] This criticism has been repeated and accepted by the American Law Institute and by countless commentators.[12]

Analysis of the case law shows, however, that there is no rule of law that a planned act is insufficient—not even in the states which cast the "control" rule in terms of "irresistible impulse." Evidence of mental condition is freely admitted, even as it is under *M'Naghten;* experts are not prevented from explaining what they mean by the words of the "control" tests, though they tend here too to assume that a psychosis automatically qualifies for the defense; and the jury is *not* told that the insanity defense requires proof of sudden, un-planned action.[13] If the loss of control is attributable to "mental disease," with all the variation that phrase permits, then the defense is established.

I have already noted that most states present the rule to the jury in terms of the capacity for self-control or free choice and do not even refer to an "impulse." In such states, the words do not connote suddenness at all. Moreover, the practice makes it evident that the defense can be asserted in cases where it is clear that the crime was planned long in advance. For example, in *State v. Reidell,*[14] the defendant alleged he suffered from what appeared to be a classic case of melan-cholia. He had killed his wife and child, believing they would be better off dead, and then failed in an effort to take his own life. The trial judge described the defendant's disease to the jury in the following terms:

> There is a certain disease of the mind . . . called melan-cholia, which sometimes operates upon the power of will. Its victim, like those in the examples before given [kleptomania and mania a potu] may be entirely sound of mind in all other respects; and yet, with the knowledge of right and wrong which attends such soundness, may be unable to control his will, or resist the prompting of his disease to do what, in one having full possession of that

faculty, would be not only a wrongful, but an atrociously wicked act.[15]

It then charged the jury in the characteristically broad language of the "control" tests:

> The question for you to decide, then, is this: Was the prisoner capable of knowing, at the time he slew his wife, that his act was a wrongful one, and had he the power or control over his will to prevent him from doing it? The question is not, simply, whether one who kills another was capable, at the time, of distinguishing or knowing the difference between right and wrong with reference to his fatal act, but also whether he was then capable of controlling himself from the commission of it.[16]

If there is a narrow construction, it must exist in those jurisdictions which use the word "impulse" in charging the jury. But even in these, it is not at all clear that the word brings with it an "implication" of suddenness. No one has demonstrated empirically that jurors understand "impulse" in this particular way. Even if the demonstration were made, there would still remain the question whether the implication holds in the context of the particular cases. If it is presented as part of an instruction which also includes the *Parsons-Davis* formula, it is hardly likely that the "implication" from "impulse" will be very significant. Similarly, if jurors hear the word after they have heard a good deal of testimony about mental disease characterized by lack of control, if that testimony refers to plans long made and yet disordered, if counsel argue about it to the jury and if the judge places no prohibition on the use to which they may put such material, it is scarcely credible that the jury will feel obligated to construe the test narrowly.

Only if juries are explicitly told they must find the act to have been sudden and unplanned can the "control" tests fairly be characterized as narrow. Yet this is virtually never done. We have found only one case which says the jury is to be told that a "planned act" cannot qualify; that the act in question must be the sort which "comes upon a person rather hurriedly; it rises quickly; short of interference by a third party, it is irresistible."[17] And it is merely an opinion on a petition for habeas corpus, not on appeal from a conviction. Moreover, the evidence admitted was not restricted at all to "impulsive" behavior. Others do come close to such a standard. The military courts, for example, speak of their rule as requiring conduct which would not be inhibited even by a "policeman at the elbow" of the offender.[18] Occasionally, one finds cases which seem to impose the requirement, as in *De Jarnette v. Commonwealth,* where the court spoke of homicidal mania as if it were a paradigm of "irresistible impulse," describing it as marked by a tendency "to break out in a sudden paroxysm of violence."[19] On closer analysis, that case, and others, prove to be descriptions for the jury of the kinds of acts which will suffice in contexts which involve suddenness. They are by no means to be taken as excluding from the defense acts which are the result of plans originating in a seriously disordered mind.[20]

The situation in the "control" jurisdictions is strikingly similar to that which was found in the analysis of *M'Naghten.* While the law may not impose the requirement that an unresisted action be sudden and unplanned, the principal actors in the trial may be doing so. For example, a psychiatrist may find the defendant lacked the capacity to control his actions, but may feel that the law is only interested in sudden impulses.

The pervasiveness of this stereotype can be seen in the extent to which courts and commentators, as well as lawyers and psychiatrists, use the words "irresistible impulse" and assume the need for suddenness even in the majority of jurisdictions where the test itself is phrased solely in terms of self-control. Thus, the Royal Commission quoted passages from five so-called "irresistible impulse" jurisdictions in the United States. Yet only one of these passages contained a reference to the word "impulse."[21]

As with *M'Naghten,* words have often been assumed to have meanings fixed by law when in fact those meanings were left open, to be fixed by the testimony or by the argument of counsel or by the common sense of the jury. Participants, operating under the view that the stereotype was law, have reinforced the stereotype by providing examples of its existence. The transition from this misunderstanding of the rules to premature abandonment of the defense also parallels *M'Naghten.* If defense counsel has only the aid of a psychiatrist adhering to the narrow view, and if he is not at home in the field, he is quite likely to forgo the defense entirely, on the assumption it cannot possibly prevail. Consider, for example, the case of Dr. Wertham, who believes the defense of "irresistible impulse" is restricted entirely to obsessional-compulsive neurosis.[22] He feels such neuroses so rarely lead to serious crime that the defense is of no practical importance. Similarly, a majority of the members of the American Psychiatric Association believe the concept of irresistible impulse is not "psychiatrically and legally sound" and, therefore, presumably are reluctant to participate in trials asserting that defense. Yet 93 per cent of the members of the Group for the Advancement of Psychiatry conceded that there were cases in which offenders were "incapable of controlling . . . the impulse to commit" harm.[23]

In short, if evidence is not presented, or if experts feel themselves inhibited, or if the defense is deterred, it is not the legal formulations of the "control" tests which are at fault; rather, it is likely to be the passivity or misunderstanding of counsel and expert witnesses. Unlike *M'Naghten,* the words of most of the "control" tests are not even susceptible to restrictive interpretation.

Unquestionably, matters would be improved if a way could

be found to persuade those who participate in the trial of the insanity defense that the "control" tests are remarkably flexible. They would be improved even more if the word "impulse" could be removed from those formulations in which it now occurs, so that jurors (as well as other participants) are denied the opportunity to view the defense narrowly. If the reference to "impulse" is not deleted, the trial judge need only tell the jury that an impulse "may be the result of long periods of brooding and reflection."[24]

III

Once the "irresistible impulse" rule is seen as a group of rules inquiring broadly into the capacity of the accused to control his conduct, it would seem to solve the problems ostensibly left by *M'Naghten*. But it too has been branded as unsatisfactory by most contemporary commentators. Their reasons are varied and often inconsistent.

Professor Jerome Hall speaks for those who see the "control" tests as unnecessary if *M'Naghten* is properly construed. Starting from the premise that the human personality is integrated, he concludes that any case of impaired volition which can satisfy the "control" rule will also be marked by the failure of knowledge demanded by *M'Naghten,* provided the word "know" is given a broad construction.[25] Unfortunately, he does not tell us why it is undesirable to speak directly to the control issue. However integrated the personality may be, no one has ever suggested that illness must affect every part of it, or must affect every type of functioning in ways which mark the defendant as incapable of complying with the criminal law. It is entirely possible for a person's self-control to be impaired by illness while his rational faculties continue relatively unimpaired. It is difficult to avoid the conclusion that Hall is making exaggerated demands on the word "know." While it may undoubtedly be understood to include emotional awareness, it is probable that expanding it to include self-control would be "stretching the *M'Naghten* formula beyond the breaking point."[26]

There is another line of criticism which also starts from the assumption of an integrated personality, but uses it as a basis for an entirely different conclusion: that the "control" rules do not broaden the insanity defense enough. Professor Weihofen speaks for this view:

> Both [the *M'Naghten* and the control] tests fail to give due emphasis to the fundamental concept that the mental processes are interdependent and interrelated. Both fail particularly to provide adequate bases for judging severe psychoneurotics and others whose criminal acts seem to stem from unconscious motivation. Both fail to take account of the now-recognized fact that all persons—even the normal—are usually more influenced by their emotions than by reasoning. Although the defendant may have been conscious of only one motive, his mental attitude and his physical behavior in response to a given stimulus or situation is almost certainly the end product of a complex of psychological processes. The criminal, even more than most people, may be largely unaware of the reasons for his behavior. Of this, neither of the tests takes any cognizance whatever.[27]

In short, he is unhappy with the degree to which the two rules speak "as if" it is possible to separate the cognitive and the emotional elements of the personality. But he points to no way in which the two, in combination, are inadequate. He does not explain why the "severe psychoneurotics and others" are deterred from asserting insanity under a "control" test, even if they may be under *M'Naghten;* or why the "control" tests require that a criminal be aware "of the reasons for his behavior." Nor does he tell us of the sorts of evidence that would be excluded or the ways in which juries would be misled if they were told to apply the two tests and to construe them broadly. Weihofen's criticism is purist in tone, asking in effect that the law speak in the language of psychoanalytic psychology. Moreover, unless Weihofen takes the view that the rule is limited to sudden impulses rather than to inability to control actions, it is difficult to see why he views it as a product of an out-of-date psychology. There is nothing in the "control" tests to suggest that behavior is not "the end product of a complex of psychological processes" which include unconscious as well as conscious elements. Those tests direct the trial entirely to the effect of those forces upon the personality of the defendant and upon his ability to control his actions.

Instead of regarding the "control" tests as too restrictive, there is a third group which feels they broaden the defense far too much, making it available to psychopaths, to neurotics, perhaps to all who commit crime. This is said to follow from the impossibility of determining which acts were uncontrollable, rather than merely uncontrolled, and the attendant suspicion that the former category does not really exist; from the fact that weaknesses in self-control are to be found in most men; and from the consequent ease of asserting an inability to control one's conduct.[28] The result prophesied under a "control" test is a dramatic rise in successful insanity pleas and a marked reduction in the deterrent impact of the criminal law.

The prophecy tends to overstate the case in at least four respects. First, as to whether there is something psychiatrists can diagnose, Weihofen writes that "almost all psychiatrists" hold the view that "there are cases in which mental unsoundness results in impulsions which are largely or wholly uncontrollable." And more than ninety per cent of the members of the Group for the Advancement of Psychiatry support him in that view.[29] Second, while the issues raised by the "control" tests are hardly precise, they are not so very different from the questions of degree which arise throughout the law. Whether the issue is "control" or "knowledge" or "intent" or "negligence," it will be impossible to draw absolute lines. Third, there is no question but that a defense which is available to people who do not seem very "crazy" is probably easier to feign than one which is available only to persons who have delusions or hallucinations. But the very fact it can be feigned makes it obligatory, in a practical sense, for the defendant to present a case which will be especially persuasive. For he will have to overcome the quite natural reluctance of the jury to believe him. The defendant who cannot present the long history of uncontrolled behavior and the expert to explain its origins in disease and its consequences is not likely to be successful. In any event, it is simply untrue that there are legions of defendants waiting impatiently to assert the insanity defense and rushing in the moment the barriers are dropped. If anything, the problem is one of too few persons raising the defense—because they fear the stigma of insanity or commitment to a mental hospital or the prospect of indeterminate detention.

IV

As with *M'Naghten,* attitudes toward the "control" tests are colored by the belief that there is an "irresistible impulse" rule, that it is interpreted narrowly, that the interpretation is unchangeable and that any reforms in the insanity defense will have to be brought about by an entirely new standard of responsibility. None of these assumptions is supported by the facts. The "control" tests are sufficiently broad, and the practice under them sufficiently flexible, to encompass the widest possible range of mental conditions. At the same time, they provide a standard for relating the offender and his offense to the proper functions of the criminal law. There is a very real risk, however, that the criticism to which the "control" tests have been subjected may result in their value being underestimated and their use neglected. As in the case of *M'Naghten,* lawyers and psychiatrists may fail to see cases as appropriate for the defense, in reliance upon criteria imposed upon them by no court or legislature.

I do not mean to suggest that the "control" tests have always been well formulated or that they need no clarification. Useful work can be (and has been) done to recast the rule in contemporary language and to eliminate explicitly some of the ambiguities of phrasing. Indeed, such modernization is at the heart of some of the most widely heralded reforms of the insanity defense. An ever greater number of courts is taking the position that "the exact wording of the charge and the actual name of the test are comparatively unimportant," that the critical inquiry is whether the charge contains three "necessary elements, namely, the defendant's cognition, his volition, and his capacity to control his behavior."[30] For present purposes, however, the important point is that in the "control" tests, lawyers and reformers have available to them doctrines which reach impaired control as well as impaired cognition, which make sense to the man in the street, and which are not at all the product of an archaic psychology. Quite the contrary. They are entirely congenial to modern ego psychology.[31]

If at this late date it can still be recognized that there already exist, in a large number of jurisdictions, rules which do all or most of what the reformers are seeking, reform efforts in such jurisdictions may be directed to clarifying the rules rather than to the far more difficult task of establishing a "new rule." Even when there is no "control" test, the task of reform is likely to be easier if reliance can be placed upon doctrines of respectable lineage and relatively wide acceptance.

CHAPTER SIX

The New Rules; Insanity as Legal Standard

Efforts to "solve" the *M'Naghten* problem began almost from the date that opinion was handed down.[1] And for much of the period, reformers were pressing some form of the "control" tests upon the courts. But as soon as the tests began to gain currency, they too were found wanting. Indeed, as we have seen, the reformers may have created the very devils they were trying to exorcise—persuading generations of lawyers and psychiatrists that *M'Naghten* and the "control" tests were hopelessly inadequate. However unwarranted many of the criticisms may have been, they have led to widespread consensus among commentators that a new test of insanity is needed. In recent years, therefore, the debate has centered on which of the proposed rules would provide the best solution to the "problems" of *M'Naghten*. This debate has taken place in the case law of almost every jurisdiction and in the legislatures of many of them.

I

There was, of course, a decline in the movement for reform during the period surrounding World War II. But soon afterward, the movement revived and reached its culmination in the report of the British Royal Commission on Capital Punishment, published in 1953. The report came after protracted hearings, in the course of which the Commission listened to a great many medical and legal witnesses. There was virtual agreement among the medical men that the mind functions as an integrated whole and that it is impossible to isolate the separate functions of cognition and control.[2]

Nevertheless, most of the witnesses recommended that the *M'Naghten* rule be retained, either because no better rule could be found or because they felt that the rule was being given a broad interpretation. The Commission concluded, however, that it was unwise to rely on "interpretation" to solve the problem.[3] It recommended instead two formulations which were "preferable." The first was

> to abrogate the Rules and to leave the jury to determine whether at the time of the act the accused was suffering from disease of the mind (or mental deficiency) to such a degree that he ought not to be held responsible.[4]

As an alternative, it suggested the following:

> The jury must be satisfied that, at the time of committing the act, the accused, as a result of disease of the mind (or mental deficiency) (a) did not know the nature and quality of the act or (b) did not know that it was wrong or (c) was incapable of preventing himself from committing it.[5]

The alternative proposal was, of course, a combination of *M'Naghten* and the "control" rule. It was the first proposal, however, which excited controversy. Describing it as not a rule at all, three dissenting members argued that "the criterion of criminal responsibility . . . must be a matter of criminal law and therefore is not within the function of the jury to decide." They insisted that a standard of responsibility was necessary to limit arbitrariness on the part of the jury, to promote uniformity of decision, and to aid the jury in deciding between the conflicting testimony of the experts.[6] Even more important, though the dissenters did not make the point, the overly general standard may place too great a burden upon the jury. If the law provides no standard, members of the jury are placed in the difficult position of having to find a man responsible for no other reason than their personal

feeling about him. Whether the psyches of individual jurors
are strong enough to make that decision, or whether the "law"
should put that obligation on them, is open to serious question.
It is far easier for them to perform the role assigned to them
by legislature and courts if they know—or are able to ra-
tionalize—that their verdicts are "required" by law.

Neither of the recommendations of the Royal Commission
were adopted in England, but they played a large role in the
development of new rules in the United States. Most importantly, they tended to fix the ideology of the insanity defense as one which found *M'Naghten* and "irresistible impulse" both narrow and at odds with modern theories of how
the mind worked. Criticism which had previously seemed
suspect now became the "established" view.

DURHAM V. UNITED STATES

The influence of the Royal Commission report is manifest
in *Durham v. United States*,[7] which was the first of the
relatively contemporary cases to announce a new rule. Written by Judge Bazelon of the United States Court of Appeals
for the District of Columbia, the opinion drew upon the
report again and again as it set forth the premises which were,
in its view, forcing it to abandon the District's blend of
M'Naghten and the "control" test. The *Durham* court took
as its fundamental principle that the mind of man was a
functional unit. It followed, therefore, that if the defendant
had a mental disease, his mind could not be expected to
respond properly to threats of sanction; he was not a "fit"
object of anger and blame; and he belonged in a hospital
rather than a prison. It would be a mistake, the court reasoned,
to try to identify types of malfunctioning or groups of
symptoms which would disable a person from complying with
the criminal law because an "integrated personality" could
not be only partially diseased; and because symptom tests
would tend to freeze the law in conventional patterns and

make it difficult for psychiatric witnesses to introduce new clusters of symptoms that might be equally disabling. The test of insanity should, therefore, be quite simple. In the words of the court, "an accused is not criminally responsible if his unlawful act was the product of mental disease or mental defect."[8] The court was convinced not only that this rule was substantively sound but that it would usher in a new era of harmony between psychiatrists and lawyers. Psychiatrists would now be able to "inform the jury of the character of [the defendant's] mental disease" and juries would be "guided by wider horizons of knowledge concerning mental life."[9] Only Maine and the Virgin Islands have adopted the *Durham* rule but it has had a tremendous and continuing impact upon the course of the debate.[10]

It should be apparent from what has already been said that *Durham's* construction of *M'Naghten* and of the "control" tests was somewhat naïve. There was nothing in the law which had grown up under either rule which need have inhibited the flow of expert testimony. But inhibited it unquestionably had been. *Durham* served the important function for the District of Columbia of directing the attention of lawyers and psychiatrists to the charade which was too often being played in the trial of the insanity defense. It sounded a call to the bar and to the community to participate more fully not only in the development of the defense but also in coping with the broader problems of crime and mental illness.

The call was taken seriously, in part because *Durham* created a feeling of ferment, in part because distinguished counsel were regularly appointed to represent indigent accused in cases touching the insanity issue. Case after case presented to the court the sorts of issues which had lain dormant for a very long time. The District of Columbia became a veritable laboratory for consideration of the details of insanity, in its fullest substantive and procedural ramifications. There was far greater alertness than ever before to the de-

fendant's mental condition; pre-trial psychiatric examinations
became fairly routine; the insanity issue came to be presented
more fully; and there was a marked rise in acquittals by
reason of insanity, though there is reason to believe the rise
was the result of a redirection into the insanity defense of
individuals who had previously been held incompetent to
stand trial.[11] I shall consider here, however, only the substantive aspects, principally the manner in which the words
"mental disease" and "product" developed.

The principal criticism of *Durham* was that it, like the
Royal Commission's first proposal, was really a "non-rule." It
was said to provide the jury with no standard by which to
judge the evidence, directing it to no pathological factors
which were relevant to the law's concerns—impairment of
reason and control. The jury was seemingly left entirely
dependent upon the expert's classification of conduct as the
"product" of "mental disease." Moreover it was said that the
"product" requirement assumed a compartmentalized mind—
just as *Durham* said *M'Naghten* had done—because it implied
that mental disease "caused" some unlawful acts and not
others.[12]

The essential flaw in *Durham* was its tacit assumption
that the concept of mental disease would provide a better
framework for expert testimony than the earlier tests. Though
the opinion is by no means clear on the point, the court seems
to have assumed that mental disease and psychosis were
virtually synonymous. Many of the sources referred to by the
court made that assumption. And the court's criticisms of
both *M'Naghten* and "irresistible impulse" draw upon instances of psychoses which were assumed to fall outside the
reach of those rules.[13] The court was unwilling, however, to
equate mental disease with psychosis. It deliberately chose to
leave the phrase virtually undefined so that the insanity
defense might draw upon anything medicine could bring
to it.[14] If a psychiatrist was willing to class "emotionally

unstable personality" as "mental disease," then the issue
would pass to the jury. And the same was true of psychopathy,
sociopathy, and narcotics addiction.[15] Similarly, if a particular illness fitted the older rules, they might be given to
the jury in addition to the newer language. In practical effect,
therefore, *Durham* shifted the courtroom controversy from
the words of the insanity test to the nature of the particular
disease, leaving it to each case to explore for the jury how
that disease was related to the crime.[16] The insanity issue
was to be presented to the jury in almost colloquial form in
an effort to make it easier for the jurors to assimilate the case,
and the issue, to their own experience.

At the very time when *Durham* was decided, the concept
of mental disease was being subjected to devastating attack.
It was becoming apparent that "mental disease" is as much a
social concept as a psychiatric one, that its content is affected
by the ends for which the diagnosis is being made. As a
result, when the test cases began to come to the District of
Columbia court, raising questions as to whether psychopathy
or neurosis or narcotics addiction were mental diseases, disputes about nomenclature arose which were strikingly reminiscent of those which had previously characterized trials
under *M'Naghten*.[17] Psychiatrists for the prosecution tended
to class the defendant's behavior as not psychotic and, for that
reason, not the product of a mental disease. Those testifying
for the defense tended either to urge that it was psychotic or
the product of a lesser mental disorder which nevertheless
qualified as "mental disease." Where there was agreement on
the existence of mental disease, the controversy shifted to
"product." Was it the sort of disease which would have had
this particular crime as its product? Could it be said of any
crime that it was not the product of a mental illness then
existing? The kinds of questions asked in order to determine
whether it was the sort of disease which would produce the
crime in question were again reminiscent of those which had

been asked under the older rules. The reason was obvious. Whatever the form of words used to define the ultimate issue, it was necessary to bring them within the common experience of the jury. That experience made critical the issues of control ("did the disease make him less able to control his conduct in activity A than in activity B, so that A could be said to be a 'product' of crime while B could not?") and understanding of the nature and consequences of his acts ("did his disease make him think she was already dead?").

In 1962, the court concluded that some effort should be made to explain what was meant by "mental disease," as a guide to experts, lawyers, judges, and jurors. In *McDonald v. United States,* it said,

> neither the court nor the jury is bound by ad hoc defini-
> tions or conclusions as to what experts state is a disease
> or defect. . . . The jury should be told that a mental
> disease or defect includes any abnormal condition of the
> mind which substantially affects mental or emotional
> processes and substantially impairs behavior controls.
> The jury would consider testimony concerning the de-
> velopment, adaptation and functioning of these processes
> and controls.[18]

In short, *Durham* had traveled a remarkably circuitous path toward the conclusion that the jury needed some guidance, that words like "mental disease" and "product" were in-adequate, and that the standard would have to incorporate somehow a description of the sorts of effects of disease that were relevant to compliance with the criminal law. Those effects, inevitably, were very much like the ones which were central to the broadened *M'Naghten* and "control" tests.

The ALI Rule

Durham had been in existence for one year when the American Law Institute (ALI) made its recommendations on

insanity for its Model Penal Code. Rejecting the advice of
its psychiatric advisory committee, which endorsed *Durham,*
it adopted a test that was very much like the Royal Commission's alternative proposal. The ALI formulation provides:

> (1) A person is not responsible for criminal conduct
> if at the time of such conduct as a result of mental disease
> or defect he lacks substantial capacity either to appreciate
> the criminality of his conduct or to conform his conduct
> to the requirements of law.
> (2) As used in this Article, the terms "mental disease
> or defect" do not include an abnormality manifested
> only by repeated criminal or otherwise antisocial con-
> duct.[19]

This test is a modernized and much improved rendition of
M'Naghten and the "control" tests. It substitutes "appreciate"
for "know," thereby indicating a preference for the view that
a sane offender must be emotionally as well as intellectually
aware of the significance of his conduct. And it uses the word
"conform" instead of "control," while avoiding any reference
to the misleading words "irresistible impulse." In addition, it
requires only "substantial" incapacity, thereby eliminating
the occasional references in the older cases to "complete" or
"total" destruction of the normal capacity of the defendant.
It has been suggested, of course, that the words "substantial"
and "appreciate" are vague, that the test assumes a compartmentalized mind, that mental disease is largely undefined.[20] But the *Durham* experience has taken much of the
bite from such criticisms. It is now apparent that a precise
definition of insanity is impossible, that the effort to eliminate
functional definitions deprives the jury of an essential con-
creteness of statement and that it is entirely sensible to leave
"mental disease" undefined, at least so long as it is modified
by a statement of minimal conditions for being held to account under a system of criminal law.

The principal criticisms that have been made of the ALI proposal, apart from those who oppose adding the "control" test to *M'Naghten,* have been directed at Section 2. Some have felt it represents an inadvisable effort to bar psychopaths from the insanity defense. Others have felt the effort was advisable because it was essential to keep the defense from swallowing up the whole of criminal liability, as it might if all recidivists could qualify for the defense merely by being labeled psychopaths.[21] It is probable, however, that the effort has not been successful because psychopathy is never "manifested only by repeated criminal . . . conduct. Psychiatrists—not just mountebanks, but the most honest ones—would invariably testify that any psychopath would show some other symptom of his psychopathy, even though his antisocial conduct might be its principal outcropping."[22]

The ALI test has already been adopted in five states and two federal circuits.[23] New York has adopted the "appreciate" portion of the rule in lieu of its previous reliance on *M'Naghten.*[24] And the United States Court of Appeals for the Third Circuit has adopted a variant of the "conform" portion, as a substitute for a formula which had combined *M'Naghten* and the "control" tests. In his opinion in *United States v. Currens,* Judge Biggs placed his failure to adopt the ALI rule in toto on the fact that it made cognition too prominent and, presumably, aggravated the risk that jurors might use it to restore *M'Naghten* in the jury room.[25] By deleting it, however, he seems to have denied to jurors a ground for finding insanity when the capacity for self-control is intact but the defendant did not "appreciate the criminality of his conduct."

II

Much of the misunderstanding which has marked the criticism of the old and the new rules may be traced to the assumption that the test questions call for specific psychological facts. The critics of existing rules, believing that the wrong facts were being sought, devoted their energies to finding the "correct" questions, questions which would enable the psychiatric witness to testify fully and meaningfully. Hence, the revival in the twenties of the "control" tests and the support in more recent times for the *Durham* rule. But every new rule has brought disappointment with it. Even under *Durham*, the phrase "mental disease" has begun to look less and less medical, more and more normative, as close attention has been directed to it. And the ALI rule has already been attacked by Weihofen on the ground that it will force experts to testify "in terms of artificially isolated capacities for social conformity about which they have no special claim to knowledge."[26]

The explanation for the misunderstanding lies in the fact that the insanity test is not really intended to raise medical questions. "The law has no separate concept of a legally acceptable ailment which *per se* excuses the sufferers from criminal liability."[27] As used in criminal law, the concept of insanity has many offices to perform. First, it serves as a statement of the circumstances under which persons who commit criminal acts should be condemned. Because the law can more easily identify *why* it wants to relieve people of responsibility than *who* should be relieved, it has generally defined the class by reference to the functions of criminal law. In essence, it has asked whether the defendant is one who excites blame or compassion in the minds of reasonable men. Though it has always used the concept of mental disease as a point of departure, the central issue has been relating the medical part of the formula to the social functions which could alone justify exemption from criminal liability. It has never seemed enough merely to make the coexistence of mental disease and crime determinative—principally because mentally ill people may be as responsive to the threat of sanctions as those who are well;

and being so, entirely appropriate subjects of anger and blame. As Waelder has pointed out,

> The concept of mental disease is well-defined and beyond controversial interpretation only in a central core of the concept, i.e. with regard to such conditions in which the sense of reality is crudely impaired, and inaccessible to the corrective influence of experience—for example, when people are confused or disoriented or suffer from hallucinations or delusions. That is the case in organic psychoses, in schizophrenia, in manic-depressive psychosis. Their characterization as diseases of the mind is not open to reasonable doubt.
>
> But outside of this inner core, there is a vast fringe area of conditions which may, or may not, be considered to be diseases of the mind. Are psychopathies, psychoneuroses (like kleptomania) or perversions (like exhibitionism) diseases of the mind? . . . Whether or not a psychiatrist is willing to classify any one of these conditions as diseases of the mind depends more on his philosophy than on any factual question that can be settled by observation and reasoning.[28]

The real problem has been to find a formula that keeps the exemption closely attuned to what the public can accept. One which pushed too far ahead of such acceptance would be met with refusals of juries to apply it, just as would a formula which was too repressive. The key to the insanity defense is probably to be found in the extent to which it must serve as a bridge, for a lay jury, between medical science and the complex social objectives described in Chapter Two. This has meant that the exemption from criminal responsibility could not be stated in medical terms alone, until the public had reached a point where it was willing to pass the insanity question entirely to the psychiatrists. That the public has been unwilling to do so has been evident in the attitudes of legislators, judges, and the bar generally. The farthest they have gone in this direction has been *Durham,* but even there, the "product" requirement was introduced as a concession to traditional notions and the concept of "mental disease" unquestionably conceals competing social purposes.[29]

So long as we do not know what really "causes" crime, the insanity defense will have to be framed in a way which permits juries to express the feelings of the community on the subject of responsibility. Perhaps when there are experts who do know, the matter can be given over entirely to them, or the question can be framed for the jury in precise terms. But in the long meanwhile, we shall have to be content with a concept of insanity very much like the one we now have. That concept treats insanity as a legal standard, a loosely framed guide for a process in which particular cases are reconciled with the hard-to-state purposes of the substantive law. Those purposes are, in turn, fixed by bodies which are authorized, through a political process, to speak for the society—legislatures in some instances, courts in others, and juries ultimately. Stated another way, legislatures and courts have fixed the insanity standard in ways which enable jurors to make moral judgments about blame, but informed as much as possible by relevant fact and medical opinion. And because moral judgments are involved about matters calling for widespread acceptance by the public, it is entirely fitting that they be made by a jury. Thus viewed, the insanity test is merely the organizing principle of a process of decision which uses a "political" solution to advance subtle social objectives. It is a normative standard applied to conflicting clusters of fact and opinion by a jury, an institution which is the traditional embodiment of community morality and, therefore, well suited to determining whether a particular defendant, and his act, warrant condemnation rather than compassion.

Examination of each of the tests of insanity supports the

foregoing interpretation. Each of them proves, on careful analysis, to have evolved as a *standard,* after initial efforts to treat them as describing medical entities. This has been done by developing a pattern of accommodation which left the rules verbally unchanged but allowed evidence to come in freely under them, experts to testify freely, and gave counsel great latitude in argument to the jury. The only point in the trial process at which the insanity tests have played an important part is at the stage of instructing the jury. And even there, no effort has been made to require the jury to find some entity specifically known to psychiatry. Instead, the jury is simply told the words of *M'Naghten* or the "control" tests and asked to apply those words to the facts of the particular case. This has also happened under *Durham* and will surely happen under the ALI rule.

III

After *Durham* was decided, there was a resurgence of hope among psychiatrists, and among many others who sought the reform of criminal law, that the courts could be persuaded to abandon *M'Naghten* and/or the "control" tests. But the hope has remained largely unfulfilled. Court after court has refused to adopt the *Durham* rule, using the occasion to reaffirm its faith in "free will" and deterrence, its hostility to psychiatry and the "deterministic" view of human behavior, its skepticism about psychiatry's status as a science,[30] its fear that the concept of mental disease was so broad that it might encompass all or most serious crime, and especially the psychopath. The ALI rule has been much more successful. It has already been adopted, either by judicial decision or by statute, in several jurisdictions. And it has been recommended for adoption in several more. The success of the ALI rule is, in part, a reaction of the legal profession against the degree to which

Durham has been championed by the psychiatrists, in part a result of the widespread acceptance of the stereotyped view of *M'Naghten* and "irresistible impulse"—a view which *Durham* did a great deal to intensify. Even as recently as the *Currens* case, we find defense counsel arguing—in a jurisdiction using both *M'Naghten* and a broad "control" test—that since he had "no evidence . . . that [the defendant] did not know right from wrong," he could raise the defense only by winning adoption of the *Durham* rule. Yet the defendant had been diagnosed as a psychopathic personality with schizophrenic tendency. It finally fell to the trial judge, on his own initiative, to charge the jury under a combination of *M'Naghten* and the "control" tests. On appeal, Judge Biggs was as quick as defense counsel had been to treat the insanity defense as if it consisted only of a narrow *M'Naghten* and to plunge ahead to a "new rule."

The ALI rule will undoubtedly gain even wider acceptance as bench and bar come to think of it as a sensible "compromise" between those who endorse existing rules and those who favor the radical-appearing *Durham* rule. It is not entirely clear, however, why a new rule is necessary. Neither *M'Naghten* nor the "control" tests are as narrow as the critics would have it. Far less effort would probably be required to rehabilitate the existing rules, hopefully in combination, than to win the adoption of an entirely new one. It has long been apparent that judges, legislators, and lawyers have been reluctant to tamper with the insanity defense, perhaps because it relates to issues of great importance which they cannot quite understand. Their reluctance is reinforced by those critics of the new rules who delight in stressing how much they depart from precedent and how often they have been rejected. Pressing for an expansion of the insanity defense by broad interpretation of its words would not involve a radical departure from precedent; it would represent no more than a

continued expansion of the law within its present framework
and yet it would be an important supplement to the current
movement for reform. Such an approach has recently been
taken by a number of federal circuit courts which find any
insanity charge sufficient if it requires findings "as to three
necessary elements, namely, the defendant's cognition, his
volition and his capacity to control his behavior."[31]

It remains true, however, that the mistaken view of the
older rules is widely held, that practice has tended to conform
to stereotype and that it may be extremely difficult to rescue
them from their history. Adoption of a "new" rule may seem
to be the only practical device for restoring vitality to the insanity defense. Yet if what I have said about the processes
of proof which underlie each of the older tests is correct,
it is unlikely that the new tests will change matters very
much. It is true that they will provide a new instruction for
the jury and that such an instruction will be especially important when it adds the "control" test to *M'Naghten*. But
they will authorize the admission of no more evidence than
could have been proffered in the past; the amount of evidence
needed to carry a case to the jury will be much the same; the
problems of presenting effective expert testimony will remain.
Unless an extraordinary effort is made, lawyers will probably continue to put only conclusionary questions to experts,
usually cast in the words of the insanity test itself. And experts
will come to believe "the law" is not interested in a detailed
description of the defendant's mental state but only in the
answers to the test questions. There would seem to be no
reason why a lawyer or a judge who has in the past insisted
on testimony framed in the language of the rules will not continue to do so under the new rules. (e.g. "Did the defendant
have a mental disease?" "Was the act a product of the
disease?" "Did he appreciate the criminality of his conduct?"
"Was he able to conform his conduct to the law?") This shade
from the past is already evident even under *Durham*. In a

recent case, a defendant objected to the fact that expert testimony had been presented *only* in the form of conclusions as to whether his actions were a "product" of this disease. This led one judge to note that the court had become more a prisoner of labels than ever before, that it was still being denied the "wider horizons of knowledge" about the minds of defendants which *Durham* was to bring with it.[32]

IV

The new rules which appeared on the scene in the 1950s represented a flight from law. They swung from the extreme of abandoning the effort to frame a legal standard, giving the matter entirely to the jury, to the opposite extreme of trying to give the matter almost entirely to the psychiatrists. The first never won favor; the second has seen the medical-seeming standard shaped by an adversary system into something as much legal as medical. In reaction against both extremes, the American Law Institute resumed the effort to frame a standard which joins medical science and social purpose. Its proposal solves most of the problems generally associated with the older rules while at the same time representing the same line of historical development. As a result, it is likely to become the formula for the immediate future in the United States.

It is doubtful, however, that any of the new rules will be able to claim exclusive, or even principal, credit for a higher rate of acquittals by reason of insanity, or for more intelligent trials of the insanity defense. Those are likely to come as a result of factors much larger than any within the control of the insanity formula. It is unreasonable to assume that any legal standard, operating within the existing framework of "blame" and a jury system, can affect the situation very much. Public attitudes toward crime and mental illness inevitably limit the impact of any legal rule. Within the existing framework, however, a good deal can reasonably be expected from changes in the way the insanity issue is handled by counsel, by psychiatric witnesses, and by trial judge, and from changes in the procedures which apply after the defendant has been acquitted by reason of insanity. It is to problems of this order that attention has begun to shift in recent years—to the quite practical questions of implementing the defense and of controlling its consequences.

CHAPTER SEVEN

A Note on Expert Opinion and the Test Questions

The description of insanity as a legal standard rather than a medical fact has direct application to a technical question which has long intrigued students of the insanity defense: may the expert witness be asked the test questions—did the defendant know right from wrong, could he control his conduct, was his act the product of mental disease? If he may, is it desirable that the questions be put to him?

There is widespread agreement that an expert witness may not be asked whether the defendant was "responsible." The reason for treating the question as improper is fairly clear. Like negligence or testamentary capacity, it is felt to be a legal question which is to be answered only through a process of decision which has the jury hearing evidence, the judge giving the jury the law's definition of responsibility, and the jury applying the law to the facts. The concept of responsibility is made up so inextricably of psychiatric, legal, and moral issues that it is regarded as too complex to put to any individual. On the other hand, psychiatrists are permitted to say whether the defendant was "sane," or whether he knew right from wrong, or acted from an irresistible impulse, or whether his crime was the product of mental disease. Indeed, even a lay witness may ordinarily express opinions on sanity and, on occasion, on the test questions.[1] The usual justification is that these are matters falling within the area of a psychiatrist's special competence or a layman's special opportunity to observe over a period of time. Under this view, sanity or insanity is a condition that can be observed and described. Even when the condition has not been observed, the expert witness (albeit

not the layman) may be permitted to give his opinion upon
facts presented to him in a hypothetical question. Similarly,
questions under the *M'Naghten* or other rules are treated as if
they call for descriptions of observable entities which can be
presented to a jury in the same way as other "facts" perceived
by witnesses.

In recent years, the pervasiveness of the general practice
has tended to conceal a strong undercurrent of concern lest
the objections which have been made to testimony on "responsibility" turn out to be equally applicable to the answers
to the test questions. This concern is now beginning to be reflected in the cases, but the authorities offer little guidance on
how the matter should be resolved.

I

In *M'Naghten*, we find a statement that a medical witness,
who had not examined the accused but who was present
throughout the trial, could not give "his opinion as to the state
of the prisoner's mind at the time of the commission of the
alleged crime, or his opinion whether the prisoner was conscious, at the time of doing the act that he was acting contrary to law, or whether he was laboring under any and what
delusion at the time." The opinion left itself open to two
quite different constructions. One was that the witness would
be permitted to express such opinions if he had personally
examined the defendant, or if the facts regarding the defendant had been presented to him in a hypothetical question.
Otherwise, he would in effect be determining "the truth of the
facts deposed to, which it is for the jury to decide." The other
was that he would be permitted to answer only "questions
upon a matter of science," that opinions on the test questions
were addressed not so much to science as to the ultimate
issues of the case and these were for the jury alone.[2] Archbold
appears to have construed the opinion in the latter sense, as

did a number of the early cases. They held such questions improper because "the very points to be decided by the jury" are whether the defendant could distinguish right from wrong in doing the act charged as criminal. An expert could not be allowed to usurp the province and functions of the triers of the facts.[3]

The bulk of the cases have either supported the first construction or have found other reasons for rejecting the "ultimate issue" objection. *United States v. Guiteau,* the earliest American case on the subject, took its position squarely in favor of opinions on the test questions. In this trial of President Garfield's assassin, the court concluded:

> If a witness is competent to give his opinion as to the mental condition of the accused, he is competent to state his opinion as to the degree of capacity, or of incapacity, by reason of disorder, and whether the disorder seemed to have reached such a degree as to deprive him of the knowledge of right and wrong. That capacity or incapacity is itself a question as to the extent of the disorder, if disorder exists, and is not a conclusion to be drawn from the existence of insanity. These witnesses were competent to speak to the question of sanity or insanity, and, therefore, as to this question as to one of its degrees.[4]

The court said nothing, however, as to whether the testimony trenched too far on the jury's prerogatives, or on the judge's, which were the bases for the "ultimate issue" objection.

State v. Roselair was the first American case to deal with the "ultimate issue" objection, put explicitly in those terms. It came out on the side of *Guiteau.* The prosecution called as a witness a doctor who had personally examined the defendant several days after the homicide. The trial judge permitted him to say that the defendant "knew right from wrong, and appreciated the consequences of his acts and the nature and quality of his acts." On appeal, defendant urged "that the duty of determining whether or not the defendant could distinguish between right and wrong devolved on the jury, whose functions were erroneously usurped by permitting the medical expert to decide that question for them." The appellate court held the answer admissible because it was necessary, and useful to jurors, "to adapt the language of the [expert] witness to the understanding of men of ordinary intelligence," even when the answers "would seem almost to trench upon an issue that the jury were called upon to determine."[5]

This position has been approved by the commentators. Wigmore early concluded, somewhat too sweepingly perhaps, that "an inquiry whether . . . [the defendant] knew the difference between right and wrong, or whether his will could control his actions, would be proper." Weihofen agreed, because "to deprive the jury of . . . [the] help [of experts] is to require them to decide this crucial question solely upon their own blundering conjectures."[6] Yet Wigmore's analysis of the problem lends support to a revival of the "ultimate issue" objection, but this time based upon safeguarding the judge's function rather than the jury's. He considered questions on "responsibility" improper because they depended "upon a legal definition; . . . it would . . . [be] improper to ask for the witness' testimony without first eliminating the element of law from the question." But Wigmore did not carry his analysis to the point of considering whether the test questions might themselves involve an "element of law" which could not be eliminated.[7]

Guttmacher and Weihofen are the only major commentators who have explicitly considered the "conclusion of law" objection. Though they purport to reject the objection on the ground that "a fact question" is involved, they also assert that a psychiatrist may decline to "give an opinion in terms of knowledge of right and wrong, or of responsibility, competency, or any other legal concept which he may consider outside his own special competence."[8] The two positions are, of course, inconsistent. They represent, in a single article, both the earlier assumption that the test questions are "essentially" questions of fact falling within the range of the psychiatrist's special competence and the more recent reservations about whether they call for facts at all.

II

The operative assumption of the opinions rejecting the "ultimate issue" objection has been that the test questions call for information which a psychiatrist can supply and which will advance the jury's inquiry. Yet psychiatrists are coming increasingly to believe they are not especially competent to answer such questions. "It may be contended," noted the Group for the Advancement of Psychiatry, "that the test questions exact only medical opinion as to the right and wrong, and 'knowledge,' from the psychiatrist and that from his answers the jury formulates the verdict. This is indeed the intention, but there is no escaping the fact that the moment the psychiatrist answers the issue of 'knowledge' he has simultaneously answered to the jury on a non-medical issue of legal responsibility." By doing so, he has become invested with "the juryman's function."[9] The GAP position, however, runs deeper: the test questions call not only for facts which are dispositive of the insanity issue, but also for value judgments which the psychiatrist thinks he has no special competence to make. According to this view, the *M'Naghten* questions do not carry "a precise psychological or psychiatric meaning." "No one," says Dr. Guttmacher, "has even suggested a test or a method for measuring the specific capacity of the individual to make ethical judgments." In the great majority of cases, even when schizophrenics are involved, the psychiatrist can "do little more than conjecture." Indeed, the reason so many psychiatrists equate psychosis with irresponsibility is because they feel themselves unable to treat questions regarding knowledge of right and wrong as if they called for medical facts.[10] In the wake of these disclaimers, the view is beginning to be widely held that psychiatric testimony on the test questions should be prohibited.

It has been suggested, however, particularly by Professor Jerome Hall, that the disclaimers of competence have been carried much too far. Conceding that the issue of criminal responsibility turns on "whether the accused in fact was competent to make a moral decision," Hall insists that a thorough clinical examination provides the psychiatrist with a great deal more insight into his patient's value-system, his awareness of the consequences of his actions to himself and to others, and his ability to act on his awareness than anyone else is likely to have.[11] In this, Hall is so clearly right that one must look for deeper reasons for the effort of psychiatrists to back away from the test question. The probability is that the psychiatric disclaimers come less from a feeling of incompetence than from a deep hostility both to M'Naghten and to the imposition of criminal liability. GAP, and others, speak quite openly of defying "legal" requirements in order to communicate "psychiatric truth," of answering the test questions in accordance with a "tacit convention" which gets the result the psychiatrist thinks desirable. Moreover, in the advice to avoid "value judgments, viz., statements imputing the rightness or wrongness of behavior, of dislike, disapproval or disgust, or of defense, approval or acceptance,"[12] one senses the view that therapeutic effectiveness may ultimately be impaired if psychiatrists participate too freely in the criminal process.

Until recently, it was expected that the problems which have arisen with regard to the test questions would disappear when M'Naghten was abandoned and a new test adopted which accorded more with current psychology. The Durham rule was created, in substantial part, to frame questions which were "meaningful" to psychiatrists. Even under Durham,

however, objections have begun to arise that the test questions
—was the act a product of mental disease?—seek "conclusions
of law and represent an improper intrusion upon the jury's
province." Judge Bazelon, author of *Durham,* has warned
against permitting the psychiatrist to usurp the jury's role of
determining whether a defendant (in this case, a psychopath)
is sufficiently "mentally diseased" to relieve him of guilt.[13]

Nevertheless, lawyers continue to want to put the test
questions to psychiatrists. The most recent instance is the
proposal of the Model Penal Code, which provides that a
court-appointed psychiatrist shall report to the court, and
testify, in the language of the test of criminal responsibility.
He is to give his "opinion as to the extent, if any, to which
the capacity of the defendant to appreciate the criminality of
his conduct or to conform his conduct to the requirements of
law was impaired at the time of the criminal conduct
charged."[14] The reason, undoubtedly, is that the draftsmen
believe they have redefined the test of criminal responsibility
in terms which are psychiatrically valid or nearly so. While
recognizing more than earlier commentators that the test
questions are not entirely medical in nature, they feel the
psychiatrist can still be useful, particularly if the limits of his
competence are noted and he is permitted to testify in terms
of probabilities. Yet by requiring answers to the test questions, they have ignored the experience under *Durham* and
retreated from their general view that the test of criminal
responsibility is more normative than it is medical.

III

The essential vice of allowing the test questions is that they
tend to supplant the factual detail upon which the decision on
responsibility should ideally be based. Too often, psychiatric
testimony consists of little else, as the test questions convert
the insanity issue into what seems to be a search for something

the psychiatric witnesses can "see"—like speed or weather, some seeing it one way and some another. The issue is treated as little more than a matter of credibility: which of the witnesses is to be believed? Which of them had a better vantage point, sharper eyes, less bias, etc.? The jury is left with the impression that it must choose between the experts, because it is not told enough about the defendant's mental life to enable it to make an intelligent judgment about *him*, rather than about the psychiatric witnesses.

It is not so much that the test questions take the psychiatric witness outside the bounds of what might be useful testimony. And it is not at all that the psychiatrist's opinion "is likely so to dominate as to make him rather than the jury, the decider of responsibility."[15] Rather, it is that the conclusions are less important than the details upon which they are based. If the test questions are barred, counsel and witness will have no alternative but to present the details of the psychiatric investigation, placing the emphasis on the defendant rather than upon the psychiatrist or the legal formula. At the same time, the psychiatrist will be spared the discomfiture he feels when he is asked to speak in judgmental terms and the trial will be relieved of the bickering about the meaning of the words of the insanity defense. Given the extent to which the test questions have served as an irritant in the past and given the probability that the answers add little to the jury's understanding of the defendant and the issues, it would probably be best not to put the test questions to witnesses. There are indications from a number of courts that the law may soon reflect that position.[16]

An important consequence of barring the test questions would be that witnesses would no longer have occasion to present their differing constructions of words like "know," "nature and quality," etc. Since this has been one of the principal ways of mitigating the rigors of *M'Naghten*, compensatory steps would have to be taken in *M'Naghten* jurisdictions to assure that the present balance is maintained. This could be done in one of three ways: first, and most desirable, the trial judge could instruct the jury to construe the word "know" broadly; second, testimony could be encouraged on the nature of perception, understanding, appreciation of consequence, etc.; third, the trial judge could instruct the jurors on the several meanings, leaving the choice explicitly to them.

CHAPTER EIGHT

Pleading, Proof, and Presumptions

The direction of the argument to this point has been that the substantive law of insanity may not be as important as the procedures through which the issue is presented. Nevertheless, procedure rarely reaches the level of high drama. Its province is the gritty managerial detail through which the formal inquiry into insanity is made—the way in which the inquiry is defined, whether by the judge or the parties or both; the manner in which evidence is offered; the amount and quality of evidence which must be presented before the judge will be required to let the jury pass on the issue; and the rules for guiding the jury's deliberations.

It is impossible to understand the insanity defense in any real detail without a mastery of the structural framework surrounding it. For the most part, the structure—the procedural rules—is the same for criminal as for civil cases. The rules of evidence and the rules regarding the qualifications and obligations of judge, jury, and counsel are virtually identical. There are, however, certain respects in which criminal procedure differs from civil procedure and in which special rules have been devised for the insanity defense. The most important of these cluster around the problems of pleading, proof, and presumptions.

I

Most lawyers have little experience or education in criminal procedure. As a result, they tend to assume the criminal trial follows the civil model. That model, in the federal system

and in an increasing number of states, is a thoroughly en-
lightened one. The parties exchange documents, called pleadings, whose function is to put them on notice of the positions
each intends to take at trial. If either feels such notice is
inadequate and wishes to take the deposition of the other party
or of witnesses, or to subpoena documents, he may do so.
The operative assumption is that each party should come to
trial well prepared to develop his own position and to con-
trovert the position of his opponent. This is regarded as
sensible not only because it makes for a fuller exploration of
the issues but also because it keeps the trial moving with
relative efficiency. Since there are few surprises, there are
likely to be few interruptions of the trial while proofs are
accumulated to deal with new issues.

In criminal procedure, the situation is usually quite different. Though the initial pleading (indictment or information) is very much like the civil complaint in setting out the
nature of the charge, the defendant need file only a cursory
response. If he chooses to contest the charge, he need ordinarily do no more than plead not guilty. As a result, the exchange of pleadings will leave both the prosecutor and the
court wholly uninformed as to the nature of the defense. In
theory, they will not know whether it is to be alibi or entrapment, self-defense or insanity. If the defense should prove
to be at all complex and unanticipated by the prosecution,
a continuance may have to be sought while the prosecution
gathers rebutting evidence, with consequent inconvenience to
all concerned.

In practice, however, the prosecutor has at his disposal a
wide variety of devices by which he can learn what the defense
will be. First, he has the results of the police investigation,
often supplemented by his own. This may turn up circumstances surrounding the crime, or a psychiatric history, which
will alert him to the prospect of an insanity defense. If he
wishes to pursue the matter further, he may use the grand

jury's subpoena power to examine all those who might have knowledge of the defendant and his crime, except perhaps the defendant himself. And finally, if he is willing to assert that the accused may not be competent to stand trial, he will ordinarily be able to persuade the court to order a psychiatric examination. Indeed, since the accused is often unrepresented, or represented in name only, at these early stages, he may consent to an examination and make a court order unnecessary. The results of such examinations, though ostensibly addressed to the competency question, will tell the prosecutor a great deal about whether an insanity defense may be in the offing. Even if he does not learn of the defense through his own initiative, the prosecutor may learn of it through that of the defendant. This may occur during the "plea bargain" stage as the defendant, in hope of advantage to himself, may try to persuade the prosecutor that he has defenses which will make the prosecutor's task a difficult one. Or it may become apparent when the defendant, lacking the resources to develop an adequate defense, asks the court before trial to appoint a psychiatrist to examine him.[1]

Though these informal mechanisms tend to soften the inequality of notice afforded by the rules of pleading, their general effect is to leave to chance that the prosecution will learn of an insanity defense. This has been widely regarded as unsatisfactory, principally because the insanity issue requires considerable preparation before trial. As a result, a large number of states have enacted statutes which require the defendant to state in advance that he intends to rely upon the defense. Some require the defendant to provide, in addition, a list of witnesses to be presented on the issue, together with the substance of their testimony. If these rules of advance notice are disregarded, the defense is treated as waived: "no evidence of insanity can be introduced, no argument made, and instructions . . . need not be given." There are, of course, leavening provisions which temper the rules in practice. The failure to plead at the proper time may be excused provided there is "good cause" for doing so. Or the prosecutor may, if he wishes, consent to the belated entry of the plea.[2] Thus construed, the "special plea" procedure has been regarded as an entirely sensible way to regulate the manner in which the insanity defense might be presented.

The decisions regarding the special plea are merely particular instances of the general problem of notice in the trial process. Strict application of the notice requirement makes it far too easy for the insanity defense to be abandoned too soon by defense lawyers who come into a case late, or who do not really learn the details of a case until they are ready for trial, or who (because of inadequate discovery procedures and inadequate resources) may not learn much about the case until they hear the prosecution's witnesses. The defendant who has an insanity defense, and who wishes to assert it, should not be barred from doing so because of inadequate procedures or inadequate lawyers. The only way to assure he will not is to discard the fiction that all defendants come equally well equipped to make the decisions, and the choices, called for by procedural rules; and to adopt a liberal view of "good cause" —one which takes into account the difficulties most defendants face in obtaining counsel, in investigating their cases fully before trial, and in having their choices clearly explained to them.

An entirely different question, and a far more complex one, arises when a defendant does not wish to plead insanity and prosecutor or judge try to assert the defense on his behalf. The question is most likely to arise when the defendant seeks to plead guilty and will be discussed in conjunction with that problem. For present purposes, it is sufficient to note that the trend of the cases is that the defense may not be raised over defendant's objection.[3]

II

In the criminal trial, even where there is a special plea statute, the process of defining issues in detail does not really begin until the proofs are presented. The first step in the process is the prosecutor's opening statement to the jury. In it, he describes in outline what each of his witnesses will say and how their testimony will support the allegations of the indictment or information. He will probably not, however, say anything about the issue of insanity. That is a matter of defense which will first be raised by defense counsel in his opening statement. Increasingly, however, defendants defer their statements until the prosecution has completed its entire case. There are substantial reasons for doing so. As I noted earlier, pleadings and discovery procedure in criminal cases are so rudimentary that the defendant may not know in any detail what he must rebut until he hears the prosecution's evidence. He will not, therefore, wish to fix in the minds of jurors lines of defense which may prove unnecessary or confusing. He may also be genuinely undecided as to the defense he should pursue. If, for example, he has been in doubt as to whether he should even raise the insanity defense, he may wish to defer his decision until he sees whether the government can prove the criminal act against him.

When the government proceeds to trial, it will call witnesses to prove every element of the offense charged. If its evidence is "sufficient" to carry the case to the jury and if the defendant offers no evidence in defense, the jury will be asked to decide the case entirely on whether the allegations of the indictment have been proved beyond a reasonable doubt. It is conceivable, however, that the defense will be held to have been "raised" by testimony elicited by the prosecutor from his own witnesses, or by the defense on cross-examination, or by both in combination.[4]

The insanity issue will ordinarily have to be introduced

by the defendant, first through his opening statement and then through his evidence. Since he is under no obligation to make an opening statement, it may not become apparent that he is asserting the defense until he requests an instruction to the jury or until he begins to call witnesses testifying to the issue of mental condition. In any event, he must ultimately take the initiative in showing he was not sane because he is everywhere *presumed* to be sane.[5] The concepts which define how much he must show, and to whom, are subdivisions of the general problem of burden of proof. They distinguish between the burden of going forward with the evidence (the "production burden") and the burden of persuading the jury (the "persuasion burden").[6] Failure to carry the production burden may lead either to a directed verdict, if the issue in question is dispositive of the entire case, or to an instruction to the jury which reflects that failure. For example, if the "production burden" is on the prosecution with regard to the sanity issue, and it introduces only lay testimony to rebut the defendant's undisputed expert testimony, a judgment of acquittal by reason of insanity may be entered by the trial judge.[7] If the "production burden" is on the defense and the evidentiary situation is comparable, the trial judge is likely to submit the case to the jury rather than enter a judgment for the defendant.

In half the states, the production burden is on the defendant. He must produce enough to permit a reasonable jury to conclude that the evidence preponderates in favor of insanity. The production burden having been satisfied, he must then carry the "persuasion burden"—that is, he must convince the jury to find that the preponderance of the evidence is with him on the issue. In the other half and in the federal courts, the "production burden" is initially on the defendant but then passes to the prosecution. By introducing "some evidence" of insanity, the defendant shifts the burden to the prosecution which must then present "sufficient" evidence so that reasonable men could find the defendant sane beyond reasonable doubt. The prosecution must also carry the "persuasion burden," proving to the jury beyond a reasonable doubt that the defendant was sane.[8]

There is some dispute, in the second group of jurisdictions, whether in order to warrant a jury instruction, the defendant's evidence must raise a reasonable doubt of his sanity; or whether something less would be sufficient—e.g. "some evidence" or "slight evidence" or "any evidence."[9] A rule which shifts the "production burden" to the prosecution upon proof which would not raise a reasonable doubt leads to difficult questions. For example, if the state produces no evidence of sanity, must the trial judge enter a directed verdict of not guilty by reason of insanity? If he does not, must he submit the defense to the jury? Two cases illustrate the conflicting approaches. In *Fitts v. United States,* the defendant introduced psychiatric evidence of chronic alcoholism and of the disturbed mental condition resulting from it. He did so to prove he lacked the "necessary intent required" for the offense of interstate transportation of a stolen motor vehicle. The government rested its case without producing any evidence of sanity. The jury convicted but the appellate court reversed. It said the trial judge should have directed a verdict of not guilty by reason of insanity, though defendant made no such request and offered no evidence explicitly addressed to the issue. Once the presumption of sanity was dispelled by "some evidence," the court said, the defendant's sanity became an "essential element" to be proved by the government beyond a reasonable doubt. The failure of the government to introduce evidence of the defendant's sanity left "no factual issue for the jury" and made a judgment of acquittal inevitable.[10] *McDonald v. United States* held, on the other hand, that "It does not follow . . . that whenever there is any testimony which may be said to constitute 'some evidence' of mental disorder, the Government must present affirmative rebuttal evidence or suffer a directed verdict. A directed verdict requires not merely 'some evidence,' but proof sufficient to compel a reasonable juror to entertain a reasonable doubt." The only consequence of defendant's putting in "some evidence" is to require that the insanity defense be given to the jury with appropriate instructions.[11]

The implication of both cases is that "some evidence" will at least suffice to carry the defense to the jury. This may, in theory, result in a jury acquittal on grounds of insanity when there is not enough evidence to sustain a reasonable doubt of sanity. The cases seem content to leave the anomaly unresolved, saying only that it is for the jury to assess the weight and credibility of the evidence and whether it warrants acquittal.

Though a great deal of attention has been devoted to the rules regarding "production burden," the cases demonstrate that it does not take very much evidence to satisfy them; and that there is no discernible difference between the amount or quality of evidence demanded when the burden is on the defendant or when it is on the prosecution. Nowhere, for example, is psychiatric testimony required. Lay testimony is regarded as sufficient even when the witness is not especially familiar with the accused and testifies in the broadest of generalizations—e.g. "he seemed abnormal," or "he was in a sort of a trance." And little or no effort is made to require evidence which addresses itself to the test questions themselves. Indeed, the cases leave the strong impression that the setting in which the defense ordinarily arises—involving a serious crime with high dramatic overtones—makes judges little inclined to take the case from the jury.[12]

That is not to say, however, that the "some evidence" rule is no aid to the defendant. But the aid is more a matter of emphasis than anything which can be identified and traced. In such jurisdictions, the production burden will pass to the prosecution if anything at all is produced which points to some form of mental aberration at the time of the crime. The evidence need not even come from the defense. It may come in as part of the prosecution's case, often in connection with issues having little or nothing to do with sanity.

When "production burdens" have been satisfied, it remains for the parties to persuade the jury that the defendant is guilty or that he should be acquitted by reason of insanity. The process of persuasion will, of course, have begun with the opening statement and will have continued through the examination and cross-examination of witnesses. The jury will have heard counsel for each side promise to prove conflicting states of fact. Witnesses will have been presented in support of each version: on one side, policemen will have told how "normal" the defendant "looked" to them, employers will have described satisfactory work records, acquaintances will have spoken of adequate performance in day-to-day living; on the other, members of the defendant's family will have told of odd behavior previously kept secret of emotional problems in school and psychiatric clinic. Psychiatrists will probably have testified to entirely different inferences from the examination of the defendant and from his prior history. And before their own eyes, the jurors will have seen in the defendant an apparently rational man who asserts he was insane at some prior time.

The law offers very little assistance to the jury in resolving these issues. It leaves them very much to their own devices in appraising the conflicts in credibility, in choosing among the experts and their testimony. The little help they get comes to them at the close of the trial through the judge's instructions—those dealing with the insanity defense itself and those dealing with burden of proof and with presumptions.

The jurors are told for the first time what the definition of insanity is and who bears the risk of non-persuasion. That risk usually follows the production burden, which we have already discussed. But it is the jury which now administers the standard. In the majority of states the defendant must prove his insanity "by a preponderance of the evidence." In the others, if "some evidence" of insanity has been introduced, the prosecution must prove the defendant's sanity beyond a reasonable doubt.[13]

III

The words of the test questions apart, the jury is given surprisingly little guidance in resolving the insanity issue. Among the few efforts which have been made are those contained in the large body of law dealing with the presumptions of sanity and insanity. Instructions on the insanity defense regularly refer to the presumption of sanity. Jurors are told it is a matter of common sense to assume men are sane unless evidence is introduced to prove they are not. Yet no one can say with any confidence how many offenders are sane, or insane, when they commit their crimes. The reference to a "presumption of sanity" directs the jury to approach its task with a preliminary generalization about the very issue it must decide. This is unquestionably part of a weighting process which expresses a preference for the criminal sanction. The underlying assumption is that if errors are to be made about who is sane and who is not, they should be made in favor of sanity, and that by doing so the principles of deterrence and retribution are reinforced as often as reasonably possible.

While the presumption of sanity needs no evidence to support it, the presumption of insanity will arise, and become the subject of an instruction, only if the defendant can prove he was insane recently enough to warrant the inference that the insanity continued to the time of the crime. There are, however, some limiting conditions. In a number of states, the presumption is said to arise only if there has been an adjudication. The reference to adjudication is, of course, based on considerations of economy. A prior judicial finding makes it unnecessary to determine anew, at the time of trial, whether there was insanity in the past. Nevertheless, the requirement is much too formalistic. *McGee v. State* illustrates the ridiculous lengths to which the rule has been carried. The defendant had been diagnosed by an Army board of medical officers as suffering from "dementia praecox" (an historical term for schizophrenia) and discharged. He was then committed to a Veterans Administration Hospital for ninety days for observation and treatment. Several months later, the defendant engaged in the conduct which led to a charge of murder. At his trial, the court held he was not entitled to a charge on the presumption of continued insanity because he had not been "adjudicated a lunatic or person of unsound mind . . . by the verdict of a jury."[14] No effort was made to examine the underlying facts to determine whether they warranted an instruction on the presumption. Yet surely the critical consideration should be the existence of the requisite mental condition in the past, not the accident of an adjudication.

The central problem is whether it is reasonable to infer from the prior state of insanity that the defendant was insane at the time of the crime. The prior adjudication, for example, may have been made in a civil commitment proceeding or as part of a finding of incompetency to stand trial or in a judgment of acquittal by reason of insanity. The civil commitment adjudication decides only the questions essential to that process —as, for example, whether the defendant was then in "need of hospitalization for mental illness" or whether he constituted a danger to himself or to society. The determination of incompetency to stand trial is based upon a finding that he could not understand the nature of the proceedings or assist in his defense. Only the prior acquittal by reason of insanity deals with issues like those in the current criminal case—and then only if the insanity standard used in the earlier case is identical with the one to be used in the current case and the illnesses in the two instances were somehow related. Moreover, the prior acquittal may properly be taken as proof of a prior state of insanity only in jurisdictions which place the burden of proof on the defendant to prove he was insane. In others, the acquittal means only that the jury had a reasonable doubt about the defendant's sanity. Nevertheless, these distinctions are usually ignored.

The question whether it is reasonable to infer continued insanity is, of course, not restricted to the jurisdictions which require prior adjudications. It may arise in the others whenever there has been proof of a prior mental illness. Should the judge, for example, tell the jury the defendant is to be presumed insane at the time of the crime because he had in the past suffered from schizophrenia? The cases have usually said he must, without inquiring into whether the prior illness met the criminal law's definition of insanity or whether the prior illness and the one presently alleged are in any way related.[15]

The one limitation applied fairly consistently by both "adjudication" and "nonadjudication" jurisdictions is that the prior condition must have been "permanent" or "chronic." A "temporary," even a "recurrent," condition will not suffice. It is not at all clear, however, which forms of insanity will be deemed permanent and which temporary or recurrent. For example, proof of epileptic seizures has been held in a number of states to require that the instruction be given. Yet epileptics have long been considered competent when not in the throes of a seizure and would be among the first instances coming to mind of "recurrent" as opposed to "permanent" insanity.[16]

In some jurisdictions, special rules have been devised for something which sounds suspiciously like "recurrent" insanity: "permanent" insanity marked by "lucid intervals." Those rules follow the general pattern of tilting the procedural balance against insanity. The jury is told to presume that the offending act was committed during the lucid period.[17] There are, however, a handful of cases in which the jury is told to presume the contrary.[18] Both positions ask the jury to draw inferences which are too broad. The question on which the presumption should turn is whether *this* defendant, suffering from a disease having certain characteristics, was probably lucid at the time the crime took place. It seems absurd, for example, to use the same presumption for a prior condition of epilepsy as for advanced hebephrenic schizophrenia. The one is marked by seizures which are widely separated, allowing ample time for causative factors other than continued insanity. The other, in contrast, is characterized by so few moments of "lucidity" that the presumption of continued insanity seems an inevitable one. The problem is rendered even more complex by the fact that psychoses are so often in remission, or seem to be, particularly as the increasing use of tranquilizers makes it more probable that seriously ill people will look remarkably well. How are the presumptions to fare under such circumstances? Clearly, the "laws" of each illness will have to be used to shape the balance of probabilities.

Since the instruction on the presumption is based on a prior condition of insanity, the basis is eliminated if the defendant was cured before the crime. The issue arises most often when the defendant has been treated and then discharged from a mental hospital. If the discharge was conditional, it will be left to the trial judge to decide whether the reasons for the discharge should eliminate the presumption. He may find, for example, that the defendant was released because it was felt that exposure to society would be therapeutically desirable or because there were needier cases, or because he no longer seemed dangerous. Though all of these may bear on the presumption of continued insanity, they cannot be said to eliminate the basis for it without further inquiry. And this is generally recognized. But if the discharge was final in nature, the trial judge will usually deny the benefit of the presumption, without any further inquiry. Yet what I have said about the conditional discharge is equally applicable to the final one.[19] The absurdity of equating a final discharge with cure is dramatically apparent in the case of persons who are finally discharged because they do not return from conditional release. Many hospitals conduct no follow-up before classing such discharges as "final." As a result, a very sick man may be treated, for purposes of the presumption, as if he had been restored to sanity.

It seems quite clear, from the foregoing discussion, that the presumption of continuing insanity has developed without adequate appreciation of the variety of mental illnesses which may exist and the myriad patterns they may take. The fact of "insanity," once proved, has been taken to signify more than is warranted by either logic or psychiatry. Even when the doctrine becomes more refined, as in the case of the permanent-temporary distinction of the "lucid interval," it remains unsatisfactory. For we now know how often psychotics may be in remission—appearing temporarily insane but being permanently so, appearing "lucid" but in fact being terribly sick.

If an instruction on continued insanity is to be given at all, a more qualitative approach is needed. The language of presumption might well be used as a way of educating the jury, provided it is drawn from factors such as the characteristics of the former insanity, the relation they bear to the insanity defense, the amount of time which has elapsed between the prior insanity and the time of the offending act, and the manner in which that time was spent.

The plain fact, however, is that the presumptions of sanity and insanity have played a more important part in appellate disputations than they have in practice. The presumptions are rebuttable by other evidence, as judges regularly tell jurors. The presumption of sanity may be rebutted by evidence offered by the defendant as he tries to prove he was insane. And the presumption of insanity may as easily be rebutted by the prosecution. The rebuttal may take the form of evidence as to how the defendant behaved at or near the time of the crime; it may come through the testimony of a psychiatrist that sanity had been regained, or that the defendant was "lucid" at the time of the crime. In short, the presumptions of sanity and insanity do little more than tell the jury what common sense teaches, guiding them to inferences they would probably draw in any event. Rarely are they regarded as strong enough, without a great deal more, to support a directed verdict.

IV

From the very beginning of the trial, the tension between procedure and substance begins to be felt. Efficiency dictates that the insanity defense be pleaded long before trial; substance requires that the decision not be made before the facts are in hand. To reconcile the two, it is essential that the defendant have counsel, that counsel have time to investigate the matter fully, and that investigative and expert resources are adequate to the task at hand. If these conditions do not exist, the procedural rule may become an instrument for distorting substantive policy. It avails the defendant little that he might have had an insanity defense if he fails to raise the defense properly. The advisability of requiring a "special plea" becomes, therefore, part of the larger problem of determining whether there are institutions and resources to support it. If they are absent, the special plea may become a way of choking off a valid defense.

The question of burden of proof is an even more dramatic example of the interrelation of procedure and substance. By presuming sanity in the absence of evidence initiated by the defendant, the law weights the scales against the insanity defense. The defendant who is unrepresented by counsel, or who is inadequately represented, may well leave the issue unnoticed and untried, and "the law" will do nothing to go behind the presumption. This is done not because it is demonstrable that most offenders are sane but because judges would prefer to err on the side of a policy which imposes criminal responsibility. This same spirit moves those who are reluctant to use the presumption of insanity, or who place upon the defendant both the production burden and the persuasion burden of proving insanity.

An entirely different view of the process underlies the "some evidence" rule which, in effect, places both the production burden and the persuasion burden on the prosecution to prove sanity. It assumes that persons who commit serious crimes are probably mentally ill; that it will serve both the offender and society for such persons to be sent to a hospital without being blamed; and that if errors are to be made, they should be in the direction of the fullest exploration of the defendant's mental condition. Since the state has (or should provide) the resources to carry out the necessary investigation, it seems entirely sensible, in the light of these assumptions, that the burden of proof rest with the prosecution. A striking illustration of the link between procedure and substance is afforded by *State v. Shoffner*. In that case, the Wisconsin court held that the defendant could have the benefit of the ALI standard if he were willing to assume the burden of proof on the issue. Otherwise, the state would have to prove sanity but the standard would be *M'Naghten*.[20]

Rules regarding pleading, proof, and presumptions are only superficially "technical." Underlying their concern for order and the efficient dispatch of judicial business are policies which point the trial toward one result rather than another. The success or failure of the insanity defense, in the particular case and as an instrument of social policy, may depend in large part upon questions of pleading and burden of proof and presumptions; and, perhaps even more critically, upon whether the parties are adequately equipped to keep procedural rules from interfering with substantive policy.

Expert Witnesses and an Effective Defense; The Special Problem of the Indigent Accused

A great deal has been said in earlier chapters about the opportunities which exist in an adversary process and the frequent failure of defendants to take advantage of those opportunities. Too often, the insanity defense is not raised when it might have been or, if raised, is not presented to court and jury as it should be. There are, of course, occasions when the defense should not be raised even when it could be— but that decision should be made with full awareness of the available alternatives, not out of a feeling that there are none. Intelligent decisions cannot be made, however, unless the accused has the resources with which to make them. And those resources must be sufficient to meet the requirements of the adversary system in which the decisions will be made. That system operates on the assumption that men who are shaped by different backgrounds, value systems, personalities, and perceptual equipment are inevitably "biased." This "bias" leads the parties to present "their" witnesses, "their" versions of events, "their" theories of law—thereby making it essential that a process of correction be built into the system. Witnesses must be penetratingly cross-examined, opposing versions of events must be comprehensively presented and conflicting legal theories must be crisply propounded. The system takes its ultimate justification from a faith, reminiscent of the more recent learning about games theory and role-playing, that the flow of information and intelligence is maximized by having parties who are specially motivated at every stage to make the most of their point of view. In order for the system to work, however, the parties must be comparable in litigating resources. At a minimum, each must be represented by counsel and each must have investigative and expert aid to assure that the representation is effective.

Until recently, the problem of counsel seemed an insuperable one. Though the state was amply represented at every point in the criminal process, the accused often was not. For one thing, there was no right to counsel at all at the early, informal stages of the criminal process. For another, there was no provision for appointing counsel for the poor, who comprise the bulk of defendants, at many of the points at which the "right" to counsel was recognized, such as the preliminary hearing. And finally, the provisions for appointment which did exist were patently inadequate.

This is about to change dramatically. It is now fairly well established that there is a constitutional right to appointed counsel, in both federal and state courts, at least from the time the defendant is called upon to plead guilty or not guilty. The right to representation, and to appointment, will probably soon be recognized as well at the preliminary hearing and at every point prior thereto at which police or prosecutor comes into important contact with the accused.[1] Indeed, matters are advancing so quickly that the current focus of concern is less on the right to counsel than on implementation of the right. There is increasing disenchantment with the assigned-counsel system which has so long dominated the scene, because it ordinarily pits against prosecutor and police an inexperienced defense counsel, ill-versed in the trial of criminal cases and lacking investigative assistance. It is becoming apparent that effective representation is likely to come only from counsel who are experienced in the trial of criminal cases, or from professionalized defender systems, provided they are paid adequately for their services.[2]

Even then, however, the defense would be genuinely comparable with the prosecution only if it were equally well provided with investigators and experts. The problem is, of course, not limited to the insanity defense. The experts needed are as likely to be ballistics and handwriting specialists as psychiatrists. Whatever the need, defendants are not yet likely to be able to meet them. Law and practice regarding expert assistance for the accused are still quite rudimentary. In what follows, I shall consider the problem in the context of the insanity defense, exploring whether the aid of a psychiatrist is essential, what the nature of his participation should be, and what methods have been devised to make his services available.

I

Though the cases say again and again that expert testimony is not "essential" to raise the insanity defense, it is clear that a persuasive case is unlikely to be made on lay testimony alone. Only the grossest of aberrations are likely to be noted by such witnesses or symptoms of mental illness.[3] Moreover, the person alleging insanity is not likely to appear very aberrant at the time of trial. For at the very moment when he is trying to persuade the jury of his past "insanity," he is probably "competent to stand trial"—that is, he is sufficiently rational to understand the proceedings and to cooperate in his defense.[4] To persuade jurors that someone who behaves much as they do was insane at some prior date is incredibly difficult. In most cases, the defendant cannot possibly hope to succeed unless he can present an expert witness to bridge the gap between past unreason and present reason. This is particularly true because the prosecution will usually present its expert to describe as "normal" what defendant's laymen are characterizing as "abnormal"; the psychiatrist for the prosecution will be testifying, with a ring of authority which no layman can duplicate, that the defendant "knew right from wrong" or that he "knew the nature and quality of his act," or that he could control his conduct. In practical terms, a successful defense without expert testimony will be made only in cases so extreme, or so compelling in sympathy for the defendant, that the prosecutor is unlikely to bring them at all.

It is far easier to agree on the importance of the psychiatric witness to the defense than on the functions he should perform. Too often, it is assumed that he is needed only to examine the accused before trial and to appear as a witness at the trial.[5] Yet if the issues are to be clearly defined and developed by the parties, it will be necessary to do much more. Problems of communication between lawyer and psychiatrist will have to be met and overcome. Stereotypes will have to be dispelled, assumptions and workways explored and understood. The very first contact between lawyer and psychiatrist, the request that a mental examination be performed, provides a useful illustration. If, for example, the purpose is to ascertain competence to stand trial, different procedures may be indicated than if the purpose is to determine sanity at the time of the crime or to determine whether civil commitment is presently warranted. Moreover, the purpose of the examination will inevitably affect the length and nature of the interviews, the need for psychological and neurological tests, and what is selected from the defendant's life history—which of his school and work experiences, which of his contacts with courts and clinics.[6] Again, if the purpose is to determine insanity and the lawyer is not precise in defining the sort of information he seeks, he may get a report framed in conclusionary terms and based upon the psychiatrist's assumption that only certain psychoses can qualify. Unless each has some sense of the purpose of the examination, it will not be a satisfactory one.

Whatever the issue, the lawyer will be able to use the experts effectively only if he understands where a psychiatrist's competence ends and that of a psychologist, a neurologist, and a social worker begins. The more familiar the lawyer becomes with the point at which knowledge slides into conjecture, the more skillful he will be in examining both his own and his adversary's witnesses and the more intelligent will be his decisions about the kinds of witnesses he needs to prove or disprove various illnesses. The process is by no means an easy one. It requires familiarity with the usage of terms like "schizoid" or "paranoid," their relation to the psychoses of schizophrenia or paranoia, the distinction between an acute state and a state of remission, an understanding of the psychotic's often rational behavior, and the manner in which hallucinations and delusions differ from daydreams and firm convictions. In short, the lawyer must learn the points of genuine disagreement among psychiatrists and how much ought properly to be made of them.[7] Similarly, the experts will be useful and effective only if they understand enough about a trial and about the nature of their assignment to appreciate the role they are to play. Each must learn, for example, that his testimony is merely one stage in a series of phased presentations of material; that the objective of his testimony (and of the rules of evidence that control its presentation) is the portrayal of this defendant and his act in terms meaningful to judge or jury.

This degree of familiarity with law and psychiatry can be achieved only if the lawyer and his psychiatric expert are freely available to each other and have enough time and contact to develop a close working relationship. In such a relationship, the psychiatrist can play a very real part, not only in sharpening his own testimony but in suggesting other lines of testimony—lay and expert—and in clarifying the issues which should be explored at trial. Even legal issues are better defined when both psychiatrist and lawyer analyze rigorously what the law requires from the psychiatrist—whether, for example, the insanity defense can usefully be grounded in the concept of "mental disease," whether explicit reliance might be placed upon a concept like psychosis, etc.

If an accused is to raise an effective insanity defense, it is clear that he will need the psychiatrist as a witness. He will need his aid in determining the kinds of testimony to be elicited, the specialists to be consulted, and the areas to be explored on cross-examination of opposing psychiatrists. And he may need him as a creative contributor to the development of the law.[8]

II

The indigent accused seeking psychiatric assistance will find several patterns of case and statute law. In some states, his plea of insanity will bring into play provisions for appointment by the court of "impartial experts" to examine him without regard to his indigence. In others, he may petition the court to appoint a psychiatrist of his choice at state expense. Where there is a public defender, a fund may be available for the payment of expert witnesses. In some states several of these procedures may be available, either alternatively, or in combination.

THE GENERAL SUBPOENA POWER

In the states which have no specialized procedure,[9] and in the rest of the states as well, counsel may call as witnesses the persons who have dealt with the accused in the course of what is often an extensive psychiatric history. The accused may have been involved with school authorities, clinics, family service agencies, mental hospitals, and juvenile authorities, leaving behind him reports of psychiatrists, neurologists, clinical psychologists, and social workers. The authors of such reports need be paid no more than a nominal witness fee. In the case of the indigent, even that fee will often be paid by the state. When subpoenaed, these experts may be required to testify to the details of their relationship with the defendant, their test findings, their diagnoses, and the like.[10] This testimony may, without more, persuade judge or jury to infer from the prior history that the accused was insane at the time of the crime.

There will, however, be cases in which the time gap between the past condition and the crime is so great that a jury could not properly infer that the condition persisted. Expert testimony will be needed to show that the prior condition would ordinarily have persisted up to the time of the crime; or that the past condition, though not in itself sufficiently serious, would have deteriorated by the time of the crime. Such testimony may be obtained from a psychiatrist who is already testifying (because of his prior relationship with the accused), provided he can supply it without additional preparation. The court will, in effect, compel him to supply a spot diagnosis based upon the facts already known to him.[11] A slight variation of this approach involves putting the missing facts into evidence through other witnesses and then presenting a summary of these facts to the expert as part of a hypothetical question. If he is already a fact witness, there is some authority for requiring the expert to answer such a question.[12]

For psychiatrists who have already been involved in the life of the defendant, the time required to serve such limited additional functions is hardly an undue burden. But when the witness summoned by the defendant has had no prior contact with him, or when his prior contact does not lend itself to current use on the witness stand, the cases reach a different conclusion. They hold that such an expert need not prepare himself to testify. He need conduct no examinations, tests, or research.

Between the two extremes, there may be a middle ground which would make only limited use of the psychiatrist, without paying him. The psychiatrist who is entirely new to the case might have information regarding defendant's mental condition supplied by a hypothetical question; or he might be able to testify regarding psychiatric matters without relating them specifically to the accused; or he might be asked to attend the proceedings, listen to the evidence, and render an opinion on the basis of observations in court. Before such uses could be made of the psychiatrist under the general subpoena power, it would be necessary to expand the case law considerably. The psychiatrist who had "witnessed" the materials in his field of expertise would have to be regarded as being as much amenable to process as those who have witnessed "facts" at some time in the past.[13]

Though there are some cases which require an expert who is not a fact witness to answer hypothetical questions,[14] the more usual position restricts the use of compulsory process to the psychiatrist who is a fact witness. If he is not, the argument runs, he is merely one of too large a class of persons to have a public duty to come forward. The argument is not persuasive. If a witness were needed to testify to the weather at a particular time and place, he could hardly resist subpoena merely because he was a member of a large class. The same is true of a person testifying to another's reputation, or of an eyewitness who may have been only one of a large number who observed the event.

The real basis for the distinction between fact witnesses and others is the reluctance to impose a substantial burden on a limited class of persons, particularly when services are involved for which substantial payment is traditionally made. Yet there are at least two situations in which persons are required to make comparable sacrifices. First, in most states, lawyers may be assigned to represent indigent defendants—usually without fee, except in capital cases. They must devote considerable time in preparing and presenting the case, often paying investigative, secretarial, and other incidental expenses from their own pockets.[15] The attorney's status as an officer of the court has been said to impose upon him the obligation to aid the court, or he has been said to share in a general obligation to assist in the administration of justice.[16] Second, citizens are everywhere required to perform jury duty with little or no compensation. Such service requires not only thought and concentration for sustained periods; for many, it entails considerable loss of earnings. Yet the Supreme Court has described jury service as a duty of citizenship which "cannot be shirked on a plea of inconvenience or decreased earning power."[17]

These analogies suggest that the state's interest in resolving disputes may require that certain groups—particularly those possessed of specially useful information—donate some of their time to the administration of justice. There are, however, compelling reasons why the analogies should not be pressed to furnish psychiatric assistance through an expansion of the general subpoena power. It is not alone that lawyers bear a special responsibility for the administration of justice; or that jurors are drawn from so large a group that burdens can be distributed equitably. There are just not enough psychiatrists to support the luxury of a free market approach to the problem.[18] There are fewer than ten thousand practicing psychiatrists in the United States and they are distributed very unevenly. Of these, a relatively small proportion are dynamically oriented psychiatrists, who might well be the experts of choice for the accused. Five cities alone—New York, Chicago, Los Angeles, Boston, and Washington—account for 63 per cent of the total number of psychoanalysts. In the few urban centers where the supply might meet the demand, too many defendants might summon the services of too few psychiatrists. Though this problem might be solved administratively —for example, by creating panels to distribute the burden— the resulting system would still not be very desirable. Economic considerations apart, the psychiatrist so summoned is likely to be both hostile and grudging of his time. Indeed, this is so potent a factor that it has deprived of any force the few statutes which seem to require the expert to testify when he has no personal knowledge of the case.[19]

Clearly, the indigent accused supplied only with counsel and relying solely upon the general subpoena power is not in a position to present an effective insanity defense. Only if he has a substantial psychiatric history in the jurisdiction in which he is tried is he likely to be able to present psychiatric testimony. Even then, he may encounter problems in bringing the history up to date or in eliciting more generalized opinions. Moreover, he cannot expect any substantial commitment of time from a psychiatrist in preparing for trial.

THE IMPARTIAL EXPERT STATUTES

In thirty-one states and the District of Columbia, statutes provide for court appointment of a psychiatrist in cases involving insanity or incompetency.[20] These statutes do not turn on indigence. Their original objective was to eliminate the so-called "battle of experts" by introducing impartial experts.[21] Nevertheless, by authorizing the appointment of a psychiatrist at government expense, they may make available a witness to the defense where there would otherwise be none.

Appointment under these statutes may come when either the prosecutor, the court, or the defense asserts that the defendant is not competent to stand trial. Or it may come when the accused interposes the insanity defense.[22] In either event, two types of examination procedures may come into play. The first involves commitment to a mental hospital, the second, designation by the court of a psychiatrist to examine the accused either in the jail or in his office or in a court clinic. Whichever one is used (and in some places both are available), the examination is ordinarily made by a psychiatrist employed by the government, either because the statutes require it or because a government psychiatrist is the only one available.[23]

Typically, the statutes contain no statement of minimum qualifications for the examiner. Either state hospital personnel will be used or the examiner will be selected by the judge, assisted by suggestions from counsel or by lists prepared in cooperation with the local medical association. Nor is any detail provided as to the kind of examination to be conducted. The judge is neither obligated, nor likely, to instruct the expert on the questions his examination should prepare him to answer. At most, the applicable test of competency or responsibility will be explained.[24] The duration of the examinations outside hospitals may vary from one-half hour to twelve hours. In mental hospitals, the commitment period ranges from thirty to ninety days, but this tells little about the proportion of that period actually devoted to examination of the accused. When the examination is completed, reports must be made and copies furnished to the court, the prosecution, and defense counsel. Again little or no guidance is given by the courts as to what the reports should contain.[25] And for the most part, only conclusions are presented.

None of the statutes makes any provision for psychiatric assistance to the defendant in preparing his defense before trial.[26] Their entire concern is with having the accused examined for the purpose of testimony at trial. This last may prove to be quite enough, if the court-appointed expert supports the defense. But if he should support the prosecutor's case, then the indigent accused will remain without any psychiatrist to bolster his defense. Indeed, he may be worse off since the prosecution may now have as witnesses both the "impartial" expert and its own psychiatrist.

The "impartial expert" procedure is, of course, not restricted to cases involving the indigent. It must, therefore, be appraised in order to determine whether it is generally useful, even if only incidentally and occasionally beneficial to the indigent accused. The most important and dramatic feature of the procedure is the added credibility which accrues to the "impartial" expert appointed by the court. Judge and jury tend to believe him. Prosecutors dismiss proceedings and defense counsel forego reliance on the insanity defense in accordance with his opinion. Indeed, advocates of the procedure rely heavily upon this very fact in arguing it is needed to correct the "partisan" battle of experts.*

If this added credibility coincided with an added ability to present the "truth," it would be difficult to reject the method which produced it. The impartial expert does not, however, bring "truth" with him. Certainly, the fact that he is not paid by the parties would hardly seem to warrant attaching additional weight to his testimony. There is no evidence to suggest that the ethics of the profession are so low or psychiatrists' incomes so inadequate. Nor is there very much to the more sophisticated justification—that a court-appointed expert's judgment would not be clouded by identification with one of two adversaries. The testimony of all witnesses is subject to the very same process of distortion. It hardly seems reasonable to insulate from the adversary process the psychiatrist, who is perhaps the one among them who has been trained to minimize the effect of identification upon his perception and judgment.[28]

An impartial expert, and the added credibility he brings with him, could be justified only if there was a high degree of consensus among psychiatrists on the answers to questions likely to arise in the courtroom, on the qualifications of persons competent to present such answers and on the techniques to be used at the various stages of examination. No such consensus can be said to exist.

The court-appointed expert may not be a qualified psychiatrist at all. Under many statutes, courts are free to choose *any* physician and they often do, without regard to whether he has had special training or experience in psychiatry, because psychiatrists are in short supply. Even when the ex-

*Though most statutes do not explicitly provide for designating the witness as court appointed, such designation occurs virtually everywhere. Responses to questionnaires indicate that court-appointed experts rarely have to testify at trial because their reports tend to be taken as conclusive. And in almost all contested cases, the fact-finders agreed with the court's expert.[27]

amination is to be conducted by a mental hospital, the short-
age of personnel is so serious that the examination may be
administered by staff psychiatrists who either lack experience
or who are not certified by the appropriate professional
board.[29]

So far as disagreements among psychiatrists are concerned,
there is little or no prospect that they will disappear unless
they are masked over. The so-called "battle of experts" arises
because psychiatrists' diagnoses and testimony reflect the work
ways, the value systems, and the tenets of differing schools
of psychiatry.[30] The organically oriented psychiatrist will
often find himself eliciting and reading a patient's history and
symptoms differently from the dynamically oriented psychiatrist. What is psychosis to one may be neurosis to another,
what some call psychopathy may be interpreted by others as a
failure of communication between a psychiatrist of a high
social class and an offender from the lower rungs of society.[31]
With the best will in the world, the testimony of each cannot
represent more than a series of estimates drawn from various
clues—some from the patient's life history, some from his per-
formances in clinical tests, some from the nature of the situation in which he found himself on the occasion in question.
These estimates will then become the basis for inferences
about a defendant who will almost invariably present a
borderline case. For the jury will probably be deciding long
after the offense, whether a psychotic who is often rational
was not rational on a given date, and whether the act in
question can properly be traced to his illness. In short, the
nature of the usual situation is such that disagreement is
to be expected and is quite proper.

If a rational appraisal is to be made of the testimony of any
psychiatrist, whatever his persuasion and whether he is "partial" or "impartial," a great deal should be known about the
methods he used to arrive at his conclusions, the kinds of
evidence upon which he relied, the techniques he used to

elicit it and to test its accuracy. Yet these factors will remain unknown to the jury unless defense counsel is able to elicit them on cross-examination or to present his own expert. Differences which may exist among the "impartial" examining physicians are not likely to be brought to light. And it is rare indeed for hospital reports to present the minority views which may have been held by some members of the staff.[32]

It may be suggested that there is no need to scrap the impartial expert in order to insure that these matters will be aired. Why not build disagreement into a board of experts? Why not, for example, authorize the defendant to name one of the psychiatrists to serve on such a board? This already occurs in several states. In Ohio, the defendant is examined by two government psychiatrists employed by a court clinic, but he may have a psychiatrist of his choice appointed to the examining commission. In Connecticut, judges appoint an examining board made up of two or three psychiatrists and often choose them upon recommendations from the state's attorney and defense counsel.[33] Such a procedure would seem to give the defendant all the benefits he could receive from appointment of the witness as his own, except that the expert he designates may not support his defense. It is hardly arguable, however, that he should have experts appointed at government expense until one takes the position he wants. Nevertheless, problems remain. If the board consists of nominees of the prosecution, the defense, and the court, the "court" expert is likely to prevail because only he will seem to be "impartial." If there are only two members, one for the prosecution and one for the defense, controversy may take place within the board. But because the board would examine and deliberate together and perhaps even file a joint report, much of the disagreement now aired in the "battle of experts" would be muted. The factual issues and normative problems calling most for decision by a jury would be screened out by the board before they ever reached the jury.

The impartial expert procedure is especially unsatisfactory when it is seen against the backdrop of an adversary system. For the affluent defendant, it places the imprimatur of impartiality upon a witness who is all too likely to testify against him. For the indigent, there is not even the comfort that he will have available the resources with which to place the testimony in proper perspective. Without his own expert to aid him—before and during trial—he will have to rely entirely on challenging the professional standing of the impartial experts, their competence, the thoroughness of their examination, and the bona fides of their impartiality. However artfully these devices may be used, they are not as likely to assure him of an effective defense as would his own expert.[34]

SUBSIDIZING THE DEFENSE

Though courts have on occasion asserted an inherent power to appoint a psychiatrist for the accused and have him paid by the state, the more common view is that defense experts will not be paid.[35] There are, however, a number of statutory patterns which deal explicitly with the problem or which may be used in an attempt to meet the need.

Most common are the statutes which provide for state compensation to witnesses called by an indigent accused. They usually refer merely to "witnesses," leaving for decision whether expert witnesses may be paid expert fees.[36] Unfortunately, there is virtually no appellate case law on the question. But at the trial level, these statutes have been construed broadly. In at least seven of the ten states having such legislation, judges and court clerks frequently pay more than the ordinary witness fee to experts.[37]

Only a handful of states have statutes directed to the problem of state payment for expert aid.[38] Their objective is to deal with "what is a matter of common knowledge, that upon the trial of certain issues, such as insanity or forgery, experts are often necessary both for prosecution and for defense . . . [A] defendant may be at an unfair disadvantage if he is unable because of poverty to parry by his own witnesses the thrusts of those against him."[39] Rhode Island, for example, has a statute providing that "In criminal cases in the discretion of the court, on the request of the defendant, expert witnesses may be furnished for the defendant at the expense of the state, on such terms and conditions as may be prescribed by the court." On motion of the defendant, the court will appoint a psychiatrist selected by the state and pay him $100 for an examination and $100 for each day of testimony.[40] California's statute and practice are similar. New York's, however, is much more restrictive. It is applicable only to capital cases and limits both the number of experts the accused may use and the amount which may be expended.[41] In a few states, general provisions for reimbursement of assigned counsel for expenses incurred in conducting the defense are sometimes construed to authorize reimbursement for funds spent on experts. In Massachusetts, defense requests for appointment of a psychiatrist in capital cases are routinely granted under such a provision. Recently, Congress has entered the field with a carefully drawn statute for the federal courts which makes provision for "investigative, expert, and other services necessary to an adequate defense."[42]

These statutory schemes are an attempt to work within and to subsidize the adversary process. They exist alongside the system of assigned counsel or public defender or private legal aid and may be used by any of these in the effort to provide an effective defense. But they are not adequate. In most cases, permission to hire an expert must be obtained from the court, but only upon a showing of special need; sums requested may be pared down; counsel may be required to justify in advance his pursuit of avenues of cross-examination and defense. The statutes leave unsettled the kinds of services which the defense may obtain from a psychiatrist and the extent to which other specialists may be used; they leave to the court the determination of the expert's fees on a case-by-case basis. In

short, they involve the court entirely too much in what should
be defense counsel's business, keeping him from having
assistance at the moment the need arises. In a small number
of cities, these problems are met through providing the public
defender or legal aid agency with appropriations large enough
so that they can go their own way. Instead of the petition to
the court for subsidy in each case, funds are provided annually
and investigative or expert assistance is obtained as needed.[43]
In such places, the defense office is as independent of the court
and as free to control its operations as the office of the
prosecution.

III

Neither the legislatures nor the bar have been very en-
ergetic in assuring an effective defense to persons accused of
crime. Nor, for that matter, have the state courts. It was not
until the Supreme Court turned its attention to criminal
procedure that the winds of change began to blow. In one area
after another, the court has imposed upon the states the
obligation to raise their standards. As a result, the processes
of criminal justice are evolving from a relatively "pure" adversary system that leaves state and accused unequal to one
that recognizes public responsibility for all facets of the
administration of criminal justice. This evolution began with
judicial insistence that the prosecution assume a divided role,
not only as adversary party but also as protector of the
processes of justice. It gathered momentum with increasing
recognition by judges that they too had an obligation to
assure a fair trial, particularly in criminal cases. But it has not
resulted in anything like the European experience, where
the state's interest in every aspect of the trial has often led to
oppression. Instead, a creative accommodation has occurred
in which the adversary trial is retained but in which the system's ultimate function is not lost. Decisions dealing with the
right to counsel, appeals by the indigent, and discovery are
particular instances of such accommodation. Still largely

unresolved, however, is the extent to which the state should assure to those it prosecutes, particularly the indigent, the opportunity to present the fullest possible defense. It was to be expected, however, that the currents of change would eventually be channeled to the indigent accused seeking expert aid.

The problem was first considered in *McGarty v. O'Brien* and *United States ex rel. Smith v. Baldi,* both of which involved examinations by court-appointed psychiatrists.[44] Defendants in both cases claimed that the denial of a psychiatrist of their own choice, paid by the state, deprived them of the "fair trial" guaranteed by the fourteenth amendment. In rejecting defendant's claim, the *Baldi* majority held there was no right "to receive at public expense all the collateral assistance needed to make" a defense. Such a principle, once established, would extend not only "to psychiatric consultation ... [but also] to consultation with ballistics experts, chemists, engineers, biologists, or any type of expert whose help in a particular case might be relevant." The dissenting judges, on the other hand, refused to class psychiatric assistance as "collateral." "[If] ... there are grave indicia of mental disease, and it appears as well that counsel cannot prepare his client's case properly without the aid of a psychiatrist, one must be appointed by the court if due process is to be had."[45]

The court in *McGarty* took a more moderate position. Decisions would have to be made on a case-by-case basis to determine "how far the state, having the obligation to afford to the accused a fair trial, a fair opportunity to make his defense, is required under the due process clause to minimize this disadvantage [of not having his own psychiatrist]." In the case before it, the court found a system of examination by a state psychiatrist to be constitutionally adequate. The state has no "constitutional obligation to promote ... a battle of experts by supplying defense counsel with funds wherewith to hunt for other experts who may be willing, as witnesses for the defense, to offer the opinion that the accused is criminally insane."[46]

Five years after *Baldi* and *McGarty,* the Supreme Court decided *Griffin v. Illinois.* The court held that an indigent defendant, seeking to perfect an appeal, had been deprived of equal protection of the laws when he was denied a transcript of his trial without charge. According to Justice Black, speaking for the court, "There can be no equal justice where the kind of trial a man gets depends on the amount of money he has."[47] *Griffin* undercut sharply the earlier positions. *McGarty* and *Baldi* had dealt more with due process than with equal protection, more with minimal standards of fairness than with assuring the poor "the kind of trial" a wealthy man gets. With the shift in emphasis to equal protection, the existence of a procedure for court appointment, so crucial to the earlier cases, becomes less determinative of the issue. Such a procedure cannot assure substantial equality in presenting the insanity defense. The indigent defendant remains without "his" psychiatrist to assist him in preparing and trying his case. And he may remain without the psychiatrist whose orientation will make the issue appear to the jury to be a substantial one. Yet these are clearly available to persons of means.[48]

Though the principle underlying *Griffin* has not yet been applied to an indigent accused asserting a right to expert assistance, the mood of the times makes it probable that it soon will be done. The legislatures, bar associations, and foundations are already pressing toward a day when the state, either directly or through subsidy, will assume the obligation of assuring an effective defense, and are considering the manner in which the obligation should ideally be fulfilled. Most recently, the Federal Office of Economic Opportunity has begun to encourage legal services programs and the report of the President's Commission on Law Enforcement has given important emphasis to the problem. At the present time, however, counsel representing the indigent accused still finds a patchwork of procedures upon which to draw in his effort to present an adequate defense.

PART III

Competing Themes

CHAPTER TEN

Acquittal as Preventive Detention: The Problem of Release

In Part II, the insanity defense was discussed on its own terms, as if it were indeed a defense and a defendant would be well served if he could persuade a jury to accept it. But the most conspicuous fact about insanity is its last-ditch quality. It is ordinarily asserted when no other course is open. In this Part, I shall consider, first, the principal reason for this phenomenon, the fact that an acquittal by reason of insanity is not an acquittal at all because in most instances it brings no freedom with it. I shall then examine the processes and defenses which compete with insanity for the mentally ill offender.

I

In at least twelve states, acquittal by reason of insanity is followed by mandatory commitment to a mental hospital. In most others, the trial judge (or a jury) must determine whether the acquitted defendant is presently in need of commitment and may, in discharging this function, commit the defendant for a limited period for observation and diagnosis. In the remaining handful of jurisdictions where no explicit provision is made for commitment within the criminal process, the prosecutor will consider whether to initiate civil commitment proceedings. The place of confinement is usually a mental hospital and most often, a maximum security unit within it.[1] In virtually all jurisdictions, the jurors are told nothing at all about the prospect of commitment or release following upon an acquittal by reason of insanity, just as they are told nothing about the sentences which may follow upon a guilty verdict. Yet the issue unquestionably nags when the insanity defense is under consideration. Unless told otherwise, the jury may be under the impression that it is being asked to release a man who has established both his incapacity and his dangerousness. Only in the District of Columbia, however, is the trial judge required to eliminate the ambiguity and tell the jury that there will be a commitment and release process administered by court and mental hospital. In a small number of other jurisdictions, the trial judge may advise the jury of these details if he chooses to do so.[2]

The operative assumption of the post-trial commitment procedures, whether mandatory or discretionary, is that the trial of the insanity defense has established something about the defendant which marks him as someone who must be, or probably should be, kept in custody. In practical terms, he is treated as if the crime had been proved against him, as if he had been proved insane at the time of the crime and as if the insanity continued to the time of disposition after trial. In the mandatory commitment jurisdictions, these assumptions present difficult problems for legal theory. For one thing, there is ordinarily no explicit finding by the jury that the defendant would have been guilty of the crime but for the insanity.[3] For another, in half the states, an acquittal by reason of insanity does not mean that the defendant was proved insane. It means only that there was a reasonable doubt on the question. Even in jurisdictions where the defendant must prove his insanity to win acquittal, the presumption of continuity is applied across the board without regard to whether the insanity was of the sort which is likely to have continued. The inflexibility of the presumption is made dramatically evident by the fact that the defendant who has just won his acquittal is presumably competent to stand trial and, therefore, at least superficially "sane."[4]

In the "discretionary" jurisdictions, the operative assumptions are entirely sensible bases for holding what is, in effect, a civil commitment hearing. The finding of "not guilty by reason of insanity" becomes a trigger for determining whether the defendant is still insane and whether discharging him would be dangerous to the public. And, in most cases, commitment is ordered, almost certainly for diagnosis and usually for treatment as well. Operationally, therefore, commitment practice in the "discretionary" jurisdictions tends to assume a mandatory form.

Several justifications are offered for some form of commitment procedure. Perhaps the most common one is that society would find it too upsetting to see a man released who had only recently committed a seriously harmful act; that some incubation period is necessary to allow time for public outrage to be dissipated, particularly in the kinds of cases which involve the insanity defense. An element of prediction is also involved. Legal niceties aside, the acquitted defendant has probably not only demonstrated his inability to conform; the fact that such inability is attributable to mental disease justifies the prediction, at least for preliminary and limited purposes, that the disease may render him unable to conform in the future. Finally, the fact of mental disease provides an apparent cause for the misconduct and a hope that the cause can be eliminated by treating and curing the disease. In addition to these entirely sensible reasons for some form of commitment, there are two others which are of dubious validity but which are nevertheless widely held: there is the feeling, first, that the threat of commitment may deter spurious claims of insanity; and second, that a bit of punishment (in the form of commitment) might not be such a bad thing, even for the insane offender.

Despite the many reasons offered for commitment, the dominant mood, after an acquittal by reason of insanity, is one which regards the offender as mentally ill and in need of treatment. The form such treatment has traditionally taken has been commitment to a mental hospital for a wholly indeterminate period. The issue of blame having been eliminated, there no longer seems to be any need for a fixed sentence reflecting either the gravity of the harm or the outrage of the victim. The sole concern is now said to be therapeutic. The erstwhile defendant, now patient, will be released as soon as he has recovered and is safe to be at large.

II

The critical issue is not so much that of commitment but that of release. The manner in which it is handled determines whether the commitment is entirely therapeutic, whether it is an elaborate mask for preventive detention, or whether it is an awkward accommodation of the two objectives.

Some of the defendants committed to mental hospitals under mandatory commitment statutes may qualify for release almost at once. The crimes charged against them may have occurred long ago; and the fact that they were competent to stand trial is at least one indication that they may no longer be insane. Others will enter upon a course of treatment within the hospital which may make them candidates for early release. And others are likely to remain in the hospital for an extended period. Whether they will fall in one or the other of these categories will depend not only upon the kinds of diseases from which they suffer but also upon the institutions in which they find themselves and the standards set by the law for determining whether they are to be released.

Generally, the hospital administrator, aided by whatever administrative procedures he may devise, decides when the indeterminate commitment will come to a close. In some places, his decision to release the patient will have to be approved by the court before he can carry it out. But for the most part, such approval is unnecessary. The decision may

be initiated by the administration itself or it may come by
way of response to a petition for release.[5]

STANDARDS FOR RELEASE

The standards governing both the administrative and the
judicial decisions whether or not to release the patient fall
into four groups, each of which addresses itself differently to
the pervasive themes of sanity and danger: (1) Is the patient
sane? (2) Is he dangerous? (3) Is he sane *and* not dangerous?
(4) Is he sane *or* not dangerous?

Sanity[6]

The particular formulations vary. Some ask whether the applicant is no longer mentally ill, or whether he is cured, or
restored to sanity. Others ask whether he is "entirely and
permanently recovered," or whether he has recovered "sufficiently . . . to be released," or whether a recurrence of insanity
is improbable, or whether he is sane and unjustly deprived of
his liberty.

When the word "sanity" is used alone, there is virtually
nothing to explain it: whether, for example, it requires cure;
And cure of what—the condition which led to acquittal under
M'Naghten or some other illness? If the patient is psychotic,
but the disease is in remission, will he qualify for release?
What if the hospital finds him to be a psychopath or a neurotic? And how "complete" or "permanent" must his recovery
be?

Some of the statutes address themselves to one or the other
of these problems but rarely to enough of them to eliminate a
pervasive ambiguity. For example, Maryland authorizes release for temporary as well as permanent recovery. But it
provides no guide for determining what the patient must have
recovered from. Kentucky says he must have "recovered" but
fails to identify whether he must be cured of the condition
which led to his insanity defense or of mental illness generally.[7]

Whatever the statutory formulae, they are usually broad enough to allow administrators free rein in the first instance and to give reviewing courts little guidance. Judicial decisions appear to be made on an ad hoc basis, with little pattern or trend discernible. Most significantly, the cases tell us little or nothing about the role of the patient's dangerousness in the administration of the sanity standard. When it is discussed, it is treated simply as part of the issue of mental condition and not as an independent ground for denying release.

Dangerousness[8]

The second group of statutes makes no reference whatever to "sanity" or to the mental condition of the patient. They ask only whether continued detention is necessary for the safety of the patient or the public. The patient who is not dangerous is to be released, even if he is mentally ill. Conversely, release will be denied to a person who is not mentally ill if he is regarded as dangerous. In these jurisdictions, the therapeutic basis for the commitment is virtually abandoned and its roots in preventive detention are made most explicit.

Though dangerousness seems, on its face, to be more susceptible to definition than "recovery" or "sanity"—because it carries with it the implication of objectively identifiable wrongdoing—it proves on reflection to be almost as ambiguous. The ambiguity comes not only from the fact that a prediction is involved. The concept of "dangerous behavior" is itself incredibly vague. Professors J. Goldstein and Katz have suggested that the concept may be construed to include: (1) only the crime for which the insanity defense was successfully raised; (2) all crimes; (3) only felonious crimes; (4) only crimes for which a given maximum sentence or more is authorized; (5) only crimes categorized as violent; (6) only crimes categorized as harmful, physical or psychological, reparable or irreparable, to the victim; (7) any conduct, even if not labeled criminal, categorized as violent, harmful, or threatening; (8) any conduct which may produce violent retaliatory acts; (9) any physical violence toward oneself; (10) any combination of these.[9]

Despite the variety of meanings which may be given to the word "dangerous," the cases have addressed themselves to it hardly at all. Even the Model Penal Code, which uses the concept in its section on release, fails to define it either in its proposed statute or in the Comments.[10] Only the District of Columbia court (which uses a standard combining sanity *and* dangerousness) has dealt with the matter in any detail. Judge Fahy has suggested, in a concurring opinion, that the question of dangerousness should turn upon the nature of the offense with which the defendant was originally charged. Under this view, continued confinement would depend on whether release posed "a danger comparable to the seriousness of the offense of which the committed person was acquitted. And if that offense is of a nonviolent character a more lenient approach to the question of danger is in order."[11] Judge Fahy does not, however, provide any further guidelines. Nor does he address himself to the situation where the patient was originally convicted of a minor offense and is now likely to commit a more serious crime. In any event, his suggestion was rejected by the court in *Overholser v. Russell,* which involved the nonviolent crime of writing false checks. Said the court,

> The danger to the public need not be possible physical violence or a crime of violence. It is enough if there is competent evidence that he may commit any criminal act, for any such act will injure others and will expose the person to arrest, trial and conviction. There is always the additional possible danger—not to be discounted even if remote—that a non-violent criminal act may expose the perpetrator to violent retaliatory acts by the victim of the crime.[12]

Sanity and Danger; Sanity or Danger

In several states, release will be ordered only if the applicant is both sane and not dangerous. The formulations vary but they all reflect a combination of the two themes we have already considered. The patient is to remain in custody if he is (a) sane but dangerous or (b) insane but not dangerous.[13]

Finally, some states make release depend upon proof of either sanity *or* lack of dangerousness. A dangerous person can compel his release, provided he is sane; an insane one may win release if he is not dangerous.[14] This last group of statutes builds on one of the two sets of assumptions. The first is that the sane person will not be dangerous while the insane one probably will be, unless he can prove the contrary. The second is that only persons who are both dangerous and insane should be subjected to continued confinement.

CONDITIONAL RELEASE

In two thirds of the states provision exists for releasing the patient conditionally, in accordance with procedures very much like those described above.[15] No statutory limit is ordinarily placed on the conditions which may be imposed, so that they may be fixed by the hospital superintendent, the court, or both. This intermediate device, which resembles parole, seems to make the decision on release a less critical one because, in theory, some control may be kept over the patient while he adjusts to life outside the hospital setting. If he should violate the conditions imposed, he may be brought back into custody.

The conditional release procedures do not, however, bring with them any refinement of release standards. Some use "public safety" as a criterion of release. Others authorize conditional release if the patient is "improved" or if it will serve his "best interest." Some beg the question entirely, requiring that the patient be "eligible for probationary release." Moreover, their implicit promise of supervision during the conditional period proves to be illusory. Nevertheless, these procedures provide a testing occasion which may be used for persons who cannot be released outright.

ADMINISTRATIVE PRACTICE

The statutory standards for release are general and overlapping. The one thing which is clear about them is that they are neither clear nor well-established. Even more than the words of *M'Naghten*, they are waiting to be shaped by the courts. But remarkably little shaping is being done, probably because few patients petition for release or seek judicial relief when their petitions are denied. Whatever meaning is given to the standards for release is to be found in administrative practices within the mental hospitals. These are, of course, largely informal. Reasoned statements by hospital superintendents as to why they decided to release particular patients are virtually nonexistent. The entire matter is approached more in managerial fashion than as an administrative procedure involving important questions of liberty.

Except where he is specifically admonished to use only the criterion of dangerousness, the superintendent's first concern should be whether it is desirable, from a psychiatric point of view, for the patient to be returned to the community. This should lead to fairly liberal release procedures, for several reasons: The number of patients so far exceeds the available resources that there is considerable pressure to release, if only to make room for new admissions. There is a quite separate feeling that it is therapeutically desirable for the patient to return to the community as quickly as possible, in order to avoid the risks of dependence upon too protected an environment.[16] Tranquilizers have made such early release far more feasible than in the past. Medically, therefore, the patient who is not seriously depressed and who can function in most day-to-day situations would ordinarily be discharged fairly quickly, often in a matter of weeks or months.[17]

When the patient has been committed after a charge of serious crime, however, the medical aspects of the problem are inevitably affected by the public or "legal" aspects. The more serious the crime charged against the patient in the past, the greater is the responsibility felt by the person who must decide whether or not to release. He cannot help but wonder whether criminal behavior will recur and, if it does, what the effect will be not only upon society, but also on his own reputation and that of his institution. If the hospital is a state agency, as it will be in most instances, his concern will run even to the effects of a "mistake" upon his relations with the legislature or with those higher in the administrative hierarchy.

The psychiatrist making the decision will, therefore, find it difficult to consider his patient's welfare alone. He will feel himself pressed, more than good medical practice would ordinarily dictate, to estimate the probability that his patient will repeat his criminal conduct upon release. Unfortunately, the job of prediction is no easy matter. "The disappearance of a symptom, . . . the subjective report of happiness, the subjective absence of conflict are no reliable indices of recovery."[18] The only reliable evidence of "cure" is the absence of observable symptoms over a period of years. As a result, psychiatrists will be sorely tempted to "play it safe" and to wait out the years, giving greater weight to nonmedical considerations than would be the case if a criminal charge had not been involved. It will be easy for them to do so because no calculus lies ready at hand to weigh the competing considerations, to balance the interest of the patient in his liberty against the interest of society in protecting itself against him. And none has been supplied either by legislatures or courts. The problem tends to be resolved, uneasily and pragmatically, in each hospital by a particular therapist or by a staff conference. Little more can be said than that the therapeutic value of release will be given little or no effect if the probability is high that the patient will commit a serious crime shortly after release, particularly one involving physical violence. But as the probability of crime becomes lower, or the nature of the probable crime less serious, therapeutic considerations will be given greater weight.[19]

JUDICIAL ATTITUDES; BURDEN OF PROOF

In virtually all jurisdictions, the patient who wishes to challenge his continued detention has the burden of persuading the court that he should be released. To do so, he must ordinarily prove he is sane or will pose no threat to the community. In theory, this burden should not be encumbered at all by considerations of blame. And some courts follow the theory, imposing no heavier burden than they would upon any mentally ill patient.[20] But a surprisingly large number treat persons acquitted as insane as members of an "exceptional class," requiring stricter standards for release than the general run of mental patients. The class is sometimes said to be made up of "guilty persons" who should not "go unwhipped of justice."[21] There are undercurrents of suspicion that the defense has been feigned and that the patient's past behavior is strong evidence that he will be dangerous to the community if he is released. As one trial judge said, "I am not going to take the responsibility of releasing a man who had alcoholic hallucinations and killed somebody and may have them again, and you say it is a possibility."

The opinions of the District of Columbia courts are typical of the genre. If a hospital superintendent does not issue a certificate of release, the petitioner must persuade the court that the superintendent's action was "arbitrary and capricious." It is not enough for the patient to show he had improved materially and appeared to be a good prospect for restoration to society. "If an 'abnormal mental condition' renders him potentially dangerous, reasonable ... doubts are to be resolved in favor of the public."[22] Even when the superintendent decides in favor of release, the applicant must persuade the court (whose approval is necessary for the release to become final) that "he has become sane to the degree that it is reasonably certain that his enlargement now will be without menace to the public peace or safety." The evidence of recovery must lead to a "substantial degree of certainty" that he will not be dangerous, perhaps even to proof beyond a reasonable doubt. Yet his mandatory commitment in the District of Columbia comes as a result *not* of a finding that he was insane but only that there was a reasonable doubt as to his sanity.[23]

Hospital administrators and judges tend too often, in their decisions on release, to express a fundamental distrust of the insanity defense. To the extent that they bring considerations of blame and punishment to bear, rather than therapeutic factors alone, they usurp roles and functions which constitutions and legislatures have delegated to juries. The consequence is not only to undercut the trial process. For the defendant, it raises the prospect that indeterminate commitment will become nearly permanent detention.

II

The power to detain indefinitely is unquestionably the most important issue associated with the insanity defense. Yet it has received remarkably little consideration. The comment which does exist is dominated by labels. If the detention is "therapeutic" in its objectives, it is assumed that it may be indefinite in duration. If it is "punitive," it must have limits. The underlying assumption seems to be that there is no need to fear excess from a medical disposition, but only from a criminal one. Where blame has been eliminated and only "treatment" is involved, detention will continue only if the patient's welfare requires it. Moreover, the very fact of indeterminacy is regarded as an incentive to patients to improve more quickly so that they can be released sooner.

However benign the purpose of indeterminate detention may be, it brings serious problems with it. I have already noted the ease with which it may become the instrument for abuse of power by those who refuse to accept the insanity defense as dispositive of the issue of blame and punishment, or who are unduly fearful of public reaction to release decisions. Patients falling into the hands of such persons will find little comfort in the underlying theory. Indeed, their fear that the detention power will be abused may have seriously adverse effects on the course of treatment.

But even if ways could be found to purge retributive feelings and to make officials more courageous, fundamental problems would remain which raise the question whether a successful insanity defense should bring with it a power to detain the offender indefinitely. The problem is raised in its starkest form by the person who cannot be "treated" in the present state of knowledge and resources.[24] For him, acquittal by reason of insanity may bring with it a period of detention far in excess of what would have ensued if he had been convicted. This will occur because he will not be able to satisfy the existing criteria of release. Where sanity is the key, it will be difficult to say it has been restored, or that the offender has been cured. If danger is the key, there will be substituted for the question of "cure" that of probable danger. The problem will become even more acute if the insanity defense is applied to include psychopaths, alcoholics, and narcotics addicts. Though they will seem more capable of functioning in society than many psychotics, they may be less curable and more dangerous. Broadening the insanity defense may, therefore, not be the humane gesture many reformers have in mind. Instead, it may become a device for luring offenders to forego the relative security of a sentence of limited duration for a potentially unlimited one.

The heart of the problem is the issue of probable danger. Detention beyond the limits fixed by the criminal code—which expresses the legislative judgment as to what is needed to satisfy retributive and deterrent and, on occasion, rehabilitative factors—can be justified only if such detention will serve the patient's welfare or that of society. It can serve the welfare of the patient who is treatable only if there is some assurance that he can be treated successfully in the period beyond what a sentence would provide; and that the possibility of successful treatment is more important than his liberty during the interim. In the cases of persons who are untreatable, continued detention is clearly based on a concern for the social welfare. It is entirely a device for preventive detention, a way of protecting society from the risk that new crimes will be committed by the patients upon their release.

The underlying assumption, with both the treatable and the untreatable, is that the risk is so much greater than in the case of the criminal, the probable ensuing damage so much more serious, as to justify extraordinary measures of restraint. The model upon which the law builds seems to be the stereotypical madman of public imagination: the rapist, the murderer, the man of violence. He must be restrained at all costs, lest he perpetrate a new outrage the moment he is loosed upon society. However, the power conferred is a general one and can be exercised without regard to the type of offense originally charged, or the type threatened. Any crime which may be in prospect will ordinarily satisfy the criterion of danger. Moreover, the state is under no obligation to prove the patient will commit these crimes in the future; the burden is on the patient to prove he will not.

The power to detain indefinitely is an extreme remedy designed for facts which are only occasionally likely to exist. For one thing, most offenders bear little resemblance to the man of passion or violence. More than 65 per cent offend only against property. They are embezzlers, car thieves, forgers, con-men, shoplifters, at worst burglars. Their release may be indicated even if one could predict with confidence that they would offend again—both because the threat they pose is relatively insubstantial when compared to the cost and consequences of indefinite detention, and because insurance and other devices may be available to mitigate the loss. It may be argued, however, that the property offender plays little or no part in the problem of indeterminate detention because he will not expose himself to the risk of it; that he will refrain from asserting the insanity defense because the criminal sanction he faces is relatively insubstantial. This argument overlooks the extent to which relatively mild offenses may become the basis for very severe sentences through "multiple offender" laws and cumulative sentencing practices; or the possibility that defendants, their families, and their lawyers may become persuaded by a psychiatry-conscious culture that it is in the defendant's best interest to assert the insanity defense, because of its promise of treatment.

Even in the case of the untreatable man of violence, for whom the power to detain indefinitely is most clearly indicated, there are serious questions. Though the class of crime he threatens seems to justify precautionary measures, the problem of prediction remains. Is it possible to predict with a fair degree of accuracy how soon and how often he would be violent again? How probable is it, for example, that he will find a target on the day when he is likely to be violent? How likely is it that he will be successful if he should locate a target? Will the police intervene? Will the victim successfully defend himself? Once the probabilities are established, they must be weighed against his freedom—not only in moral but in pragmatic terms. For example, should his economic contribution during each day he is *not* likely to be violent be weighed against the harm he may do on the days when he will be? What of his emotional and social contribution to his wife, children, and friends? And what of the possibility that what happens to him after release may facilitate his "cure" in ways unanticipated by his therapists? If the issue of preventive detention, and probable danger, is to be considered seriously each case would have to be analyzed along lines like those I have described. Such analyses would reveal in short order how little we really know and how difficult it is to predict who is likely to do what under which circumstances.

The criminal law provides few analogies that bear directly on the problem of preventive detention, probably because much of our current ideology comes from the struggle to establish upper limits on detention and to civilize the social appetite for retribution and deterrence. There are, however, important themes which sound cautionary notes. The closest analogy comes from the law of attempts, which expresses a fundamental distrust of the possibilities of predicting crime from evil intentions alone, much less from past crimes. Some sort of action pointing very clearly toward a crime soon to be committed is regarded as an essential precondition for invoking the harsh sanction of the criminal law.

A second analogy is to be found in the manner in which the law of homicide balances the interest in preserving life against competing social interests. When a highway is built, we know that many deaths will result from its use. Yet we do not penalize the highway builders. This is because a social consensus supports the building of highways, even if it means loss of life. Again, when a railroad is built through a wilderness, we can expect the rigors involved will result in deaths, injuries, and illnesses. But we tolerate, indeed encourage, the activity because we see a railroad's utility to society. In both instances, economic and social benefit is held to outweigh the cost in lives. If a similar approach were applied to the problem of the probable offender, some disturbing questions would have to be faced. Though it can be assumed that he may threaten society, how often is he likely to do so? How seriously? How certainly? And what weight should be assigned to the social interest in individual freedom? The moral to be drawn from the law of homicide is that a viable society involves the balancing of risks, often quite serious ones, but that risk-taking often brings with it substantial rewards. A system of indefinite detention tries to act "as if" it is possible to eliminate risk, to give the appearance of scientific precision to judgments which are all too human and too fallible. The unhappy fact is that a system of indefinite detention can be justified only if we are confident we can achieve cure or predict the degree and frequency of danger. Until we do, such a system invites the timid, the punitive, or the unconcerned to sacrifice individual liberty at the altar of security.

At present, the law of release is entirely too general in its approach. Statutory criteria treat all persons acquitted by reason of insanity in identical fashion, regardless of the nature of their crime or the kind and degree of danger they pose. And the courts have done little or nothing to deal with the problem in more discriminating fashion. Even the psychiatric literature is relatively silent. It has contented itself with urging the expansion of the insanity defense, so that more offenders might be brought into the mental hospitals, and has neglected almost entirely the gnawing question of what should be done with those who cannot be treated successfully. Yet for those who cannot be "treated," there is a covertly punitive quality in the power to detain indefinitely. It is difficult to avoid the impression that psychiatrists, and mental health professionals generally, are so anxious to treat the curable ones that they are willing to sacrifice the incurable by promising society greater protection from them than may be necessary.

III

When solutions to the problem of indeterminate detention have been discussed, they have taken one of two forms. The first would limit the time the offender could be hospitalized to the maximum possible sentence he would have served had he not been "acquitted" by reason of insanity, so that his "treatment" would not become a way of imposing even greater punishment than he would have suffered if he had been convicted."* If the state should desire to hold the offender longer, it would be forced to bring civil commitment proceedings for this purpose.[25] The second would treat him as "acquitted" but would require the state at once to initiate civil commitment proceedings. This last is, in essence, what is done in those states which authorize, but do not require, the trial court to commit a person acquitted by reason of insanity. Both proposals are built on the assumption that the civil commitment process has developed standards which would protect the rights of the patient and rescue the issue from the ambiguity found on the criminal side. "Dangerousness" is presumably given substance and men are confined only as long as therapeutically necessary. If the assumptions are correct, then not only might explicit use of civil commitment be desirable, but its procedures and its standards might be incorporated into the body of law dealing with the release of persons acquitted by reason of insanity.

The assumptions are only partially warranted. At present, the special virtue of civil commitment lies more in its procedure than its substance.[26] It deals with the issue of continued detention in a separate proceeding which is, in theory, freed of any special obligation to the criminal law. This is reflected in the fact that the erstwhile defendant is now explicitly a prospective patient. The burden of proof is on the state to show his detention is necessary, not upon him to show it is *not* necessary. Freedom, in short, is presumptively his, to be taken from him only if exceptional circumstances are proved to exist. Since the question of "sanity" or "dangerous-

---

*This may provide illusory maximum limits where the criminal statutes provide for a great range between minimum and maximum limits.

ness" is often close factually and ambiguous legally, the location of the burden of proof may make the critical difference between confinement and release. Its importance, therefore, should not be minimized.

The hope of the reformers, however, is for guidance from the substantive law of civil commitment, particularly on the question of probable danger. Unfortunately, the statutes offer little aid. Contrary to popular belief, they are not generally keyed to the question of potential danger. They run the gamut from mental illness to public danger to whether the patient is "in need of care and treatment" in a mental hospital and "lacks sufficient insight" to make the decision on his own. A relatively small number of jurisdictions put the "danger" issue explicitly on the scales.[27] The case law is more promising, albeit still in its infancy. A brief examination of the currents which have developed in it may provide us with some standards for approaching the problem on the criminal side of the court.

In the cases most analogous to those which arise in the criminal court, the individual is usually committed, just as he would have been retained in custody had he gone the criminal route. These are the instances where he has already engaged in violence—as by a murder already committed, or by driving recklessly or discharging a pistol in public, or by beating wife and family.[28] More important for our purposes, however, are the situations which involve no current violence at all, but only the threat of it. In such cases, the committing court is called upon to make a prediction of dangerousness. The problem is presented most clearly by persons diagnosed as paranoiac, or as paranoid schizophrenic. Such persons often have delusions of persecution. As a result, they tend to be readier than most to "strike back" at their imagined persecutors. A wife's hands, for example, may be regarded as "poison" and provoke "paranoid reactions" which are aggressively defensive in nature. Some courts have used a standard of imminent danger, very much like the act requirement in the law of attempts, as a basis for concluding there should be no commitment. Others have looked to "potential danger." The nature of the disagreement between the two positions is illustrated by *Warner v. State,* which involved an emergency commitment rather than a general one. The majority of the court noted that though "a paranoid condition may sometimes erupt suddenly in some dangerous act, it may . . . slumber indefinitely; one who suffers from it may conduct himself for years, throughout life even, peaceably and quietly, with no symptom other than a belief that he is being persecuted." Finding that "Warner had committed no overt act forecasting danger to himself or others," the court concluded that it was improper for him to be subjected to summary arrest. To justify such action, it was necessary for him to present an "imminent and immediate danger of harm." To the dissenters, it was enough that he was a member of a class of persons regarded as dangerous by experts. In their words, "Qualified persons thought he was a paranoiac. Paranoia is a psychosis and persons suffering therefrom are psychotics who need medical treatment and sometimes show sudden and unpredictable outbursts of violence . . . 'perhaps the most dangerous of the so-called insane.' " The test they urged was that of potential danger, even if it had not yet been realized in actions harmful to the community.[29]

The attitude of the dissenters is widely held, not only by courts but by committing psychiatrists. It moves far too quickly and casually from the diagnosis of paranoia to the conclusion of probable harm to the community. *Brock v. Southern Pacific Co.* provides a revealing illustration of such a process at work. The doctor who had participated in commitment proceedings testified in the malicious prosecution case (subsequently brought by Brock) that Brock

> had certain paranoid delusions, feelings of persecution to the extent that he felt his life had been jeopardized on

> numerous occasions . . . Knowing that he was suffering
> from a mental disease, I felt that there was a reasonable
> possibility that he would seek redress for his persecution
> and knowing, again, that he had, was suffering from
> mental illness, I had no assurance that such redress would
> be of an orderly or lawful type and therefore I felt that he
> might seek redress of a violent nature.

From the fact of paranoia, he had inferred a "reasonable possibility" that Brock "might seek redress of a violent nature."
And having no assurance that he would not, he saw commitment as the only way out. Yet the relevant commitment
statute required that the patient be a "menace to himself or
society." The witness conceded that the statutory standard
had been ignored. "Actually, he need not have been much of
a menace to himself and society. That is the current phrase
used by anybody we feel needs hospital care, whether he wants
it or not."[30]

When the danger posed by the patient is not physical
violence but property damage or some more abstract harm,
the weighting process tends to change. Where the prospect of
violence brings the assumption that it must be avoided even
at the expense of liberty, the prospect of lesser injuries brings
solicitude for the liberty of the patient. For example, when
the paranoia is characterized by harassment and litigiousness,
the courts may treat the harm as *de minimis* and refuse to
commit. The same is true when they are faced with persons
who are "insane" but who are at worst nuisances, such as
cranks, religious fanatics, and pathological liars.[31]

There is another line of authority, however, which points
in a different direction. In these cases, most often involving the
sexually irresponsible and the senile, the issue of probable
danger tends to recede from view and "protection" of the
patient becomes the dominant theme, so much so that the
requirement of mental illness is sometimes ignored.[32] *Ex
parte Bowyer* offers a troublesome illustration. Its central

character was a twenty-two-year-old girl. She had borne two illegitimate children by the time she was twenty and had led a "totally immoral" life. Though she was not psychotic, it appeared that she was a moron, that her parents were helpless to control her and that, if released, she would again prostitute herself. The court refused to order her release, saying,

> A woman who . . . is very much oversexed and has only the mentality and will power of a child of tender years to control her appetites and passions is insane and not only insane but also a danger to herself and to the community. . . . The provisions of the law relating to the confinement of insane persons are by no means limited to the case of maniacs who will slay others and injure themselves, but apply as well to those unfortunates who for their own sake as well as in the interests of the community are dangerous to be at large.

The court explicitly rejected the argument that "this girl is her own master and her body is her own to use and to abuse as she sees fit," saying only that "liberty to resume her reckless life will mean further disaster." The nature of the disaster was not identified; the use of alternatives to commitment was not considered; the interest in personal liberty, however squalid, was given short shrift.[33]

The language of paternalism has not been confined to the senile or the sexually irresponsible. In *Paul v. Longino,* a schizophrenic young woman had taken to sitting by the roadside at night, several miles from home. She subsequently became a member of Jehovah's Witnesses and spent many days away from home, knocking on strange doors. Her sister testified that it was not safe for her "to travel on foot through the country, remaining away from home until after dark, and going into houses of all sorts of people." No evidence was offered to establish that she was likely to do herself or anyone else serious harm. Nevertheless, her commitment was upheld.[34]

Thus far, I have dealt with the issue of probable danger only as it arises in cases where the courts assume the individuals in question are "insane." Usually they fall into a group generally regarded as psychotics, because it is only for them that psychiatrists will ordinarily use civil commitment. Yet, as is true of the insanity defense, the language of most civil commitment statutes is sufficiently broad to encompass "lesser" ailments like psychopathy.[35] And psychopaths are more apt to seem dangerous than any other category of the mentally ill. Yet I have found only one case which considers the problem in any detail under the general commitment statutes. *In re Williams* involved a man who had been arrested in 1949 for the crime of assault with a deadly weapon. In the next eight years, he was tried five different times for that offense, two trials ending in mistrials and three in convictions. All three convictions were reversed by the Court of Appeals and the last time they ordered him freed. The United States Attorney then attempted to have him committed civilly, not because he was mentally ill *and* dangerous but on the theory that his dangerousness alone was an adequate basis for commitment. At the commitment hearing, two psychiatrists testified. Both agreed Williams was not then psychotic but that there had been psychotic thinking in the past. They also agreed that his release would present a real physical danger to the community. This conclusion was based upon a long pattern of drinking, gambling, fighting, frequent arrests for carrying dangerous weapons, absence of any regular occupational adjustment, persistent difficulties with the law, an attitude of suspiciousness and resentment toward authority, refusal to admit or accept responsibility for his crimes, apparent lack of anxiety or remorse over his past pattern of antisocial behavior. The court refused to order the commitment. In its view, no matter how great the probable "danger" from

Williams, he could not be committed unless he was presently insane; for some reason, the government had made no effort to establish that a psychopath fitted the designation.[36]

Williams was a clear attempt to use civil commitment to accomplish preventive detention. But the significance of its failure should not be exaggerated. If the government had pressed the point that Williams was a psychopath or that he had a conduct disorder and that these are mental illnesses, it might well have prevailed. The extent to which phrases like "mental disease" and "mental disorder" have expanded in meaning in recent years suggests they are not likely for long to set significant limits on civil commitment.

The substantive law of civil commitment provides no ready guide for release policy after acquittal by reason of insanity. Though it has begun to deal directly with the issue of probable danger, it has not advanced very far. Indeed, the complexity of the "danger" issue may well account for the fact that so many states have eliminated the question of probable danger from their civil commitment statutes and have substituted standards like: is the patient a "fit subject for care and treatment?"; or does he have the "capacity or insight to make responsible decisions concerning hospitalization?" Instead of clarifying the issue of control over the mentally ill, these succeed in masking difficult issues of social policy behind what are ostensibly medical judgments. They leave unanswered why a sane man who merely threatens harm, even if he is a recidivist, may not be detained at all while the insane man may be detained forever; or why the sane man may go from door to door exercising his right of free speech by proselytizing for Jehovah's Witnesses, while the insane man may be incarcerated for doing the same thing; or why the sane man or woman may fornicate with abandon while the insane may not.

There is a more specialized body of civil commitment statutes which also involve detention for an indeterminate period—the statutes addressed to sexual psychopaths and to defective delinquents. Though some come into play only upon conviction of crime, others turn on the charge of crime alone or upon a showing of the designated condition. But in their detention and release provisions, they pose again the problems I have already convassed. The only difference is that, in theory, the legislature has restricted the drastic remedy of indeterminate detention to a defined class which is presumably dangerous.[37]

IV

The problem of release is important for two quite separate reasons. The first, which I have considered in some detail, is the threat to liberty involved in indeterminate detention. The second, which I have touched upon hardly at all, is the relation between such detention and the insanity defense itself.

I noted earlier that the insanity defense is raised so rarely as to make questionable assigning it an important role in the criminal law. That problem will continue as long as the defense brings with it the specter of indeterminate detention. Defense counsel would be derelict in his duty if he failed to ask how the consequences of criminality compare with those of insanity. Since he will find that as much stigma is suffered from one as from the other, that employers are equally likely to hesitate about hiring persons in either category, he will quickly turn to the question of length of incarceration. The defendant who does not assert the insanity defense will probably be convicted and sentenced to a term of years fixed by the legislature, or to a range with minimum and maximum limits. These may be suspended by the court, or he may be released on probation. Even if he is sent to prison, his sentence may be reduced by allowance of time off for good behavior or by release on parole. However, if he should successfully assert the insanity defense, he would probably be committed for a wholly indefinite period. This may prove to be longer, or shorter, than the period he would have served if he had been convicted.

The insanity route is likely to be chosen only where conviction would bring with it a sufficiently long sentence to override the anxiety and fear excited by a wholly indefinite term. But as the probable sentence decreases, the risks inhering in an indefinite term will seem more forbidding and the insanity defense will be correspondingly inhibited. At present, the lawyer's inclination in the bulk of criminal cases is, unquestionably, to keep his client within the conventional criminal process—because he is more familiar with it, because he can make educated guesses about what will happen to his client at various stages, and because the fixed maximum sentence allays the haunting fear of a detention which may never end.

It may well be that this attitude will change as lawyers become more proficient in handling criminal cases. In time, they may be able to predict with reasonable accuracy—through their own experience or through the publication of statistics on release—just what the prospects of release may be after a successful insanity defense and to compare them with the probable periods of detention after conviction. Matters may develop so far that account will be taken of the therapeutic aspects of the problem: Will the offender be helped more by the mental hospital or by the prison? Is he suffering from a mental illness which can be treated? How long will the treatment take? Do the state's institutions for the criminally insane have the personnel and the facilities to provide the treatment indicated? Are such facilities equally likely to be available in the prisons, or somewhere else within the Department of Corrections? Is it possible for someone within the prison system to be treated within the mental hospital system and yet not have to be committed for an indefinite term? What is release policy for the insane? And how does it compare with parole policy for prisoners?

Until we arrive at a day when questions of this sort can be answered with relative precision, and the ability to treat successfully makes the answers comport with a decent concern for individual liberty, it is essential that something be done about the problem of completely indeterminate detention. One approach, which has been taken recently in *Rouse v. Cameron,* is to hold the state to its promise of treatment, upon which the indeterminate detention is ordinarily based, and to release patients if the promise is not fulfilled.[38] That approach is so easily avoided, however, by legislative action to withdraw the promise of treatment and to base the detention instead on probable danger, that it is not likely to serve for long. Moreover, it would assign too great a role to litigation and to the judiciary to superintend treatment processes.

A second, and more attractive, approach would be to have the acquittal by reason of insanity result, initially, in a limited commitment for the purpose of determining whether the offender is currently dangerous, with the burden of proof on that issue placed upon the state. If commitment should then be ordered, a cutoff point should be fixed at the outset, the outer limit of which would be the sentence that might have been imposed, because that period represents the "political" judgment as to how much detention is needed to serve legitimate deterrent or retributive functions. Detention for "treatment" should not continue beyond that period unless it can be shown that it is highly probable that the offender's release would be dangerous to life or person in the reasonably near future. Even for this limited class, detention should not be as indeterminate as it now is. The state should be required to apply periodically (e.g. annually) to a court or board for renewal of the commitment, with the patient represented by counsel and findings required.[39] Unfortunately, however, these proposals still beg the question of detailed substantive standards of commitment and release which would have to be faced either by the civil commitment process or by the renewal procedure. Those are likely to develop only if the new procedures force case-by-case consideration of the problems raised in this chapter or if counsel moves aggressively into this field of law.

CHAPTER ELEVEN

Competing Processes and Attrition Before Trial

American society is increasingly disposed to view crime as merely one form of antisocial behavior which may originate in mental illness. Each instance of such behavior, therefore, presents a choice between treating the offending act as a crime or a symptom of mental illness. Each response moves the offender toward an entirely different process for deciding whether he is in fact a criminal or a patient and for dealing with him after that fact has been determined.

The criterion for choosing between the two processes is, of course, what the insanity defense is about. But the defense arises almost at the end of the law enforcement process, at a time when few offenders are left to be measured by it. Only about 10 per cent of those charged with crime ever contest their guilt at trial. Some 90 per cent plead guilty and untold numbers of others drop out of the criminal process without being charged at all. There can be little doubt that these two groups include large numbers of mentally ill persons who could assert the insanity defense but who either make no effort to do so, or are diverted elsewhere by the agencies of law enforcement. In this chapter, I shall consider the points at which the decision is made as to whether they will be diverted or will remain in the criminal process—and the ways in which policies and procedures relevant to the insanity defense should be brought to bear before trial on the police, the prosecutor, the magistrate, and the grand jury.

I

The policeman is principally concerned with the enforcement of criminal law, and with the processes of investigation and arrest traditionally associated with such enforcement. But he is also authorized to initiate a wide variety of "civil" processes. The most important of them is the traditional procedure for committing the insane; in addition, twenty-seven states provide for commitment of sexual psychopaths, ten states provide for commitment of "defective delinquents," and many states provide for commitment of alcoholics, narcotics addicts, the mentally retarded, and the juvenile offender. Though some of these come into play only after a conviction of crime, others may be invoked either at the point of arrest or formal charge, or even in advance of either. These last are sufficiently broad to make them genuinely competitive with the criminal process.[1] As the most visible and available agent of the state's power—the one who is most likely to be called when there are events which disturb the peace of the community—the policeman must decide whether the events should be treated as crimes or whether the offending behavior should be ignored entirely or whether the offender should be directed to one of the myriad "helping" agencies, or whether some form of civil commitment should be sought. The events themselves—acts of violence, thefts, sexual misconduct, drunkenness, or vagrancy—will not point him inevitably in one direction or the other. Nor will the memory traces left from the lectures on mental illness to which he is increasingly exposed. They will, however, have impressed upon him the fact that there are very real risks in subjecting the mentally ill to the processes of arrest, interrogation, fingerprinting, line-up, detention in a jail, and bail-setting. More often than in the past, therefore, he is likely to pause and put to himself the question how he should proceed.

There is very little available to tell us how the police actually respond to the choices before them. We know only that the law surrounds the police with a large discretion which is virtually unreviewable in the courts. As a result, they are free to act on almost any grounds but the most arbitrary. It is not that the law makes no effort to set standards. Quite the contrary. Statutes in a great many states require the police to prosecute *all* crimes coming to their notice. But nowhere are such statutes taken seriously. The police are regarded in such states, and elsewhere, as having a broad discretion to arrest or not.[2]

Their authority to detain for civil commitment purposes is comparably broad. The most popular of the statutory formulae authorizes confinement if a person is mentally ill and in need of care and treatment. Others do so if he is "mentally ill" and it is in his "own and others' welfare" for him to be hospitalized. And only one fourth of the states require any showing that the patient is dangerous. Similar criteria are to be found in the more specialized commitment procedures. These civil and criminal processes serve some of the same objectives and deal with an overlapping population. But for the most part they take little note of each other. Priorities between the two processes are not established; provisions for movement from one to the other are largely non-existent, except in some of the newer procedures like those dealing with sexual psychopaths and defective delinquents. In a particular case, the choice among them is left to police and prosecutor.[3]

The special difficulty of the choice inheres in the fact that it must be made almost intuitively at the very beginning of a process whose very purpose is to make the choice deliberately. If, for example, the police officer should decide not to charge a man with assault, because he regards the man as insane, he would be determining at the outset the very question the insanity defense is designed to reach at a later stage. If he should charge him, he creates the risk of harm to the individual which medical considerations would have him avoid. Yet the increasing concern about "labeling" a man as a criminal—with the attending stigma and the influence it may have on fixing him in that role—presses toward making the choice as early as possible. The police stage, when a decision must be made whether to charge crime or not, is thus moved toward becoming adjudicative in nature. It is not at all clear, however, that it is possible at so early a stage to make a sensible choice between a criminal process and a civil one. For one thing, the facts are not yet in and cannot possibly be. For another, the policeman is hardly cast ideally to make the decision on medical grounds, or moral grounds, or even on grounds of deterrence or retribution.

The police tend to regard antisocial behavior as crime rather than sickness and to err in the direction of moving the offender along the criminal route. The more serious the offense, the more likely it is that the offender will be charged criminally rather than proceeded against civilly. Even with minor offenses, the criminal course seems to be favored. The arrest process may, however, become a conduit toward civil commitment, particularly for lower-class persons.[4] A study of New Haven reports that the police tend to book lower-class persons who are mentally disturbed, and causing trouble, on a criminal charge of breach of the peace, noting that "this is a mental case." The notation ordinarily leads the City Attorney to order a psychiatric examination. If the offender is found to be "incompetent," he will be committed to a state mental hospital. This device passes the critical decision from the police to the City Attorney, who utilizes the psychiatric examination as an aid in the exercise of his discretion.[5]

Until now, I have written as if the criminal and civil processes were neatly coordinated and the need for a choice between them always present in the case of the mentally ill offender. The fact, however, is that the insanity defense looks to the past, the time of the crime, while the civil processes look to the present. As a result, the man who could have proved his insanity may have recovered and there will be no real alternative to the criminal charge (except perhaps to dismiss it entirely). Even if the offender is still mentally ill, his illness may seem appropriate for civil commitment but not for an insanity defense. Again, if the offender is not regarded as suitable for civil commitment but yet as someone who is dangerous, the criminal arrest may seem the only way to assure the detention. This pattern is especially conspicuous in the case of alcoholics and narcotics addicts and psychopaths; and all those who might be able to raise the insanity defense but who choose not to do so.

The manner in which the police resolve these choices and dilemmas may affect the insanity defense in three ways: first, to the extent that the conduct in question is seen as a symptom of mental illness, the offender may be removed from the criminal process, thereby reducing the pool of offenders from whom the defense may come; second, the offender may be kept in the criminal process and the police officer may alert others to the probable existence of mental illness so that the prosecutor may take it into account either in preparing to rebut the defense, or by raising the question of competency to stand trial, or by initiating civil commitment proceedings; third, it offers the police the opportunity to institute proceedings looking toward indeterminate detention in those cases where the defendant elects not to assert the insanity defense and is acquitted or where the criminal sentence seems too mild.

II

The prosecutor, like the police officer, is ordinarily included among those who may institute civil commitment proceedings. And he too is not told how to choose between civil and criminal processes or the factors he should take into account. Only two states deal specifically with the matter. One makes it obligatory for him to initiate civil commitment proceedings if he should refuse to proceed criminally on grounds of insanity. Another authorizes him to seek civil commitment if he believes an offender is insane and dangerous.[6] Apart from these instances, the prosecutor's discretion to choose his course is virtually complete. When he receives the charge from the police, he may refuse to prosecute and either initiate civil commitment proceedings or leave it to others to "do something" about the offender, or he may prosecute, leaving it to the defendant to raise the insanity defense.

If he should choose not to prosecute, his decision will be virtually unreviewable by the courts. Even where there are statutes which seem to make prosecution mandatory in the case of "all crimes" or all crimes of a particular kind, the courts have held he may decline to prosecute for a wide variety of reasons—e.g. because he believes he could not prove his case in court; or because the harm to the public from the commission of the crime is not very great; or because the violation is not flagrant enough; or because tactical requirements dictate dismissal; or because some other public policy requires inaction, or because a warning is believed to be sufficient. Only in the rare instances when it can be shown that his discretion was exercised corruptly or in bad faith will the courts intrude.[7] A decision not to prosecute because the offender is mentally ill, or because civil processes are being pursued, is hardly likely to be classed as taken in bad faith.

The consequence of so much discretion is, of course, that decisions are made informally and administratively, often for reasons which are not articulated. We have already seen that the prosecutor may utilize psychiatric examinations to aid him in deciding whether to keep the offender within the criminal process or to proceed civilly. He may also devise a species of administrative probation, which keeps the charge of crime alive and unprosecuted as long as the accused obtains psychotherapy or some other form of assistance from social agencies, and which may ultimately lead to dismissal of the charge. A great deal more might be made of this device since it is the last opportunity to avoid the formal "labeling" of the offender as a criminal. And there are signs that it will be developed more systematically in the near future.[8]

Most often, however, the prosecutor, like the police before him, will use the process most familiar to him—the criminal prosecution. Trained to believe the decision regarding insanity is delicate and complex, he will be most reluctant to use his discretion to decide it prematurely. He will be inclined to leave the matter to the courts. The length to which this may be carried is illustrated by the practice described for the District of Columbia, where a prosecutor would not agree to an insanity plea even if he was persuaded that the defendant was insane at the time of the crime. Instead, he would go to trial, put on his evidence and leave it to the court to find the offender insane and to commit him.[9]

The tension already noted at the police stage thus reappears in the prosecutor's office. Both find themselves caught between overlapping statutory obligations and conflicting allegiances. They must define their role either as ministerial officers leaving to the judicial process decisions as to guilt or innocence, sanity or insanity; or as officials mindful of the discretion vested in them and the degree to which it encompasses matters broader than the criminal law; or as an uneasy accommodation of both.

III

If the accused is arrested and charged with crime, he must be brought promptly before a magistrate. If the offense is a minor one, it will be tried by the magistrate himself. If it is more serious, a preliminary hearing must be held. In that hearing, a decision must be made as to whether the accused should be held for the action of a grand jury, or for trial where there is no grand jury. My primary concern in this chapter is with the preliminary hearing. It is important to note, however, that a large number of mentally disordered offenders will pass into the penal system through conviction of offenses like vagrancy, breach of the peace, or minor sex offenses, which may be the criminal law's characterization of behavior by the mentally ill, particularly those at the lower end of the social scale. Yet, as Foote points out, the magistrate may be peculiarly ill-cast to deal with such cases. He may lack the power to "grant a suspended sentence which includes supervised probation, or commit the obviously ill to a medical institution or obtain any of the information essential to intelligent disposition of the cases. There is neither the time nor the facilities for obtaining pre-sentence reports or checking with other social agencies for information about the defendants."[10]

For serious crimes, the magistrate is the first judicial screen between state and accused; his purpose is to assure that only those who are probably guilty will be exposed to the risks, the stigma, and the inconvenience attending the charge of crime. The purpose is generally held to be satisfied if the evidence presented by police or prosecution persuades the magistrate that there is "probable cause" to believe that an offense was committed and that the accused is guilty.[11] Matters of defense, including insanity, are to be left to subsequent stages. Moreover, unlike his predecessors in the criminal process, he has no discretion to terminate the proceedings because he thinks the accused was insane—or because of general notions of justice or fairness or wise enforcement policy. However, the prosecutor retains such discretion, even after he has presented his case at the preliminary hearing, and the magistrate may informally try to persuade him to exercise it. For the magistrate, in any event, there is ordinarily no dilemma of formal choice between competing statutory obligations and competing ways of dealing with the mentally ill offender. Yet the picture is not so clear. In some jurisdictions, the magistrate may find himself administering a process which "competes" with the insanity defense. And it is not at all certain that the insanity defense has no part in the preliminary hearing.

The competing process exists in those few states in which

the issue of competency to stand trial may be considered at
the preliminary hearing. In these states, it may be raised by
the defendant or by the prosecutor or by the magistrate himself. Though its function is to remove from the trial process
persons who cannot understand the nature of the proceedings
against them until such time as their competency is restored,
it is in practical effect a civil commitment. It draws on the
same group of people, those who are currently psychotic, and
places them in a mental hospital until they can take their
places once again as active participants in a trial. But that
time may never come, either because competency is never
restored or because the defendants have been detained so
long that witnesses are no longer available and the prosecutions are dismissed.[12]

In several states the situation is more ambiguous. There is
little or no case law on the question whether a magistrate at a
preliminary hearing has the common-law power of a trial
judge to inquire into the competence of the defendant to participate in the proceeding before him. It is probable that he
does not. Yet such power probably does exist where the defendant is being tried by the magistrate for a petty offense
which does fall within his jurisdiction as a trial judge. If the
magistrate should regard the petty offender as incompetent to
stand trial, he would be able to draw the offender from the
criminal process. In some states there are statutes which might
be construed as authorizing the magistrate to deal with competency at the preliminary hearing. These provide that the
issue may be considered whenever a person has been "charged
with a crime." Though that phrase was probably intended to
refer to an indictment or information, which follows the
preliminary hearing, it is certainly broad enough to raise the
question whether it might not refer as well to the complaint
that precedes the hearing.[13] In yet others, the magistrate
might fall within language authorizing "public officials" to
institute civil commitment proceedings, unless he is con-

strained by a practice which requires criminal proceedings to be completed, once begun.

The uncertainty about the place of the insanity defense in the preliminary hearing arises from two quite separate influences. The first of these challenges the common assertion that a magistrate "could not hear" a special plea of insanity, because "it is entirely an element of defense, triable only in a court having jurisdiction of the trial of felonies." The same magistrates are obligated to permit the defendant to call witnesses and to testify in his own behalf. In some jurisdictions, they are even admonished to consider all the evidence, including matters of defense, and to make a realistic appraisal of probable guilt.[14] The second influence comes from those jurisdictions which hold that the introduction of "some evidence" of insanity places the burden upon the prosecution to prove the defendant sane beyond reasonable doubt.[15] These cases raise the question whether insanity is really a defense at all, or whether, under such circumstances, sanity must be established by the prosecution at the preliminary hearing.

It is, of course, arguable that the defendant is allowed to call witnesses only to illustrate the inferential gaps in the prosecution's case, or to demonstrate the inherent incredibility of all or part of the prosecution's case, and that trial standards of burden of proof cannot be applied literally to pretrial processes. But there is almost no experience, and even less case law, addressed to these matters. Preliminary hearings are rarely held and even more rarely reported[16]—either because most defendants are unrepresented at this early stage and therefore waive the hearing, or because the level of representation in criminal cases, even when it exists, is not very high. It is probable, however, that defense counsel will soon become a fairly regular participant in the preliminary hearing.[17] With his coming, there will be increasing pressure to make the hearing more substantial. Issues which were latent will be brought into the open for the first time, among them the place of the insanity defense at this early stage of the criminal process.

The principal argument for bringing the insanity issue into the preliminary hearing is that persons who are blameless should not have to suffer the sanctions of the criminal process for a moment longer than necessary. If they are insane, they should be withdrawn from the criminal process at once and a determination made as to whether they need treatment. And, the argument continues, the magistrate is ideally suited to decide the question. He is the first judicial officer to appear on the scene; in many jurisdictions, he is already entrusted with the closely related issue of competency to stand trial.

The argument is insufficient on several grounds. At the present time, the magistrate is likely to be a judicial officer in name only. He is often selected casually and presides over a process which is most informal. In many jurisdictions, he is neither a lawyer nor specially trained in any other way. Indeed, his general lack of qualification points more toward withdrawing the competency issue from him than adding the insanity defense to his responsibilities. Moreover, he ordinarily has no authority either to initiate a civil commitment proceeding or to commit an accused person to a mental hospital.[18] As a result, he is unable to protect the community from the possible consequences of a successful insanity defense—the release of a dangerous person. But even if magistrates were better selected and the problem of commitment could be solved, there would remain the question whether the preliminary hearing should be expanded. If the hearing were opened to defenses, including insanity, it would soon become necessary to assure a process in which the fullest presentation could be made. This, in turn, would mean that counsel would have to be provided for the accused sooner, pleading and motions practice would have to be refined, and discovery procedures would have to be accelerated. Inevitably, the time between arrest and preliminary hearing would have to be extended as the preliminary hearing came to approximate the trial itself. Its principal function, as a prompt judicial check upon the arresting officer, would soon be lost. Moreover, the insanity issue might well be tried twice, since the decision of the magistrate is not ordinarily a bar to subsequent prosecution. This could, of course, be solved but the end result might well be the distortion of the preliminary hearing in an undue effort to serve the insanity defense.

IV

The grand jury is a hybrid institution, exercising both investigatory and screening powers. In about half the states, the screening function is exercised only in extraordinary circumstances. But in the remaining half, mostly in the East, the person who is arrested may not be put to trial until an indictment has been returned against him by a grand jury. The evidentiary base for the grand jury's decision varies from "probable cause" to "substantial evidence to evidence sufficient to persuade a jury." These standards are generally held to be guides to the grand jury alone and are not enforceable by the courts. As a result, the grand jury has virtually free rein to indict or not. Ordinarily, however, it follows the lead of the prosecutor. It hears only the witnesses he chooses to present to it. And he usually presents only the government's evidence. The defendant has the right neither to be present nor to have counsel appear on his behalf, to cross-examine the state's witnesses or to present his own witnesses. The hearing is treated by all concerned as little more than an obligatory aid to the exercise of prosecutorial discretion.

Though this conventional learning is deep-rooted, there are other currents which indicate that the insanity defense may sometimes play a part in the grand jury proceeding. In several states, grand juries are admonished to pursue their inquiries as far as they lead when "they have reason to believe that there is other evidence, not presented and within reach, which would qualify or explain away the charge under investigation." Under such circumstances, they are told, "it would be their duty to order such evidence to be produced." Such admonitions invite consideration of defensive matter, including insanity, but they seem not to have been pressed very far. On the rare occasions when the question has been presented, the courts have construed the phrase "qualify or explain away" narrowly, as referring to elements of the government's case alone. This has occurred even when the defendant has been given the right to be represented by counsel and to present witnesses, as in Georgia, or when he may appear personally, as in New York. The overriding consideration has been a reluctance to convert the grand jury hearing into a trial.[19]

Despite the settled learning, and the restrictive statutory interpretation, twelve states have statutes dealing with the disposition of an accused when a grand jury fails to indict him on the grounds of insanity. Though these statutes may have been addressed to the problem of incompetency to stand trial, they speak in general terms, providing for commitment to a mental hospital if the defendant is presently dangerous or insane.[20] The mere existence of these procedures, however, cannot be taken as inviting a presentation of the insanity defense to the grand jury, much less requiring it. The statutes can be reconciled with a body of law and practice which keeps the grand jury from hearing defenses if they are regarded as providing for the unusual case in which the defendant's insanity becomes clear from the prosecution's case alone; or for the rare case when the defendant is invited to present witnesses and elects to do so.

There is one way in which the grand jury might properly play an important part in dealing with the insanity defense. It might serve as an internal administrative procedure to assist the prosecutor in exercising his discretion when he expects the insanity defense will be raised and he wishes to be in a position to agree to it or not; or when defense counsel asks him to exercise his discretion to dismiss the criminal charge and to have the defendant committed. The grand jury's subpoena power makes it possible to conduct a full investigation. Its composition makes it more representative of the community and its decision, therefore, more acceptable. Its secrecy makes it less stigmatizing and perhaps less traumatizing. It would be a mistake, however—for all the reasons already canvassed with regard to the preliminary hearing—to convert such an exceptional approach into a regular consideration of the defense by the grand jury.

V

After indictment, there are two processes which can fairly be described as "competitive" with the insanity defense. These are the procedure for determining competency to stand trial and the plea of guilty.

The question of competency to stand trial has already been discussed because it may arise before the magistrate at the preliminary hearing. It may also arise after the indictment, by means of a motion by the defense or by the prosecution to determine whether the defendant is incompetent—that is, whether he is unable to understand the nature of the proceedings against him or to assist in his defense. If he is, then the charge against him will be suspended and he will be committed to a mental hospital until his competence is restored. If he never regains his competence, then he will presumably remain in a hospital for the rest of his days. If he does regain his competence, he will be tried unless so much time has passed that the prosecution is no longer able to present a case against him. On rare occasion, the prosecutor may treat the commitment following incompetency as if it were a civil commitment and dismiss the criminal case at once, on the assumption that restoration to competence and "sanity" are roughly equivalent and that the public safety will be adequately protected in the meantime.[21]

Though the competency issue involves a great many interesting problems, two are particularly important for our purposes. First, the man who is incompetent at the time of trial is likely to have been insane at the time of the crime, particularly if too long a time has not elapsed between the two events. To the extent that his incompetence removes him from the criminal process, there is yet another reduction in the pool of persons who might assert the insanity defense. Second, a competency proceeding, unlike the insanity defense, may be initiated by the prosecution. By doing so, the state may be able to obtain an indeterminate commitment of the accused without proving a prima facie case against him, without showing that he is presently dangerous, and without showing that a restoration to competence is at all possible. Like civil commitment, therefore, it poses a very real risk of abuse and of being bent to punitive purposes. Indeed, it has recently been suggested that these procedures are fast displacing the insanity defense. Finding the defense "impracticable, time-consuming, expensive, and largely irrelevant to the concerns of appropriate disposition," officials have turned increasingly to "the ancient procedures for determining competence to stand trial." They have found such procedures "relatively easy to invoke, providing expert yet inexpensive psychiatric evaluation; . . . procedurally ambiguous enough to embrace conflicting and competing motivations and . . . flexible enough to permit a rich exercise of discretion."[22]

The plea of guilty is probably the most important of the processes competing with the insanity defense. More than 90 per cent of all formal charges of crime are resolved in this way. Since very little is known about these cases except the nature of the charge and the fact that the charge has been conceded, it is impossible to say how often they conceal defenses which might have been successfully raised. The courts screen the pleas hardly at all, limiting their inquiry to a routine effort to determine whether the plea was made "vol-

untarily." It is left almost entirely to defense counsel to assure
that any defenses which might exist have been carefully canvassed and intelligently waived. Yet it is well known that
defendants often forego defenses in return for a "plea bargain"—a reduction in the nature of the charge or a promise of
reduction of sentence.[23]

Where the insanity defense is concerned, there is a very
special motive for abandoning it. As we have seen, if it is successful it will probably be followed by indeterminate commitment. Until recently, this unwelcome prospect was sometimes offset by the fact that such commitment might be the
only avenue through which an offender could obtain treatment rather than punishment. Today, however, defense
counsel are increasingly aware that treatment may be found
in the penal system as well as in the mental hospital; and that
punishment may be found in the hospital as well as in the
prison. This turnabout is the result of two important developments: the mental hospitals lack either the facilities or the
techniques for curing many of the mentally ill offenders; the
sentencing, probation, and penal systems are being reshaped
so that they now offer, or soon will offer, diagnostic and treatment facilities and resources comparable to those found in the
mental hospitals.[24] It can be anticipated, therefore, that defense counsel will be increasingly reluctant to use the insanity
defense. The combination of pre-sentence reports and a relatively determinate sentence with either serious efforts at
rehabilitation or the availability of probation and parole
will make the plea of guilty far more attractive.

At the present time, the scales are weighted so heavily
against the insanity defense and in favor of the plea of guilty
that the balance could be restored only by taking from the
defendant the decision as to whether the defense is to be
raised. The traditional position has been that a defendant
who is competent to stand trial is also competent to decide
the lines of his defense; if he is to receive any guidance on

the matter, it should come from his counsel, not from the court. Yet if the choice is left entirely to him, he may succeed in avoiding procedures that are designed not only to protect the community but also to direct him out of the penal system and, at the same time, to affirm certain moral values.

The case which has come closest to dealing with the question is *Lynch v. Overholser*. Colonel Lynch had a long history of passing bad checks. When his case came before the Municipal Court of the District of Columbia, he wished to plead guilty. The ensuing sentence could have been no greater than one year's imprisonment. The trial judge refused to accept the plea because he thought Lynch could make out an insanity defense. At the trial which followed, the prosecution proved Lynch was insane and he was committed to St. Elizabeth's Hospital. He then petitioned for his release. The United States Court of Appeals for the District of Columbia upheld his detention, emphasizing the importance of "endeavoring to reach at the earliest possible stage . . . ideally prior to trial and sentence . . . the approach to a particular case which appears most appropriate. . . . Society has a stake in seeing to it that defendant who needs hospital care does not go to prison." The Supreme Court reversed, holding that the government had used the criminal process to effect a civil commitment and that it would have to start again, using a civil commitment procedure. The implication was that the defendant having elected not to raise the insanity defense, the prosecution could not do so.[25]

There are, however, a number of cases which point in the other direction. Some state quite explicitly that there are circumstances when the court may assert the defense even when the defendant has not—as, for example, when defense counsel thought the defense should be made[26] or where the court thought the evidence clearly sufficient to warrant an insanity defense. These last are typified by *Tatum v. United States,* in which the defendant did not plead insanity.[27] The appellate court reversed, saying it was "plain error" for his counsel not to have asserted the defense on his behalf. Since both classes of cases predate *Lynch,* their current status is in doubt. Moreover, it is not at all clear that Tatum, who faced a possible death sentence, knew the defense was available to him and freely chose to abandon it, as Lynch clearly had.

Lynch will probably emerge as authority for the proposition that neither prosecutor nor judge can assert the insanity defense when a competent defendant, who is adequately represented, has chosen not to do so. There is no more reason for the prosecutor or judge to displace defense counsel with regard to the insanity defense than there is in the case of alibi or entrapment or a coerced confession or an unlawful search. All that can reasonably be asked is that the guilty plea be supervised sufficiently closely to assure that the abandonment of defenses takes place after adequate advice.

VI

It should be apparent by now that the insanity defense is a small part of the problem presented by the mentally ill offender. Long before it appears, he has been dealt with by a variety of officials who may or may not have perceived his crime as deriving from mental illness. Choice and discretion lurk in unanticipated places and offenders do not move inexorably toward dispositions uniquely appropriate to their situations. We have no way of knowing how many persons arrested and discharged at some point before formal charge were insane when they committed the crime. Nor can we say how many were redirected into a civil commitment process, or how often the choice between civil and criminal processes was deliberately made. Even those who proceed beyond the formal charge of crime may erase the insanity defense, either by pleading guilty or by choosing to defend on some ground other than insanity. And then, of course, there are the myriad others who do not even know they might have a defense, much less exercise the choice of abandoning it.

An important substantive issue of the future will be the extent to which discretion should be controlled and choices determined by rule—particularly, whether the principles underlying the insanity defense should be brought to bear before trial. Should the policeman, for example, take them into account? Or the prosecutor? Or the magistrate? Each of them will find himself under increasing pressure to do so. The pressure will come not only from the popular culture but also from the training courses which are educating officials to the available alternatives, from defense counsel as he begins to participate in these early stages, and from the creation of new procedures authorizing offenders to be diverted from prosecution into noncriminal alternatives. This is already authorized under the English Mental Health Act, which provides that a person charged before a magistrate, and suffering from a mental illness for which hospital detention is warranted, may be committed without a conviction, if the court is satisfied he did the act. And it is the subject of a proposal by the President's Commission on Law Enforcement.[28]

Unquestionably, a policy decision on the part of police and prosecutor to use the civil process for the mentally ill offender, wherever possible, would move more offenders to mental hospitals. From a therapeutic point of view, except in unusual cases, this is probably desirable. It would enable the offender-patient to avoid the series of stigmatizing, and often traumatizing, experiences associated with the criminal process. Even more importantly, it would also avoid the risk that the mentally ill offender who goes into the penal system may find it has neither the facilities nor the personnel to treat him; and the legal or administrative structure may be such that he cannot easily be moved from prison system to hospital system.

There are, however, important factors to be placed on the other side of the scales. First, premature abandonment of the criminal process may mean that the ideal of personal responsibility will be reinforced in too few instances. Second, as the criminal process is used less often, greater use may be made of the indeterminate civil commitment processes to satisfy the felt need for detention. Third, it may not be possible to make a sensible decision—on matters so complex as the choice between a criminal and a civil process—at so early a stage. There are too many elements to be considered: the facts of mental illness, the moral sense of the community, and ways of establishing both so that the community will accept and identify with the decision.

I have gone on at such length about the currents that compete for primacy in choosing between civil and criminal processes, and about the extent to which the insanity defense tends to be swallowed up by other processes, because they illustrate what is probably its most significant characteristic: its almost accidental quality. If we once recognize how occasional an event the insanity defense is, we may be able to face up to some fundamental questions: Does it make any sense to assign it a major role in determining which offenders should go to a mental hospital and which to prison, which should be blamed and which should not? Should determined efforts be made to discover the points of "leakage" which result in mentally ill offenders remaining in the penal system? Finally, should the "leakage" be accepted as a fact of life and the penal system refashioned to take the mentally ill offender into account, either through provisions for transfer to mental hospitals or through developing its own therapeutic facilities?[29]

CHAPTER TWELVE

Competing Defenses; The Trend Toward Subjective Liability

The defendant who pleads not guilty has available to him the full range of defenses, as well as the opportunity to challenge the sufficiency of the government's case against him. But if he should wish to use his mental illness, he will ordinarily be able to do so only through the insanity defense. This is the result, as I noted earlier, of the widespread adoption of an objective theory of criminal liability. There are indications, however, that the objective theory is being eroded and that the facts of mental illness may become relevant to defenses other than insanity. If this should occur, difficult problems will be presented not only for defense counsel—who will have to decide among the competing lines of defense—but for the courts as well. Chief among them will be the divergence between "guilt" and dangerousness, for a subjective theory tends to treat some of the most dangerous among us as the least guilty.

I

The objective theory of criminal liability, described most clearly by Holmes in *The Common Law,* is responsible for excluding evidence that the defendant was mentally ill. The defendant's weaknesses and infirmities—his fearfulness, irritability, suggestibility—are ordinarily inadmissible except when offered in support of the insanity defense. "The strength of a man's mind," the courts have said, "has no bearing upon his responsibility for a criminal act, nor upon the inquiry of felonious intent, malice, and the like, if he is endowed with mind enough to discriminate between right and wrong."

"Men who are not insane or idiotic [are expected] to control their evil passions and violent tempers or brutal instincts, and if they do not do so, it is their own fault."[1] The model is that of the reasonable man, whose standard of conduct the defendant is expected to emulate.

This "objective theory" has occupied an uneasy place in a body of law which has always made much of its roots in personal immorality. Words like voluntary, malicious, intentional, willful, and *mens rea,* reference to a requirement that there be a "concurrence of an evil-meaning mind with an evil-doing hand," seem to promise an inquiry into a particular individual's mind to determine whether he deserves condemnation and imprisonment. The objective theory sees to it that the promise is largely unfulfilled. The defendant's acts, not his thoughts, become the real basis of criminal liability. "A person necessarily intends the probable and natural consequences of his own voluntary acts," said the Idaho court. "The only yardstick by which one's intent can be determined is his external acts and conduct."[2]

There are several reasons for limiting the subjective inquiry to instances when the insanity defense is pleaded. One is the reluctance to believe it is possible to know what passes through a man's mind. From this comes the feeling that acts are the only reliable indices, and with it the suspicion that the person who claims he was not "responsible" for his acts is lying. If he should win his freedom by virtue of what are probably lies, the security of society would be threatened. A second is that the use of a subjective theory would probably result in more acquittals. Yet such acquittals might bring freedom for defendants who have proved themselves less able than most men to control their conduct, thereby increasing the threat to society. The insanity defense takes both these problems into account by allowing a full presentation of the defendant's mental life while, at the same time, providing a way of keeping him in custody if it should seem necessary.

II

Pressures on the objective theory have come from a variety of sources. Most important has been the extent to which Americans have become sensitized to the problem of mental illness. In what has become a veritable "Age of Psychology," it is hardly unexpected that defense counsel are quick to find psychological explanations for deviant behavior and are strongly tempted to bring such explanations to bear on the criminal trial. The insanity defense is, of course, the most obvious route for doing so. But, as I have shown, the conventional learning is that the defense is available only under the most extreme circumstances. And those who have gone beyond the conventional learning are deterred from presenting such evidence by fear of the completely indeterminate commitment which may follow a successful defense. Persons who avoid the defense for either reason may decide to attack the objective theory directly—by offering both the evidence traditionally excluded and requests for instructions to the jury which call upon it to apply a subjective theory; or they may try to mitigate the objective theory by offering subjective evidence as probative of words like "intent," "malice," etc. Their hope will be that the evidence, once admitted, will persuade the jury to apply the words subjectively, in accordance with their apparent meaning.

Under pressures such as these, doctrines have begun to appear and gain currency which offer defense counsel the prospect that they may be able to use evidence of the defendant's mental illness and yet not have to plead the insanity defense. Some of these doctrines are entirely new, others hark back to the day when the objective theory was not yet entrenched. They appear in two general classes of cases: (1) those in which the subjective element becomes the reason for reducing the degree of guilt and the sentence following thereon —principally the homicide cases involving the issues of premeditation and provocation; (2) those which may lead to complete acquittal—the cases involving specific intent, involuntary acts, and self-defense.

It should be kept in mind that each of these issues may be raised in cases which *also* raise the insanity defense. For example, if the charge is murder or manslaughter, the defendant may urge the jury to find that he acted in self-defense, or involuntarily, in which event he would go free. He may also press upon them the view that he was provoked and acted in the "heat of passion," in which event he would be asking for the reduced sentence following upon the reduced charge. And he may also be offering the insanity defense. In such a case, the evidence of mental illness presented on the issue of insanity will be available for use by the jury in deciding the issues raised by the other defenses. Similarly, when subjective evidence has come into a murder trial on the issue of punishment, it may be used by the jury on the other issues.[0] But such uses will be covert and in violation of the judge's instructions. The issue I shall explore in subsequent sections is the extent to which such evidence may be used explicitly and with the approval of the court.

REDUCING THE GRADE OF HOMICIDE: "PARTIAL RESPONSIBILITY" AND "PROVOCATION"

The movement toward subjective liability has been most apparent in situations where the consequences seemed least critical to society and where the pressure for compassion was most keenly felt. These were the homicides. The effort to escape capital punishment led defendants to seek reductions from first degree murder to second degree murder, or from murder to manslaughter. Two doctrines became the focal point of these efforts. One was known as "partial responsibility"; the other was the more traditional plea of provocation.

The doctrine of "partial responsibility" had its origins in the cases which admitted evidence of intoxication to negate the elements of murder in the first degree. But the extension to other mitigating evidence has been slow. In 1925, only two states had adopted the more general doctrine. Today, it exists in some dozen states. Under it, evidence of mental disorder and of other subjective characteristics is admitted to prove that a defendant was incapable of the premeditation and deliberation required for first degree murder. In England, the doctrine has been called "diminished responsibility" and has been extended by statute to reduce murder to manslaughter.[4] The principal function of the doctrine is to give the jury the opportunity to find the defendant less guilty than the reasonable man, because he lacks the equipment to deal reasonably with life's stresses. But the opportunity is a restricted one. Compassion is not mistaken for absence of danger. Though the doctrine reduces the sanction that may be imposed, it leaves one severe enough to protect the public from the offender, to deter others, and to satisfy lingering impulses toward retribution.

The "partial responsibility" doctrine holds special appeal for the very class of persons that provides a principal source of the insanity defense—the defendants who face either a death sentence or a very long prison term. Since it is also framed broadly enough to include within its scope a great many cases which might also fit within the insanity defense, "partial responsibility" becomes an important alternative to the plea of insanity, particularly when the question of capital punishment is removed. The defendant facing a murder charge must then choose between, on the one hand, insanity and indeterminate commitment and, on the other, conviction and a long sentence, which may be reduced by parole. Some indication of how they choose is afforded by the recent English experience with "diminished responsibility." That plea has become so popular that it threatens to displace the insanity defense entirely.[5]

The provocation doctrine has the effect of reducing the grade of the defendant's homicide from murder to manslaughter. To qualify for it, the defendant must prove he killed under provocation and in the heat of passion. The law of provocation is an archetypical illustration of the dissonance between a subjective-sounding rule and an objective theory of liability. Though the doctrine seems to focus upon the particular defendant and his state of mind at the very moment of killing, juries are told to use a "reasonable man" standard to determine whether the provocation was adequate, or whether the passion was hot. The crime is manslaughter only if the reasonable man would have been provoked into losing his self-control or if his passions would not have subsided. Such a standard makes irrelevant any evidence that the defendant was peculiarly susceptible to provocation or passion—e.g. that he was intoxicated, or that he was mentally ill, or that he was mentally retarded, or unduly fearful or highstrung. Moreover, the passion must have been aroused entirely by provocation stemming from the conduct of the deceased. The defendant's circumstances, and the impact of the victim's conduct upon these circumstances, are not given any consideration.[6] A measure of how strictly the rule is applied is a recent English case in which an eighteen-year-old boy killed a prostitute after she had referred again and again to his impotence, jeering at, hitting, and kicking him. The court held the boy's mental condition was irrelevant for purposes of determining the adequacy of the provocation.[7]

Though the objective standard is unquestionably the general rule, it is not as universally accepted as text-writers suggest. In Utah, for example, if the defendant offers evidence that he was not a normal man, the "heat of passion" will be regarded as adequate even when there was "no evidence sufficient to cause a normal mind to be wrought up to heat of passion." Similarly, in a Tennessee case in which the defendant had killed a man who he mistakenly believed was debauching his wife, the court held that if he was convinced of his wife's infidelity and if he acted in the heat of passion under temporary mental stress, he was incapable of entertaining the malice required for murder.[8] Other states adopt a middle position which ostensibly retains the "reasonable man" standard but then undercuts it by instructing the jury to place the "reasonable man" in the situation of the defendant. The jury is to determine, for example, "whether there was sufficient cooling time for the passions to subside and reason to resume its sway . . . from the standpoint of the defendant in the light of all the facts and circumstances disclosed by the evidence." Under this approach, evidence may be admitted to show "peculiar weakness of mind or infirmity of temper," or that the defendant was "mentally and emotionally exhausted."[9] The "reasonable man" has often been endowed with so many of the defendant's characteristics as to make this standard almost indistinguishable from a completely subjective one.

The middle position has now been adopted by the American Law Institute in its Model Penal Code. A homicide is reduced from murder to non-reckless manslaughter when it "is committed under the influence of extreme mental or emotional disturbance for which there is reasonable explanation or excuse." However, "the reasonableness of such explanation or excuse [is to be determined] from the viewpoint of a person in the actor's situation under the circumstances as he believes them to be." The comments recognize that "a larger element of subjectivity" has been introduced but "the ultimate test" is said to remain objective. Illustrations are supplied in an effort to eliminate the ambiguity inherent in such a provision. It is said that the defendant's "scheme of moral values" may not be considered. If, however, he "had just suffered a traumatic injury, if he were blind or were distraught with grief, if he were experiencing an unanticipated reaction to a therapeutic drug," these factors could be taken into account.[10] Apparently, the only subjective elements to be considered are physical disabilities or emotional disturbances caused by dramatic external events. The deliberate failure of the reporters to deal specifically, in the Code or in the comments, with evidence of the defendant's personality, either by ruling it out or by making it clearly admissible, is probably an instance of purposeful ambiguity—leaving to case-by-case development the number and kind of personality traits and idiosyncrasies which will be admitted into evidence as part of "the actor's situation."

If the Code provision should win favor, there will be yet another alternative for defendants to consider in weighing whether to plead the insanity defense. The choices will be very much like those considered with regard to partial responsibility." On the side of the plea of provocation will be the prospect of a substantial term of imprisonment subject to reduction through parole; on the side of the insanity defense will be commitment to a mental hospital for an indeterminate period. Here, too, the probability is that the choice would be made against the insanity defense.

The developments I have described tend to confirm the worst fears of those who have sustained the objective theory. A subjective theory of provocation would result in reducing the length of imprisonment of the very persons who are least capable of restraining themselves under difficult circumstances and who are likely to be detained longest if they make out an insanity defense. As one court put the problem,

> while sympathy might at first glance suggest a more lenient rule for persons of low mentality or unstable emotions, the result would be disastrous . . . The rule

suggested would become a refuge for ill-tempered irresponsible citizens; it would put a premium on lack of
self-control and would penalize the reasonable man,
the average man, the prudent man because of the restraint he practices in dealing with his fellows.[11]

Yet it is difficult to believe the problem is a serious one, so
long as no more is involved than reducing the offense from
murder to manslaughter. The consequences of manslaughter
convictions are sufficiently severe to make it unlikely that they
will be much less effective as deterrents to potential offenders
than those attending convictions of murder. Moreover, the
sentence for manslaughter is usually long enough to keep
the offender in custody until he is cured or has reached an age
when the criminal tendencies of even the most dangerous are
likely to have disappeared.

THE WELLS-GORSHEN DOCTRINE

The theory underlying both the "partial responsibility"
doctrine and the subjective view of provocation is that verdict
and sentence should be tied more accurately than in the past
to the defendant's culpability. Carried to its logical extreme,
this would permit mental disorder to be used generally to
negate the mental element required for any crime. Beginning
with *People v. Wells,* the California courts have been moving
toward such a position. In *Wells,* the defendant was charged
with assaulting a prison guard "with malice aforethought," a
capital offense. He offered evidence from the prison psychiatrist that he had been suffering from nervous tensions which
made him abnormally susceptible to fear. The evidence was
excluded by the trial judge. He took the position that such
evidence could be admitted only on the issue of insanity, and
the state's procedure confined that issue to a second trial, after
"guilt" had been determined. The California Supreme Court
reversed, holding that the defendant must be permitted to

show he had committed the assault because of fear. However unjustified the fear may have been, if it existed in his mind, he "would not have committed that particular aggravated offense with which he is charged, for the essential element of 'malice aforethought' would be lacking." The court noted that "he would not be guiltless of crime," but only of the crime which requires "proof of a specific mental state, as, for example . . . murder in either degree . . . [and burglary, which] requires proof of entry with the specific 'intent to commit grand or petit larceny or any felony.'"[12] Several years later, in *People v. Gorshen,* the court held that the defendant's mental disorder could be used to negate the "malice aforethought" required not only for murder (which would be analogous to the English diminished responsibility rule) but for manslaughter as well. "It appears only fair and reasonable," said the court, "that defendant should be allowed to show that, in fact, subjectively, he did not possess the mental state or states in issue.[13]

The *Wells-Gorshen* doctrine is broad enough to make the defendant's mental illness admissible whenever he is charged with a crime requiring *mens rea.* Its reach encompasses specific intent, general intent, and recklessness. Thus far, however, it has not been applied by the California courts to any non-capital case, perhaps because it has had its most conspicuous application in the first stage of the "split-trial." But such applications have been made by the United States Court of Military Appeals. The first instance was *United States v. Higgins.*[14] The defendant was charged with willful disobedience of his superior officer. He defended on the ground that amnesia and intoxication had prevented him from knowing the man in question was his superior. The court noted that "if an accused person produces evidence of an underlying mental state [some mental derangement] which might have served to affect his intent at the time of the acts alleged, . . . [such evidence may be considered] in determining the accused's capacity to entertain premeditation, intent, or knowledge—when any of these is relevant to an offense charged." In subsequent cases, the doctrine has been applied to cases involving robbery and assault. And the court has intimated that evidence of mental disorder is admissible to negate "whatever . . . state of mind is required for the offense charged," provided it is genuinely relevant to that state of mind.[15]

More recently, the *Wells-Gorshen* doctrine has found its way into a Colorado statute which provides that "evidence of mental condition may be offered in a proper case as bearing upon the capacity of the accused to form the specific intent essential to constitute a crime."[16] And it has been used in an opinion of the United States Court of Appeals for the Fourth Circuit to hold that evidence of mental disorder is admissible to prove the defendant did not "knowingly" make false statements on his income tax returns.[17] Finally, and most importantly, the ALI's Model Penal Code provides: "Evidence that the defendant suffered from a mental disease or defect is admissible whenever it is relevant to prove that the defendant did or did not have a state of mind which is an element of the offense."[18] Though the accompanying comment purports to limit the provision to cases in which defendant is trying to negate the specific intent required for first degree murder (the "partial responsibility" doctrine), the language of the provision itself may reach to the farthest extension of *Wells-Gorshen.*

In earlier sections, I have tried to weigh the effect upon the insanity defense of other defenses which are only partial— which mitigate penalty but yet retain the offender in custody for a long time. The *Wells-Gorshen* doctrine is potentially even more erosive, for it may lead to releasing the defendant entirely. This can occur whenever evidence of mental disorder is used to negate *mens rea* in a crime which contains no lesser offense.[19] In such cases, the courts would not be able to rely on imprisonment for the lesser offense, as has been the case with "partial responsibility" and "provocation." The complete acquittal of such offenders would release from state control the very persons society should probably fear most—because their endowments are fewer, because they are more suggestible, more manipulable, more fearful. Though the problem is less critical where there are lesser-included offenses, because the state will retain some hold on the offender, it must nevertheless be taken into account because the hold may be inadequate. The subjective theory classes as less serious the offender who is less culpable; assuming him to be less "guilty," it proceeds to class him as less dangerous and either reduces the length of time he may be detained or releases him entirely. Yet his objective behavior may mark him as extremely dangerous and seriously in need not only of correction and treatment but of detention as well.

The courts have thus far been spared the complexities of the problem because the insanity defense had been virtually the only way to turn the inquiry into a subjective one and because commitment ordinarily followed. But no such protective device comes with *Wells-Gorshen* and its progeny. The state is left entirely to the civil commitment process if it should wish to detain the offender. As a result, these doctrines threaten to eliminate the insanity defense entirely for they offer the offender not only the fullest consideration of his mental illness but also the immediate prospect of freedom—at least until civil commitment or the expansion of crimes of strict liability is used to fill the breach.

COMPLETE ACQUITTAL: INVOLUNTARY ACTS AND SELF-DEFENSE

There are two instances in which traditional doctrine permits the insanity defense to be circumvented and the mentally ill offender to win his release: one is through proof that the offending act was "involuntary"; the other, in a small number of jurisdictions, is through use of a subjective standard in the law of self-defense.

Involuntary Acts

Crime is generally defined as a composite of two elements: a voluntary act proscribed by law (*actus reus*) and a state of mind which marks the offender and his act as culpable (*mens rea*). It has never been clear why a mental element need be part of the act requirement, since *mens rea* was required in any event. Nevertheless, the prevalent view is that the act must be something more than a muscular contraction. It must involve some minimal degree of purpose. This view is now codified in the Model Penal Code which defines crime as "conduct which includes a voluntary act or . . . omission" and then sets out instances of behavior which are *not* voluntary acts: "(a) a reflex or convulsion; (b) a bodily movement during unconsciousness or sleep; (c) conduct during hypnosis or resulting from hypnotic suggestion; (d) a bodily movement that otherwise is not a product of the effort or determination of the actor, either conscious or habitual."[20] The ALI view is based on cases like *Fain v. Commonwealth,* which held that a person who killed another while in a state of "somnolentia" (sleepwalking) could not be said to have acted voluntarily.[21] The same approach has been taken in cases of homicide while in an epileptic fit, or while suffering from a brain tumor, or while suffering from Ménière's syndrome, or while unconscious.[22] These instances involve diseases so clearly incapacitating as to make frivolous any effort to measure the resulting behavior by the rules of *mens rea.* The result has been outright acquittal. The insanity defense has ordinarily been regarded as inapplicable either because there was some doubt whether the conditions qualified as "mental disease" or "mental defect" or because the absence of a "voluntary" act or a "conscious" act kept the insanity issue from arising. And

civil commitment seemed inappropriate, particularly because
the defendant's general functioning seemed entirely normal.

Today, it is probable that most of the conditions which
have in the past supported a defense of "involuntary act"
would also be able to support the insanity defense. However
physical their origins, their impact on the mental state of the
affected individual seems clear. That is certainly true in the
case of epilepsy. And it is probably true in the other instances
specifically cited by the ALI. Yet, for the moment, the two
bodies of doctrine exist alongside one another, offering the
defendant the opportunity to prove one or the other, or both.
The result, in practical terms, is that the mentally ill offender
has still another way of placing his mental illness on the
scales while at the same time minimizing the risk of commitment if he should prevail. At present, there is no procedure
within the criminal process for retaining in custody persons
acquitted because their acts were "involuntary." And civil
commitment is likely to be invoked haphazardly, even though
the factors that mark these persons as blameless may also
mark them as threatening to the community and as appropriate for some form of medical supervision by the state.

Self-Defense

The law of self-defense is usually presented to the jury in
two questions: (1) did the defendant in fact kill out of an
honest fear of immediate danger to himself? (2) was his belief
reasonable under the circumstances? The first of these questions is clearly subjective in nature and invites any and all
evidence of the defendant's mental condition for the bearing
it may have on the question whether the defendant was
actually fearful. The second is entirely objective and is designed to keep the jury from using too broadly the evidence
which may come in on the first issue. There are, however,
several jurisdictions which explicitly authorize the jury to use
the subjective evidence in applying the standard of reasonable-

ness. This is done by telling the jury to appraise the situation from the standpoint of the defendant himself, rather than from that of the hypothetical reasonable man. There is very little specification, however, of the characteristics which may be attributed, though it is clear that his physical disabilities and his knowledge of the deceased may be.[23] Only rarely have the courts permitted his mental characteristics to be attributed to him. *Nelson v. Ohio* is one of these exceptional cases. Defendant, sixty years of age and not robust either physically or mentally, shot a neighbor with whom he was quarreling over damage allegedly done to his property. At the time, the neighbor was approaching him threateningly, hammer in hand. The court found that the evidence justified an instruction on self-defense, commenting that:

> the conduct of any individual is to be measured by that individual's equipment mentally and physically. He may act in self-defense, not only when a reasonable person would so act, but when one with the particular qualities that the individual himself has would do so. A nervous, timid, easily frightened individual is not measured by the same standard that a stronger, calmer, and braver man might be.[24]

The movement to an explicitly subjective standard in the law of self-defense has been a slow one, perhaps because subjective elements could come into the case in any event as bearing on the first question, the honesty of the defendant's fear. It was, therefore, possible to hold the defendant to the standard of reasonableness while mitigating it by putting before the jury the defendant's personality in all its imperfections.

The Model Penal Code would make the subjective standard the exclusive one. It has abandoned the objective part of the self-defense formula and requires only that the actor believe force is "immediately necessary for the purpose of protecting himself."[25] The risk of meeting an unreasonable response is thus placed upon the aggressor. Under such a formula, it is virtually inevitable that psychiatric testimony will be offered and received on the question whether the defendant was genuinely frightened and whether he used that degree of force which *he* believed to be "immediately necessary."

If the ALI approach is adopted, its doctrine of self-defense will provide yet another avenue for the mentally ill to avoid the insanity defense and the risk of commitment it entails. In doing so, it may free persons who respond too soon to threatened danger, or who respond disproportionately.

III

Under an objective theory of criminal liability, guiltless persons are treated as criminals because to do otherwise would be to release dangerous persons. As we begin to replace the objective with the subjective view of criminal liability, methods will have to be devised for coping with those dangerous persons we do not wish to label "guilty." Indeed, the very forces which make us loath to condemn them—because we see them as sick, as victims of adversity, as socially disadvantaged—will press us to detain them, to try to make them better or to take care of them. Traditionally, this has been done by sending such people to mental hospitals or to other treatment institutions. And the device for doing so has been either the insanity defense or civil commitment. The problem presented by the movement to subjective liability is that it may be releasing persons who cannot be committed civilly, under present practices, and who would either not prevail in an insanity defense or who choose not to raise it.

If the pressures toward a subjective theory continue to build, it may become necessary to refashion the traditional devices in order to solve the new problems. This has, of course, already begun with the insanity defense as it comes to encompass the broader conception of mental disease. But so long as the insanity defense remains an *alternative* to these other defenses which the defendant may assert or not, as he wishes, it is unreasonable to expect that very many defendants will use it. It may become necessary, therefore, to develop doctrines that will once again make the insanity defense the exclusive avenue for bringing subjective evidence into the trial. This has already occurred in England in two classes of cases: in one, evidence of "automatism," offered to prove the act was involuntary, has been held to come in only through the insanity defense; in the other, the defense of "diminished responsibility" was said to open the door to the prosecution to prove the defendant was insane. And it has occurred in a few instances in the United States without explicit consideration of the issues.[26] Alternatively, it may be desirable to fashion detention or supervision procedures explicitly directed to these offenders. Such an approach would have the virtue of scaling guilt to culpability, while providing for the dangerous. If neither approach is taken, we may see police and prosecutors pressing the broad language of the civil commitment statutes to their limits, either after the defendant has been acquitted under the new subjective doctrines or by avoiding the criminal process entirely in anticipation of such acquittal. In all of these eventualities, we may have a significant addition to the problem of preventive detention. Moreover, we may see a legislative effort to avoid the problem entirely by expanding the number of crimes which abandon *mens rea* and which impose strict liability on the offender.

PART IV

Perspectives

CHAPTER THIRTEEN

Reflections on the Insanity Defense

The insanity defense is caught in a cross-current of conflicting philosophies. Its roots are deep in a time when people spoke confidently of individual responsibility and of "blame," of the choice to do wrong. The emphasis was on the individual offender and the defense was seen as an instrument for separating the sick from the bad. It was not long, however, before ideas drawn from social utilitarianism took over the insanity defense. It was now feared that treating an offender as "sick" might weaken the deterrent effect of the criminal law. *M'Naghten* emerged as an effort to maintain the principle of the defense while at the same time keeping alive and vigorous the threat of criminal sanction. Men who knew what they were contemplating, and that it was wrong, were to be helped to help themselves and the criminal law could be used in the enterprise.

It was apparent then, as it is now, that there were people who could not control their conduct because they could not respond adequately to what they knew about consequences. But the difficulties of identifying accurately who would be affected by the threat of sanction led to a preference for *M'Naghten* over the "control" tests. It was felt that errors should be made in the direction of more sanction, rather than less, particularly in a period when the institutions of law enforcement seemed so rudimentary.

During the nineteenth century and most of the twentieth, the question of "responsibility" has dominated the literature. In the early part of the twentieth century, however, determinist influences—Darwinian, social positivist, Marxist, psychoanalytic—began to shape the criticism of the insanity defense and of criminal law generally. "Blame" began to seem an archaic concept and attention turned to finding the cause of the crime—either in the individual or in the environment—and eliminating it. It was widely assumed that the healing professions could make the offender better where punishment only made him worse; and that ultimately social reform would eliminate the conditions that led to crime. The insanity defense, more than any other concept of substantive law, felt the impact of the new enthusiasm. Reformers sought first to broaden the defense, so that more offenders could be taken in charge by the healing professions, and then to convert the criminal law entirely to a process for dealing with social danger, regardless of blame.

The advocates of reform started with the assumption that *M'Naghten* could not be bent to these objectives. As a result, they set about to destroy it. In the barrage of criticism and denunciation which ensued, they created the very devil they were trying to exorcise. Assuming *M'Naghten* to be an unusually restrictive test of insanity, they trained generations of lawyers and psychiatrists to regard it as such. The banners around which the reform forces first grouped were the "control" tests. But enthusiasm proved short-lived. For inexplicable reasons, those tests were also endowed with restrictive characteristics that the courts had not imposed, and were consigned prematurely to the waste-heap.

With the advent of *Durham,* it seemed that the "truth" had at last prevailed. What could be simpler, and more sensibly attuned to the needs of reform, than that offenders whose conduct was the product of mental disease be classed as insane and given over to mental hospitals? It soon became apparent, however, that the concept of mental disease was not a reliable guide. At the very time *Durham* was being written, psychiatrists and sociologists were subjecting the concept to withering attack. In addition, the mental hospitals were being

revealed to the public as lacking the facilities or the techniques for treating many of the mentally ill offenders. As the
insanity defense promised to encompass more of those who
were less sick, the specter of indeterminate commitment began
to move to the center of the stage.

Durham's principal contribution has been less as a "solution" to the insanity problem than as a dramatic demonstration that there are no solutions. By giving the reformers their
head, it has made apparent that a great deal of the criticism of
the insanity defense is really misplaced—that their target is
really the criminal law itself or the adversary process of trial
or the complexities of modern life. The consequence has been
highly beneficial. A retreat is at last beginning to be sounded
from what had been almost exclusive preoccupation with the
words of the insanity defense.

Nevertheless, the words in which the defense should be cast
are still receiving far more attention than they deserve. But
what is now at work is a tidying-up process. Though the debate still centers on whether *M'Naghten* should be discarded,
whether the "control" tests are adequate, whether *Durham* or
the ALI rule should be adopted, the discussions have begun to
change their form. It is slowly becoming clear that the words
of the test are a small part of a process which includes, in addition, the testimony of laymen and experts, examination and
cross-examination, argument and counter-argument. The significance of any one of the competing formulae turns on
whether one formula leads a trial judge to admit more evidence than another, or experts to testify more usefully, or
juries to acquit or convict more persons.

Measured by these standards, the various tests do not seem
very different. As matters now stand, identical evidence may be
admitted under each of them and juries tend to assign much
the same meaning to them. Even when the words themselves
are regarded as different, they come to the jury as part of a
process of proof and argument which shapes the words to the

particular case. I do not intend to minimize the difficulties which have followed from misunderstanding of either *M'Naghten* or of the "control" tests, or to suggest there is no need to follow the ALI in combining and improving upon them. The point, rather, is that reform of the insanity tests will have surprisingly modest results. In any event, before very long, defendants and their counsel will become aware of the opportunities available to them under the older rules. Both *M'Naghten* and the "control" tests will probably be construed more liberally than in the past, as the judiciary finds such courses preferable to adoption of a new rule.

I

Beyond the immediate future, the issues are much more complex and the resolutions less predictable. There will first be the problem of setting limits upon the mental conditions that can qualify for the insanity defense. After the full range of psychoses have been given a legitimate place, there will be the question of lesser mental disorders. As we have seen, the District of Columbia courts have been unable to fix any limits. The psychopath, the neurotic, the narcotics addict, the "emotionally unstable personality" have all been held to qualify for the defense, provided a psychiatrist is willing to testify that the condition in question is a "mental disease." Even the American Law Institute's deliberate effort to exclude the psychopath from the reach of the defense has proved easy to circumvent. If this trend continues, the insanity defense will become explicitly what it has long been implicitly, a free rendering to the jury of the fullest possible testimony regarding the accused. The principal objective sought for so long by the reformers will then have been attained. The defense will have been "broadened" so that experts will no longer be "hamstrung" in their testimony and, the jury willing, more mentally disordered offenders will be removed from the criminal process. The need for such a broadened standard is becoming increasingly apparent as we learn more about the degree to which jurors tend to resist the defense.

In time, the jury may come to accept the liberalized standard and to acquit in accordance with its terms, particularly if the jury is assured that its "acquittal" does not mean freedom but rather a decision that the offender is ill and will be treated.* For ever greater numbers, the prison will then be replaced by the mental hospital, punishment by treatment, harsh criminal sentences by commitment for no longer than necessary to make the offender better.

An insanity defense without limits is an attractive prospect if the consequence is prompt and successful treatment of the offender. Unfortunately, this is not likely to happen very soon. The mental hospitals do not want to receive "criminal" types, principally because psychiatry is usually unable to treat them; the few successful methods of treatment are so expensive as to make them a practical impossibility. As a result, a successful defense is too often likely to bring with it detention beyond that which will follow a criminal conviction. A broadened defense thus raises the siren song of "treatment" to draw the unwary away from a criminal law which offers, at the least, a fixed maximum sentence. The contrast between commitment and conviction is particularly acute when we note that the prisons are changing their form. The federal system, California, and other pace-setting states are creating within their correctional systems a mix of facilities roughly comparable to what one would find in a good mental health system—group counseling, psychiatric services, half-way houses, follow-up programs. These facilities, however, are usually located within a framework of relatively determinate sentences which can be leavened by the suspended sentence, probation, and parole. In short, the correctional system is at present more able than the mental health system to risk re-

*See discussion supra pp. 143–44.

leasing persons who are difficult to treat and who are most likely to be recidivists. The risk and the attendant burdens are distributed among the legislature, which fixes the maximum length of sentence, the parole board, which is made up of a representative body of citizens, and the judiciary, which is protected by centuries of tradition.

As disenchantment sets in regarding the length and effectiveness of the indeterminate commitment, there will be even greater reluctance than before to use the insanity defense. An already pronounced trend toward abandonment of the defense will thus be accentuated. For, as noted earlier, the defense has never played an important role in separating the sick from the bad. Most defendants are either drawn out of the criminal process or they plead guilty; only a small number of those who remain raise the defense. This trend will be pressed even further by the efforts of mentally ill offenders to take advantage of the alternatives afforded them by an increasingly subjective theory of criminal liability. This has already happened in England as the defense of "diminished responsibility" is coming to replace the insanity defense. Since a subjective theory means less culpability for the most dangerous, it should probably be coupled with devices for detaining persons longer than their "guilt" warrants. Until such devices are fashioned, the subjective theories may provide a way of avoiding the insanity defense and yet gaining advantage from the offender's mental illness.

The agencies of law enforcement will not find themselves powerless to respond to the avoidance of the insanity defense, even if subjective theories should take hold. They may start by urging that the defense should be the exclusive method for introducing notions of subjective liability. If that should fail, they have at hand a wide variety of civil commitment statutes which may be pressed into service to deal with the dangerous offender. These procedures, which have been given renewed vitality by the decisions in *Robinson v. California* and its

progeny,[1] include the general provisions for commitment of
the mentally ill, the more specialized ones for committing the
sexual psychopath, the defective delinquent, the alcoholic, and
the narcotics addict. Bypassing the criminal process and the
insanity defense, they take literally the positivist thesis that it
is *not* the act but the man which is important. Abandoning the
concept of blame, they usually provide for detention until
the offender is no longer dangerous. The existence of these
processes—and of the vaguely worded definitions of the
persons drawn within them—are likely to prove too tempting
to be resisted for long, if the insanity defense should be
avoided too often or if the correctional system comes to be
regarded as "too soft."

The map I have drawn of currents and cross-currents im-
pinging upon the mentally ill offender makes it very difficult to
chart a course for the insanity defense. Its vision of a benign
mental hospital releasing people sooner than a harsh correctional system is belied by the grim reality of inadequate treatment methods and resources. The situation may change, of
course, if a body of experience should develop regarding
length of detention in mental hospitals, and they should turn
out to be shorter than, or no longer than, prison sentences.
But even as such changes tilt the scales toward the insanity
defense, the correctional systems will also be changing. How,
then, is the insanity defense to be located within this stream
of competing tendencies? In the immediately foreseeable
future, it probably promises a more therapeutic orientation
for the individual offender than does a conviction. But even
that generalization may not hold for every jurisdiction. In
some places, even now, the correctional system offers a greater
prospect of treatment than the mental hospital. And where
the hospitals do offer superior treatment possibilities, they
cannot be said to offer very much.

If one probes deeply into the positions of those who urge
expansion of the insanity defense, it soon becomes apparent

that they see it more as a spur to development of treatment resources than as offering very much at present. They seem to believe that the treatment-oriented hospital administrator who receives mentally ill offenders will feel he must "do something" positive about them; or that "society" will. This rationale, and it is encountered surprisingly often, ignores the equanimity with which hospital administrators and "society" have for generations tolerated custodial facilities housing huge numbers of people lost in the back wards. So long as the prospects for "cure" in the mental hospital and in the prison are comparably poor, it is difficult to dispute the view that the balance of benevolence is at present against the medical approach—because it brings with it the specter of indeterminate commitment. Until that problem is solved, defendants will make every effort to avoid the insanity defense.

This problem of indeterminate detention may come in any one of several guises—either through an expanded insanity defense, or through avoiding the criminal law by more extensive use of civil commitment or through raising the maximum periods of detention under criminal statutes—but whatever the guise, it presents one of the central legal problems of our time. Before very long, we shall have to develop a core of meaning for concepts like treatability and potential danger, and then we shall have to face the question whether it is "fair" to hold indefinitely persons who cannot be treated successfully. The answer will depend upon how accurately we can predict dangerous behavior, rather than upon characterizations of individuals as psychopaths or defective delinquents or insane. Certainly, we cannot now make such predictions accurately in very many cases. Too many imponderables are involved, too many estimates of how often unfortunate personalities are likely to confront precipitating events.

The effort to develop a law of dangerousness is likely to take us back to the body of ideas that underlies much of classical criminal law, as reflected in the law of inchoate crimes and in the traditional calculus of sentencing. What will probably ensue is a set of doctrines which will once again emphasize how wary we must be of inferring real dangerousness from behavior which has not advanced very far toward the harm a legislature is willing to condemn, or of assuming too readily that past behavior will be repeated. If determinate periods of detention seem too restrictive, then periodic review procedures will have to be developed, with the burden on the state to justify continued detention. The principal task for the future will be to fuse such concerns into what has until now been regarded as a medical process which needed no standards and no procedural safeguards.

Several conclusions emerge from the foregoing analysis. First, the insanity defense can no longer be equated with the problem of the mentally ill offender. It is far too occasional to serve as a diagnostic device separating the sick from the bad. Unquestionably, large numbers of defendants who might be able to raise it successfully elect not to do so; or police and prosecutors direct them away from the criminal process. As a result, mentally ill offenders are as likely to move into the correctional system as to be diverted to the mental hospitals. Explicit provision must be made for such offenders in the correctional system—either by providing it with its own treatment resources or by providing for transfer to the mental health system or by merging the two systems.

Second, for those who wish to avoid being condemned as criminals and who wish to seek treatment in a mental hospital, the way must be made clear and effective, particularly during the transition period in which correctional systems may not yet serve rehabilitative ends. At a minimum, *M'Naghten* must be construed broadly and supplemented by one of the "control" tests, though adoption of the ALI rule would probably be preferable. Procedural impediments to raising the defense must be reduced and expert assistance in presenting the defense assured.

Third, there must be an end to loosely drawn authority to detain persons indefinitely, either through acquittals by reason of insanity or through civil commitment processes. For the bulk of mentally ill offenders, the period fixed for their criminal sentence is long enough to try to make them better. If that should fail, then they should be released—because the prediction that they will err again is likely to be inaccurate and because the crimes threatened are not likely to be either so imminent or so serious as to compensate for the probably inaccurate prediction. For a relatively few offenders, a detention procedure should be devised for defined and limited periods, but only after a showing that such persons are imminently and seriously dangerous to life—making appropriate discounts for the unreliability of such predictions. The procedure for such extensions of term should be one in which the burden of proof is upon the state and the offender is given every opportunity, and aid, in rebutting the charge against him.

II

It may well be suggested that these conclusions are at cross-purposes, that it makes little sense to devote very much time to the insanity defense when it cannot be expected to reach more than a relative handful of mentally ill offenders. Moreover, it raises problems of treatment and detention which cannot be passed casually on to the mental hospitals. Why not, therefore, abandon the defense entirely and substitute a system in which the courts decide only whether the offending act has occurred—and then pass the offender to a "treatment tribunal" which will take his mental condition into account in determining what is to be done with him?[2] Proponents of this view argue further that there is little purpose in trying to assess "blame" because the factors which move a man to crime are too various and too unfathomable. It no longer serves even the needs of the society because too many other forces are at work—economic, social, and political—to take seriously any longer the occasional criminal trial involving the insanity defense.

If the office of the defense is conceded to be the identification of persons whose conviction will *not* serve the functions of the criminal law, the argument for abolition grows even stronger. There are remarkably few persons who have committed seriously harmful acts whose condemnation will not serve *some* function of the criminal law. For example, the "corrective" or "educative" function can be served with all who commit serious harm, regardless of their state of mind. Similarly, it is difficult to credit the view that victims of crime—and those sufficiently identified with them to feel aggressive—will want to hold only "responsible" offenders to account. Though there may be some point at which an offender's mental condition will be so extreme as to outweigh the harm, even in the eyes of those who have been injured, the retribution function can probably be served by "condemning" all but the grossest of deviants.

Deterrence emerges from analysis in much the same way as the other functions. A prohibition on conduct, with an attending penalty, will unquestionably affect the behavior of large numbers of persons, some by the mere fact of prohibition, a greater number by their expectation that the prohibition will be enforced and the penalties imposed. For the latter group, therefore, the question is almost entirely one of how many instances of enforcement there must be to keep the threat alive, how swift and how regular the enforcement will be, how much the exigencies of the particular situation overwhelm the more remote influences emanating from a threat of prosecution. Moreover, such persons are likely to be deterred by *any* conviction of crime, noticing hardly at all whether it involved the insanity issue. If they are especially calculating, we may assume they will be deterred only by convictions which seem genuinely applicable to them. For example, the prospective burglar may be more deterred by learning of a conviction of burglary, particularly if it relates to a neighborhood and to circumstances which enable him to identify with the convicted burglar. It seems extremely implausible, however, that he will be deterred by a conviction of crime and not by a finding of insanity. Indeed, persons who are so calculating would probably know that their "acquittal" would bring with it not freedom but the prospect of a "civil" commitment at least as onerous as a criminal sentence. In sum, the insanity defense is not likely to affect the behavior of any of these groups very much.

Despite the superficial plausibility of the proposal to abolish the insanity defense, there are a great many objections to it. First, the effort to separate the offending act from the mental state of the offender has been singularly unsuccessful in the only jurisdictions which have tried it. Louisell and Hazard have recounted in detail the manner in which California's two-step trial, separating the issue of "guilt" from that of insanity, has foundered on the view that *mens rea* may not be read out of the guilt-finding part of the criminal trial.[3] Reserving the insanity defense to a separate stage is likely, therefore, to result in two trials where there was only one before. A more sustained effort might, of course, be made to eliminate all questions of mental condition from the first stage. But the California courts have intimated it would be unconstitutional to do so. And they have case law on their side. The only two attempts in our history to eliminate both the *mens rea* requirement and the insanity defense have been unsuccessful. The statutes were held by the courts of Washington and Mississippi to deny due process of law, depriving defendants of a jury trial on defenses which had "always" been passed on by the jury. "This right of trial," said the Washington courts, "must mean something more than the preservation of the mere form of trial by jury, else the Legislature could by the process of . . . defining crime or criminal procedure entirely destroy the substance of the right by limiting the questions to be submitted to the jury." The issue of insanity, the court continued, was too intrinsic to the concept of crime to permit its removal by legislation. It "is patent to all men that the status and condition in the eyes of the world, and under the law, of one convicted of crime is vastly different from one simply judged insane."[4] To convict an insane man, said the Mississippi court in tones remarkably like those of *Robinson v. California*, would be a "cruel and unusual punishment."[5]

Second, the proposal tends to sweep past the jury and toward the sentencing stage large numbers of "offenders" who would now go free, because they lacked *mens rea*, on the assumption that they would be weeded out by the "treatment tribunal." Experience suggests, however, that prematurely labeling a person an "offender" is more likely than any other single factor to confirm him in a criminal career; and that the "helping" professions tend to think they can help even when they cannot, with all that implies for keeping more people in custody or control than in the past.

Third, and most fundamentally, eliminating the insanity defense would remove from the criminal law and the public conscience the vitally important distinction between illness and evil, or would tuck it away in an administrative process. The man who wished to contest his responsibility before the public and his peers would no longer be able to do so. Instead, he would be approached entirely in social engineering terms: How has the human mechanism gone awry? What stresses does it place upon the society? How can the stresses be minimized and the mechanism put right?

This approach overlooks entirely the place of the concept of responsibility itself in keeping the mechanism in proper running order. That concept is more seriously threatened today than ever before. This is a time of anomie—of men separated from their faiths, their tribes, and their villages—and trying to achieve in a single generation what could not previously be achieved in several. Many achieve all they expect, but huge numbers do not; these vent their frustration in anger, in violence, and in theft. In an effort to patch and mend the tearing social fabric, the state is playing an increasingly paternal role, trying to help as many as possible to realize their expectations and to soothe and heal those who cannot. As this effort gains momentum, there is a very real risk it will bring with it a culture which will not make the individuals within it feel it is important to learn the discipline of moderation and conformity to communal norms.

In such a time, the insanity defense can play a part in reinforcing the sense of obligation or responsibility. Its emphasis on whether an offender is sick or bad helps to keep alive the almost forgotten drama of individual responsibility. Its weight is felt through the tremendous appeal it holds for the popular imagination, as that imagination is gripped by a dramatic trial and as the public at large identifies with the man in the dock. In this way, it becomes part of a complex of cultural forces that keep alive the moral lessons, and the myths, which are essential to the continued order of society. In short, even if we have misgivings about blaming a particular individual, because he has been shaped long ago by forces he may no longer be able to resist, the concept of "blame" may be necessary.

However much we may concentrate our attention on the individual, we rely implicitly upon the existence of a culture, and a value system, which will enable us to move the individual toward conformity or to a reasonable nonconformity. That value system, if it is to become fixed early enough, must be absorbed from parents. And it, in turn, is a reflection of the larger culture, absorbed slowly and subtly over generations, transmitted by parent to child through the child-rearing devices extant in a given society. The concept of "blame," and insanity which is its other side, is one of the ways in which the culture marks out the extremes beyond which nonconformity may not go. It is one of the complex of elements which train people so that it becomes almost intuitive not to steal or rape or kill. A society which did not set such limits would probably, in time, become a less law-abiding society. This is not to say that there is not a good deal of room for humanizing the criminal law, or the insanity defense, but only that it is essential that "blame" be retained as a spur to individual responsibility.

Finally, the heart of the distinction between conviction and acquittal by reason of insanity lies in the fact that the former represents official condemnation. Yet the acquittal is itself a sanction, bringing with it comparable stigma and the prospect of indeterminate detention. If the choice between the two sanctions is to be made in a way that will not only be acceptable to the larger community but will also serve the symbolic function we have noted, it is important that the decision be made by a democratically selected jury rather than by experts—because the public can identify with the former but not with the latter. It does not follow, however, that the decision regarding the type of facility to which a particular offender is to be sent need also be made by the jury. Once the distinction between "blame" and compassion has been made, decisions as to disposition should be made by those who are professionally qualified.

It is impossible to say with any degree of certainty how few convictions of crime are needed to sustain the threat of enforcement for those likely to be affected by such a threat. Nor can we say how often the insanity defense need be tried in order to play its long-term role of shoring up the moral order. We cannot even say very much about how the competing formulations are, in fact, understood and applied by judge, jury, counsel, and defendants. We can do little more than draw the uneven line traced by the defense as it serves first one objective, then another, and even a third, sometimes separately and sometimes together. In considerable part, this is because the defense and its implications depend so much upon institutions outside the control of the courts, which have until now played a dominant role. Judicial efforts are inevitably inhibited by the fact that the courts cannot assure either the will or the wit, the money or the men, to carry out the implications of a broadened insanity defense, or of a narrow defense which sends large numbers of convicted offenders into the correctional system. Only legislative action can provide the structure and the funds under which a thoroughgoing effort can be made to present the insanity defense effectively, to provide the full range of therapeutic facilities for mentally ill offenders (whether they find themselves in the correctional or the mental health system), and to assure that sensible limits are placed on the length of detention. Even then, long-term solutions will have to await our learning how to treat offenders and how to eliminate the causes of crime.

NOTES

CHAPTER TWO

Insanity and the Criminal Law

1. The cases are collected and discussed in Chs. 4, 5, and 6 infra. For references to the statutory or common law bases for the defense, see Keedy, "Irresistible Impulse as a Defense in Criminal Law," 100 *U. Pa. L. Rev.* 956, 976 et seq. (1952).

2. See generally Glueck, *Mental Disorder and the Criminal Law,* Ch. 5 (1925); Jones, *Lunacy, Law and Conscience,* Ch. 1 (1955); Dain, *Concepts of Insanity in the United States, 1789–1865* (1964); Deutsch, *The Mentally Ill in America,* Chs. 1 to 5 (1949); Platt and Diamond, "The Origins of the 'Right and Wrong' Test of Criminal Responsibility," 54 *Calif. L. Rev.* 1227 (1966).

3. State v. Strasburg, 110 Pac. 1020 (Wash. 1910); Sinclair v. State, 132 So. 581 (Miss. 1931). For more recent discussions of insanity in the context of constitutional law, see Leland v. Oregon, 343 U.S. 790, 800–01 (1952); State v. white, 374 P.2d 942, 965 (Wash. 1962); Dubin, "Mens Rea Reconsidered," 18 *Stan. L. Rev.* 322, 387 (1966) (discussing relation between insanity defense and Robinson v. California).

4. For an introduction to the literature, see Hart, "The Aims of the Criminal Law," 23 *Law & Contemp. Prob.* 401 (1958); Wechsler, "The Challenge of a Model Penal Code," 65 *Harv. L. Rev.* 1097 (1952); Andenaes, "General Prevention—Illusion or Reality," 43 *J. Crim. L. & Crimin.* 176 (1952); Waelder, "Psychiatry and the Problem of Criminal Responsibility," 101 *U. Pa. L. Rev.* 378 (1952). See, in addition, Ehrenzweig, "A Psychoanalysis of the Insanity Plea," 73 *Yale L. J.* 425 (1964); Alexander and Staub, *The Criminal, The Judge and The Public* (1956 ed.); Redmount, "Some Basic Considerations Regarding Penal Policy," 49 *J. Crim. L. & Crimin.* 426 (1959); Kaplan, "Barriers to the Establishment of a Deterministic Criminal Law," 46 *Ky. L. J.* 103 (1957); Lewis, "The Humanitarian Theory of Punishment," 6 *Res Judicatae* 224 (1953); DeGrazia, "Crime Without Punishment," 52 *Col. L. Rev.* 746 (1952); Cohen, "Moral Aspects of the Criminal Law," 49 *Yale L. J.* 987 (1940); Mead, "The Psychology of Punitive Justice," 23 *Am. J. Soc.* 577 (1918).

5. See the references in Ch. 4, note 3 infra; and see Guttmacher, "The Psychiatrist as an Expert Witness," 22 *U. Chi. L. Rev.* 325, 329 (1955).

6. See Holmes, *The Common Law* 41 et seq. (Howe ed. 1963); and see discussion in Ch. 12 infra.

7. See generally Joint Commission on Mental Illness and Health, *Action for Mental Health* (1961); Robinson, *Community Resources in Mental Health* (1960). Illustrative of the shifts in treatment trends is Jones, *The Therapeutic Community* (1953).

8. See generally Merton, "Social Structure and Anomie," in *Social Theory and Social Structure* 131–60 (1957); Cohen, *Delinquent Boys* (1955); Cloward and Ohlin, *Delinquency and Opportunity* (1960); Matza, *Delinquency and Drift* (1964); England, "A Theory of Middle Class Juvenile Delinquency," 50 *J. Crim. L. & Crimin.* 535 (1960).

CHAPTER THREE

The Defendant

1. See generally Newman, *Conviction: The Determination of Guilt or Innocence Without Trial* 3 et seq. (1966); Note, Guilty Plea Bargaining, 112 *U. Pa. L. Rev.* 865 (1964).

2. See Kalven and Zeisel, *The American Jury* 330–31 (1966). It is, of course, possible for heavy sentences to be imposed for less serious crimes, through cumulation of charges and sentences or through use of "habitual offender" laws. See generally Comment, "Twice in Jeopardy," 75 *Yale L. J.* 262 (1965); Brown, "The Treatment of the Recidivist in the United States," 23 *Can. B. Rev.* 640 (1945). For indications that new currents may affect the general point, see infra pp. 168–69. It should be noted that the "insane" offender who is sentenced to death may be rescued by executive clemency. See Braithwaite, "Executive Clemency in California," 1 *Issues in Criminology* 77 (1965). Where the jury has the power to impose the death penalty, evidence of mental disorder may be offered on the issue. State v. Sikora, 210 A.2d 193, 203–04 (N.J. 1965).

3. See generally Star, *The Public's Ideas About Mental Illness* (National Opinion Research Center, 1955), reprinted in part in Donnelly et al., *Criminal Law* 818–20 (1962); James, "Jurors' Assessment of Criminal Responsibility," 7 *Soc. Prob.* 58 (1959); Kalven and Zeisel, *The American Jury* 331, 404–05 (1966).

4. See generally Arieti, *American Handbook of Psychiatry*, Parts Three and Eight (1959); White, *The Abnormal Personality*, Ch. 15 (1956); Henderson and Gillespie, *A Text-Book of Psychiatry*, Ch. 10 (7th ed. 1950); Strecker and Ebaugh, *Practical Clinical Psychiatry*, Ch. 7 (1940); Strecker, *Basic Psychiatry*, Ch. 7 (1952); Hartwell, *Practical Psychiatry and Mental Hygiene*, Ch. 30 (1947); Overholser, *The Psychiatrist and the Law* 25 et seq. (1953); Cooper, "Problems in Application of the Basic Criteria of Schizophrenia," 117 *Am. J. Psychiatry* 66 (1960).

5. See Kreschner, "Simulation of Nervous and Mental Disease," 103 *J. Nerv. and Ment. Dis.* 571, 605 (1946); Srole et al., *Mental Health in the Metropolis* 130 (1962); Joint Commission on Mental Illness and Health, *Action for Mental Health* 39–46, 168 et seq. (1961); Greenblatt

et al., *From Custodial to Therapeutic Patient Care in Mental Hospitals* (1955).

6. Sullivan, *Clinical Studies in Psychiatry* 326 (1956); Mayer-Gross et al., *Clinical Psychiatry* 263 (1954).

7. The quotation is from Belknap, *Human Problems of a State Mental Hospital* 193 (1956). See also id., passim and at 164, 190–93; Chambers, "Perceptual Judgment and Associative Learning Ability of Schizophrenics and Nonpsychotics," 20 *J. Consult. Psychol.* 211 (1956); Chapman, "Distractability in the Conceptual Performance of Schizophrenics," 53 *J. Abn. and Soc. Psychol.* 286 (1956); Long, "Praise and Censure as Motivating Variables in the Motor Behavior and Learning of Schizophrenics," 63 *J. Abn. and Soc. Psychol.* 283 (1961); Robin and King, "Psychological Studies," in Bellak, ed., *Schizophrenia,* Ch. 6 (1958); Baur, "Legal Responsibility and Mental Illness," 57 *N.W.U.L. Rev.* 12, 16–17 (1962).

8. Strecker and Willey, "An Analysis of Recoverable 'Dementia Praecox' Reactions," 3 *Am. J. Psychiatry* 593, 663 (1924).

9. In addition to sources in note 4 supra, see Moody, *The Primary Psychiatric Syndromes* 253 (1956); Arieti, *Interpretation of Schizophrenia* (1955); Cameron and Magaret, *Behavior Pathology* 494 et seq. (1951); Lindsay, "Periodic Catatonia," 94 *J. Ment. Sci.* 590 (1948); Kasanin, "The Acute Schizoaffective Psychoses," 13 *Am. J. Psychiatry* 97 (1933); Gordon, "The So-Called Lucid Interval in Manic-Depressive Psychoses," 74 *Am. J. Insanity* 667 (1918); Kreschner, "Simulation of Nervous and Mental Disease," 103 *J. Nerv. and Ment. Dis.* 571, 605 (1946).

10. See Strecker, *Basic Psychiatry* 81 et seq. (1952); Henderson and Gillespie, *A Text-Book of Psychiatry,* Ch. 14 (1955).

11. See Hartwell, *Practical Psychiatry and Mental Hygiene* 179 et seq. (1947); Henderson and Gillespie, supra note 10; Skottowe, *Clinical Psychiatry* 289–92 (1953).

12. Strecker, *Basic Psychiatry,* Ch. 5 (1952); Hartwell, supra note 11, at 159 et seq.

13. See Sakel, *Epilepsy* 44–45 (1958); Henderson and Gillespie, supra note 10, at 547 et seq.; Skottowe, supra note 11, at 282 et seq.; Hartwell, supra note 11, at 191 et seq.

14. See Hartwell, supra note 11, at 222 et seq.; Skottowe, supra note 11, at 185 et seq.; Strecker, supra note 10, at 219 et seq.

15. See Strecker, supra note 10, at 183 et seq.; Skottowe, supra note 11, at 141 et seq.; Henderson and Gillespie, supra note 11, at 227 et seq.

16. See Skottowe, supra note 11, at 26; Israel and Johnson, "Discharge and Readmission Rate in 4,254 Consecutive First Admissions of Schizophrenia," 112 *Am. J. Psychiatry* 903 (1956); U.S. Public Health Service, *Patients in Mental Institutions,* Parts II, III (1957).

17. See Skottowe, supra note 11, at 208 et seq.; Moody, *The Primary Psychiatric Syndromes* 240 (1956); Arieti, *Interpretation of Schizophrenia* 326 (1955); Bellak, ed., *Schizophrenia*, Ch. 1 (1958); Bernstein, "Recurrent Psychotic Episodes in Middle Life," 110 *Am. J. Psychiatry* 377 (1953).

18. For an introduction to the literature of psychopathy, see Cleckley, *The Mask of Sanity* (1955); McCord, *Psychopathy and Delinquency* (1956); Henderson and Gillespie, *A Text-Book of Psychiatry*, Ch. 12 (1952); White, *The Abnormal Personality* 394 et seq. (1956); Levy, "The Deprived and the Indulged Forms of Psychopathic Personality," 21 *Am. J. Orthopsych.* 250 (1951). As to the general problem of communication and diagnosis, see Hollingshead and Redlich, *Social Class and Mental Illness*, Chs. 6, 8 (1958).

19. See Hunt et al., "A Theoretical and Practical Analysis of the Diagnostic Process," in Hoch and Zubin, *Current Problems of Psychiatric Diagnosis* 55 (1953); Diethelm, "The Fallacy of the Concept: Psychosis," id. at 24; Wootton, *Social Science and Social Pathology*, Ch. 7 (1959); Jahoda, *Current Concepts of Positive Mental Health* (1958); Lewis, "Health as a Social Concept," 4 *Br. J. Soc.* 109 (1953); Redlich, "The Concept of Normality," 6 *Am. J. Psychother.* 551 (1952); Bowman and Rose, "A Criticism of the Terms 'Psychosis,' 'Psychoneurosis' and 'Neurosis,'" 108 *Am. J. Psychiatry* 161 (1951).

20. See generally Flannery, "Meeting the Insanity Defense," 51 *J. Crim. L. & Crimin.* 309, 311 et seq. (1960).

21. But see Hughes v. United States, 306 F.2d 287, 289 (D.C. Cir. 1962) which says the statutory appointment procedure "does not apply if the examination is merely for the purpose of informing the United States Attorney as to the defendant's mental condition. The United States Attorney is free to use any doctor or hospital he selects to conduct such an examination." See also Judicial Conference of D.C., *Report of Committee on Problems Connected with Mental Examination of the Accused in Criminal Cases* 25 (1965); and see pages 131 et seq. infra.

22. See discussion infra pages 184–85.

23. As to reforms in the bail field which are making monetary bond less important, see Freed and Wald, *Bail in the United States* (1964); Foote, "The Coming Constitutional Crisis in Bail," 113 *U. Pa. L. Rev.* 959 (1965). A recent report describes the practice in the District of Columbia of revoking or denying bail when a motion for a mental examination is made. Judicial Conference of D.C., *Report of Committee on Problems Connected with Mental Examination of the Accused in Criminal Cases* 31 (1965).

24. The defendant may not be summoned before the grand jury. But he may appear in response to an invitation. If he is not yet a defendant, he may be summoned as a witness. In some jurisdictions, however, he

may not be summoned as a witness if he is already marked for prosecution. See generally Note, "Self Incrimination by Federal Grand Jury Witnesses," 67 *Yale L. J.* 1271 (1958).

25. See Flannery, "Meeting the Insanity Defense," 51 *J. Crim. L. & Crimin.* 309, 313 et seq. (1960).

26. Star, *The Public's Ideas About Mental Illness* 3–6 (National Opinion Research Center, 1955); James, "Juror's Assessment of Criminal Responsibility," 7 *Soc. Prob.* 58 (1959); Arens et al., "Jurors, Jury Changes and Insanity," 14 *Cath. U. L. Rev.* 1 (1965).

CHAPTER FOUR

M'Naghten: The Stereotype Challenged

1. M'Naghten's Case, 10 Clark & Fin. 200 (1843). For historical background, see Weihofen, *Mental Disorder as a Criminal Defense* 52–63 (1954); Biggs, *The Guilty Mind* 81–117 (1955). The cases are collected and discussed in Weihofen, Ch. 3 (1954). A more recent collection is to be found in Moore, "M'Naghten Is Dead—Or Is It?," 3 *Houston L. Rev.* 58, 74 et seq. (1965). Several jurisdictions still recognize the "insane delusion" test which was separately stated in *M'Naghten's* Case. Most commentators have taken the position that it adds nothing to what is commonly understood as the *M'Naghten* rule. The same is true of the "mistake of fact" portion of *M'Naghten*. See Weihofen, *Mental Disorder as a Criminal Defense* 60–63, 112–13 (1954); Perkins, *Criminal Law* 751 et seq. (1957); Williams, *Criminal Law* 521–27 (1961).

2. See Wechsler, "The Criteria of Criminal Responsibility," 22 *U. Chi. L. Rev.* 367, 374 (1955) ("So long as there is any chance that the preventive influence [of criminal law] may operate, it is essential to maintain the threat. If it is not maintained, the influence of the entire system is diminished upon those who have the requisite capacity. . . . On this analysis, the category of the irresponsible must be defined in extreme terms."); State v. White, 374 P.2d 942, 966 (Wash. 1962), cert. den. 375 U.S. 883.

3. See the references collected in Durham v. United States, 214 F.2d 862, 870–71 (D.C. Cir. 1954). In addition, see United States v. Freeman, 357 F.2d 606, 619 (2 Cir. 1966); Glueck, *Law and Psychiatry* 61–68 (1962); Weihofen, *The Urge to Punish* 29 et seq. (1956); Roche, "Criminal Responsibility," in Hoch and Zubin, *Psychiatry and the Law* 112 (1955); Group for the Advancement of Psychiatry, *Criminal Responsibility and Expert Testimony* 4 (1954) (quoting Zilboorg, *Mind, Medicine and Man* 273: "except for [the] totally deteriorated, drooling, hopeless psychotics of long standing, and congenital idiots—who seldom commit or have the opportunity to commit murder—the great majority and perhaps all murderers know what they are doing, the nature and

quality of their act and the consequences thereof, and they are therefore 'legally' sane' regardless of the opinion of any psychiatrist."); *Report of Royal Commission on Capital Punishment,* p. 80 (1953); Overholser, *The Psychiatrist and the Law* 22, 36 (1953); White, *Insanity and the Criminal Law* 99 (1923); Brancale, "More on M'Naghten: A Psychiatrist's View," 65 *Dick. L. Rev.* 277, 277–78 (1961); Carroll and Leopold, "Current Influence of Psychiatric Concepts in Determining Criminal Responsibility in Pennsylvania," 31 *Temp. L. Q.* 254, 264, 280 (1958); Waelder, "Psychiatry and the Problem of Criminal Responsibility," 101 *U. Pa. L. Rev.* 378, 380–81 (1952); Stevenson, "Insanity as a Criminal Defense: The Psychiatric Viewpoint," 25 *Can. B. Rev.* 731, 732 (1947).

4. Weihofen, *Mental Disorder as a Criminal Defense* 119 (1954); Weihofen, "The Definition of Mental Illness," 21 *Ohio St. L. J.* 1, 6 (1960); Kuh, "The Insanity Defense—An Effort to Combine Law and Reason," 110 *U. Pa. L. Rev.* 771, 785 (1962); Davidson, "The Psychiatrist's Role in the Administration of Criminal Justice," 4 *Rutgers L. Rev.* 578, 583 (1950); Wertham, "Psycho-authoritarianism and the Law," 22 *U. Chi. L. Rev.* 336, 337 (1955); Cleckley, "Psychopathic States," in 1 Arieti, *American Handbook of Psychiatry* 567, 570 (1959); Krash, "The Durham Rule and Judicial Administration of the Insanity Defense in the District of Columbia," 70 *Yale L. J.* 905, 927 (1961).

5. State v. White, 142 A.2d 65, 68 (N.J. 1958)

6. State v. Andrews, 357 P.2d 739, 744 (Kans. 1961), cert. den. 368 U.S. 868.

7. Barbour v. State, 78 So.2d 328, 340 (Ala. 1955). See also State v. Painter, 63 S.E.2d 86, 97 (W. Va. 1950); Myers v. State, 174 P.2d 395, 400 (Okla. 1946); State v. Clokey, 364 P.2d 159, 164 (Idaho, 1961); Askew v. State, 118 So.2d 219, 222 (Fla. 1960); Griffin v. State, 96 So.2d 424, 425 (Fla. 1957); Maddox v. State, 17 So.2d 283, 285 (Ala. 1944); People v. Griggs, 110 P.2d 1031, 1034 (Calif. 1941); Prather v. Comm., 287 S.W. 559, 560 (Ky. 1926); Martin v. State, 139 S.W. 1122, 1124 (Ark. 1911). Many of these cases try to distinguish between "voluntary" intoxication and intoxication caused by disease. The former can at the most reduce the grade of an offense; the latter can presumably lead either to acquittal or to the insanity defense. See discussion infra p. 203. Some tend to assimilate these cases to the rule, which exists in several states, that a "morbid propensity" to commit prohibited acts is insufficient. But if such a propensity is part of a "mental disease," it will suffice.

8. For instances when the issue was passed to the jury, see, in addition to cases in note 7 supra, State v. White, 142 A.2d 65, 68 (N.J. 1958); Griffin v. State, 96 So.2d 424, 425 (Fla. 1957); State v. Painter, 63 S.E.2d 86, 92 (W. Va. 1950). For cases where it was not, see Ruffin v. State, 123 A.2d 461, 464 (Del. 1956); Salter v. State, 264 S.W.2d 719 (Tex. 1953); Burr v. State, 114 So.2d 764, 766 (Miss. 1959); State v.

Rio, 230 P.2d 308, 314 (Wash. 1951), cert. den. 342 U.S. 867. See also
R. v. Spriggs, [1958] 1 All Eng. Rep. 300, 304 (in a diminished responsibility case, Lord Goddard said: "it has always been for the jury [in
insanity cases] to find whether or not he is suffering from a disease of the
mind. . . . I do not know how abnormality of mind can be defined").

9. As to what is ordinarily said to be the general practice, see Krash,
"The Durham Rule and Judicial Administration of the Insanity Defense
in the District of Columbia," 70 *Yale L. J.* 905, 925 (1961); *Report of
Royal Commission on Capital Punishment,* § 401, p. 139 (1953). This
practice reflects a long-existing tendency to treat insanity, mental disease,
and psychosis as synonyms. See 14 *Encyclopedia Britannica* 597 et seq.
(1910) (article on Insanity); Oppenheimer, *The Criminal Responsibility
of Lunatics* 9–10 (1909). In the military jurisdiction, "mental disease"
is defined to include the psychoses and some neurotic conditions but
probably not the character disorders, such as psychopathy. See *Manual
for Courts Martial,* p. 200 (1951); United States v. Smith, 17 CMR 314,
330 et seq. (1954). Some states still instruct juries that mental disease
must be a "disease of the brain" and define the phrase as if an organic
defect were required. See, e.g., State v. Foster, 354 P.2d 960, 972
(Hawaii, 1960); State v. Goza, 317 S.W.2d 609, 616 (Mo. 1958). But
this distinction is not taken literally. Compare R. v. Kemp, 40 Crim. App.
Rep. 121, 127 (1956) (in a case involving arteriosclerosis, Devlin, J.,
said the law is "not concerned with the origin of the disease or the cause
of it, but simply with the mental condition which has brought about the
act").

10. Bryant v. State, 115 A.2d 502, 512 (Md. 1955); Comm. v.
Krzeniak, 119 A.2d 617, 619 (Pa. 1956); State v. Byrd, 93 S.E.2d 900,
904–05 (S. Car. 1956); Washington v. State, 85 N.W.2d 509 (Neb.
1957); Nail v. State, 328 S.W.2d 836, 839–40 (Ark. 1959); State v.
Huff, 102 A.2d 8 (N.J. 1954). In several of the foregoing cases, defense
counsel may well have been able to get an instruction on insanity if he
had elicited testimony that the defendant, who was mentally defective,
could not tell right from wrong. But compare Thomas v. State, 112 A.2d
913, 915–16 (Md. 1955); Reece v. State, 94 S.E.2d 723 (Ga. 1956) (to
qualify, it was not enough that the defendant "had the mentality of a
child nine or ten years old." He must be an idiot.); Stewart v. State, 345
S.W.2d 472 (Ark. 1961); *Report of Royal Commission on Capital
Punishment* 118–24 (1953). Wootton says the feebleminded are not
included in M'Naghten, unless they were brought in by the Homicide
Act of 1957. Wootton, *Social Science and Social Pathology* 230 (1959).

11. Zilboorg, *Mind, Medicine and Man* 273 (1943).

12. Among the few appellate court references are: State v. Kirkham,
319 P.2d 859, 860 (Utah, 1958) (approving trial judge's instruction
that defendant must have been insane, inter alia, "to such an extent that

he did not know the nature of the act; that is, did not know he had a revolver, that it may be loaded, or that, if discharged, it may injure or kill." But note that Utah applies a "control" rule, so that a narrow M'Naghten rule may not be very important); State v. Andrews, 357 P.2d 739, 748 (Kans. 1960) (appellate court, after summarizing psychiatric testimony that defendant was a schizophrenic who felt no emotions and thought it was "morally" right to kill, says: "under this diagnosis, defendant should be held to be responsible for his criminal acts." The point in issue, however, was whether a jury verdict rejecting the insanity defense should be overturned. The defense had been submitted to the jury); State v. Finn, 100 N.W.2d 508 (Minn. 1960); People v. French, 87 P.2d 1014, 1019 (Calif. 1939); but cf. People v. Wolff, 394 P.2d 959, 965 et seq. (Calif. 1964); *Manual for Courts Martial*, § 120, p. 200 (1951); Rex. v. True, 16 Crim. App. Rep. 164, 167 (1922).

13. The following cases include jurisdictions which follow M'Naghten alone and those which have both M'Naghten and a "control" rule: Chase v. State, 369 P.2d. 997, 1001–02 (Alaska, 1962); State v. Schantz, 403 P.2d 521, 525 (Ariz. 1965); People v. Wolff, 394 P.2d 959, 961–62 (Calif. 1964) (the California case quoted in text); Arridy v. People, 82 P.2d 757, 761 (Colo. 1938); State v. Davies, 148 A.2d 251, 255 (Conn. 1959), cert. den. 360 U.S. 921; State v. Iverson, 289 P.2d 603, 606 (Idaho, 1955); People v. Jenko, 102 N.E.2d 783, 785 (Ill. 1952) (Ill. now has the ALI rule, see Ch. 6, note 23); Flowers v. State, 139 N.E.2d 185, 195 (Ind. 1957); State v. Beckwith, 46 N.W.2d 20, 29 (Iowa, 1951); Terry v. Comm., 371 S.W.2d 862, 865 (Ky. 1963); Thomas v. State, 112 A.2d 913, 916 (Md. 1955) (and see Trial Tr. 376–77, instruction to jury); State v. Knight, 50 Atl. 276, 277–78 (Me. 1901) (adopted Durham rule by statute, see Ch. 6, note 10); Comm. v. Rogers, 48 Mass. 500, 502 (1844) (adopted ALI rule); Johnson v. State, 76 So.2d 841, 844 (Miss. 1955), cert. den. 349 U.S. 946; State v. Noble, 384 P.2d 504, 508 (Mont. 1963); Thompson v. State, 68 N.W.2d 267, 271 (Neb. 1955); State v. Throndson, 191 N.W. 628, 634 (N.D. 1922); Dare v. State, 378 P.2d 339, 346–47 (Okla. 1963); State v. Jensen, 296 P.2d 618, 625 (Ore. 1956); Comm. v. Woodhouse, 164 A.2d 98, 103 (Pa. 1960); McCune v. State, 240 S.W.2d 305, 308 (Tex. 1951); De Jarnette v. Comm., 75 Va. 867, 878 (1881); State v. Harrison, 15 S.E. 982, 989 (W. Va 1892); State v. Esser, 145 N.W.2d 505, 521–22 (Wis. 1962) (suggesting defendant may have the choice between a broad M'Naghten rule or the ALI rule, but with different burdens of proof attaching to each); cf. State v. Shoffner, 143 N.W.2d 458, 465–66 (Wis. 1966) (Though it was not error for trial judge to deny a request that a defendant who lacked "real insight," etc. was insane, defense counsel could argue that interpretation to the jury); State v. Putzell, 242 P.2d 180, 184 (Wash. 1952); but see State v. White, 374 P.2d 942, 959 (Wash. 1962), cert. den. 375 U.S. 883; State v. Brown, 151 P.2d 950, 954 (Wyo. 1944). Where reference is made to the adoption

of the ALI or *Durham* rules, the relevant references are to be found in Ch. 6. To ascertain which of the foregoing also follow a "control" rule, see Ch. 5, note 1 infra.

14. Report of *Royal Comm. on Law of Insanity as a Defense in Criminal Cases* (Canada), pp. 12–13 (1955). See also 2 Stephen, *History of Criminal Law* 157, 166, 170–71 (1883); R. v. Davis, (1881) 14 Cox C. C. 563; Glueck, *Law and Psychiatry* 55–56 (1962); Guttmacher and Weihofen, *Psychiatry and Law* 413 (1952). See 1 Hume, *Commentaries on the Laws of Scotland* 36 (1819) ("Though . . . [a person may] have that vestige of reason which may enable him to answer in the general that murder is a crime; yet if he cannot distinguish a friend from an enemy, or a benefit from an injury, but conceives everything about him to be the reverse of what it is, and mistakes the ideas of his fancies for realities . . . these remains of intellect are of no sort of service [toward the] government of his actions, or for enabling him to form a judgment as to what is right or wrong on any particular occasion").

The Australian courts do not distinguish between "intellectual" and "emotional" knowledge. Instead, they follow a Stephen-like approach which asks whether a man can "be said to know . . . whether his act was wrong if through a disease or defect or disorder of the mind he could not think rationally of the reasons which to ordinary people make that act right or wrong." R. v. Porter, 55 Comm. L.R. 182 (High Ct. Aust. 1936); Stapleton v. R., 86 Comm. L.R. 358, 367 (High Ct. Aust. 1952) (adding reference to comprehending "the nature or significance" of the act of killing). But Wilgross v. R., 105 Comm. L.R. 295, 300–01 (High Ct. Aust. 1960) seems to say that a trial judge is not to tell a jury that insanity may be based upon a defective "appreciation of, or feeling about, the effect of his act upon other people."

15. Judge Holtzoff, quoted in Durham v. United States, 214 F.2d 862, 868 (D.C. Cir. 1954).

16. Weihofen, *Mental Disorder as a Criminal Defense* 73 (1954); with State v. Collins, 314 P.2d 660, 666 (Wash. 1957), compare United States v. Smith, 5 USMCA 314, 341–43 (1954). In the few instances in which explanations are offered, it is unclear whether "nature and quality" or "know" are being defined. See, e.g., People v. Roche, Trial Tr. 488–89, aff'd 128 N.E.2d 323 (N.Y. 1955) (the court charged the jury that "The nature of the act is knowing what a person is doing, such as hitting, or stabbing. The quality of the act refers to the knowing that he is striking a person as distinguished from striking a piece of wood, or thinking that he is striking an animal"); State v. Kirkham, note 12 supra; Hall, "Psychiatry and Criminal Responsibility," in *Studies in Jurisprudence and Criminal Theory* 281 (1958) ("'nature and quality' . . . is an ordinary way of specifying what, in part at least, is meant by the psychiatrist's 'reality principle.' It concerns knowledge of ordinary actions and their everyday consequences"). Some of the references to trial tran-

scripts in this chapter are drawn from memoranda prepared by Richard Medalie for Judge David L. Bazelon, who generously made them available to the author.

17. R. v. Codere, 12 C. A. R. 21, 26–27 (Cr. Ct. App. 1916).

18. People v. Roche, Trial Tr. 488–89, aff'd w/o opin. 128 N.E.2d 323 (N.Y. 1955); People v. Horton, Trial Tr. 1088, 3262–63, aff'd 123 N.E.2d 609 (N.Y. 1954).

19. State v. Esser, 115 N.W.2d 505, 521 (Wis. 1962); Guttmacher and Weihofen, *Psychiatry and Law* 403–04 (1952).

20. M'Naghten's Case, 10 Clark & Fin. 200, 210–11 (1843).

21. R. v. Windle, [1952] 2 All Eng. Rep. 1, 2.

22. Sauer v. United States, 241 F.2d 640, 649 (9 Cir. 1957).

23. McElroy v. State, 242 S.W. 883 (Tenn. 1922) (Insanity defense based on assertion that defendant killed in obedience to order from God. Though court refused to set conviction aside, the defense was submitted to jury); Harrison v. State, 69 S.W. 500 (Tex. 1902); State v. Andrews, 357 P.2d 739, 747 (Kans. 1961); United States v. Smith, 17 CMR 314, 341–42 (1954); People v. Nash, 338 P.2d 416, 418 (Calif. 1959); State v. Foster, 354 P.2d 960, 972 (Hawaii, 1960). This is the position taken by the American Law Institute, Model Penal Code, Proposed Official Draft § 4.01 (1) (1962).

24. People v. Schmidt, 110 N.E. 945, 948, 949–50 (N.Y. 1915); People v. Wood, 263 N.Y.S.2d 44, 50 (1962); Sauer v. United States, 241 F.2d 640, 649 (9 Cir. 1957) (seems to construe *Schmidt* as creating a subjective standard). See dissent in People v. Horton, 123 N.E.2d 609, 618–20 (N.Y. 1954) (argues for a subjective view of moral wrong).

25. See People v. Schmidt, supra at 949, where Judge Cardozo urges an expansive interpretation of "wrong," lest the rule lose "all relation to the mental health and true capacity of the criminal." See also People v. Sherwood, 3 N.E.2d 581 (N.Y. 1936); Cohen, "Criminal Responsibility and the Knowledge of Right and Wrong," 14 *Miami L. Rev.* 30, 49 et seq. (1959).

26. See note 3 supra. See, in addition, Allen, "London Letter," *N.Y. Times Book Review,* pp. 12, 14 (April 10, 1966) (quoting Truman Capote, author of *In Cold Blood,* who had replied to criticism in the *London Observer* from Kenneth Tynan: "If fifty world-famous psychiatrists had trooped into court prepared to swear that Smith and Hickock were 'paranoid schizophrenics' . . . it still would not have done a damn bit of good, because Kansas courts abide by the M'Naghten rule and would not have allowed any testimony that deviated from its confines").

27. 1 Wigmore, *Evidence,* § 228 (1940); People v. Hauser, 217 N.E.2d 470 (Ill. 1966); People v. Wolff, 394 P.2d 959, 965 et seq.

(Calif. 1964); People v. Wood, 263 N.Y.S.2d 44, 48–49 (N.Y. 1962); State v. Johnson, 124 N.E.2d 126, 127–28 (N. Car. 1962); Moody v. State, 100 So.2d 733 (Ala. 1958); State v. Wallace, 131 P.2d 222 (Ore. 1942); Baker v. State, 129 N.E. 468, 472 (Ind. 1921); Bulgar v. People, 151 Pac. 937 (Colo. 1915); Comm. v. Williams, 160 Atl. 602, 605 (Pa. 1932); see also Hall, "Psychiatry and Criminal Responsibility," 65 *Yale L. J.* 761, 774 (1956).

28. Howard v. State, 172 Ala. 402, 409 (1911).

29. The quotations are at 93 N.W.2d 354, 360–61 (Wis. 1958). The more recent case is State v. Shoffner, 143 N.W.2d 458, 463 (Wis. 1966).

30. 140 A.2d 385, 393–94 (N.J. 1958).

31. State v. Foster, 354 P.2d 960, 973 (Hawaii, 1960); see also State v. Lucas, 152 A.2d 50, 64–65 (N.J. 1959); State v. Guido, 191 A.2d 45, 51 et seq. (N.J. 1963); Brook v. State, 123 N.W.2d 535, 542 (Wis. 1963); State v. White, 374 P.2d 942, 966 (Wash. 1962) (evidence of lack of control freely admitted in a M'Naghten jurisdiction).

32. ALI, *Model Penal Code,* Tent. Dr. No. 4, App. A. to Commentary, § 4.01, p. 162 (1955); see also R. v. Codere, [1916] 12 Crim. App. Rep. 21, 24; *Att'y Gen'l for N. Ireland v. Gallagher,* [1963] A. C. 349, 372 et seq.; but cf. R. v. Wilkinson, 1 *Crim. L. Rev.* 22, 144 (1954).

33. State v. Odell, 227 P.2d 710, 719 (Wash. 1951). See also Chase v. State, 369 P.2d 997, 1001–02 (Alaska, 1962).

34. See, e.g., Sauer v. United States, 241 F.2d 640, 647 (9 Cir. 1957) (" The appellant's entire mental condition was brought to the attention of the jury [by Dr. Miller] . . . If he was verbally confined in a 'strait jacket,' it is apparent that he did not know it and that no one took the effort to inform him of it"). The foregoing occurred in a federal court, which applies a combination of *M'Naghten* and the "control" rule. But the cases do not limit the evidence to one or the other form of the rule. Compare the following, which admit evidence of psychopathy: Comm. v. Chester, 150 N.E.2d 914, 917 (Mass. 1958); State v. Davies, 148 A.2d 25 (Conn. 1957). In addition to the illustrations which follow in text, see comments by Cleckley, *Mask of Sanity* 521 (1955); Mr. Justice Frankfurter's testimony in *Report of the Royal Commission on Capital Punishment* 232–43 (1953). But see State v. Janovic, 417 P.2d 527, 529 (Ariz. 1966) (Court observes that "mental disorders less extensive than required by the rule in *M'Naghten's* Case are not admissible to a jury," but the question of admissibility of evidence was not before the court).

35. People v. Roche, Trial Tr. 382–83, 399, aff'd w/o opin., 128 N.E.2d 323 (N.Y. 1955).

36. Id. at 422.

37. Id. at 476.

38. McKenzie v. United States, Trial Tr. 200, rev'd 266 F.2d 524, 535 (10 Cir. 1959); see also State v. Lucas, 152 A.2d 50, 64–65 (N.J. 1959).

39. Comm. v. Chester, 150 N.E.2d 914, 917 (Mass. 1958) (note that Massachusetts is an "irresistible impulse" jurisdiction; the testimony quoted, however, is addressed to the M'Naghten part of the formula). See also Dusky v. United States, 271 F.2d 385, 391–92 (8 Cir. 1959) ("when a man is so severely ill the diagnosis of schizophrenia is overtly present, he would not know the difference between right and wrong by reason of delusions, disordered thinking, a misinterpretation of reality").

40. State v. Lucas, Trial Tr. 532–33, 541, aff'd 152 A.2d 50 (N.J. 1959). See also State v. Johnson, 124 S.E.2d 126, 127–28 (N. Car. 1962). (Held error to prevent psychiatrist from supplying details of defendant's case history and opinion that "in general defendant would know the difference between right and wrong but that for some specific event or thing he could not fully distinguish between right and wrong").

41. Warner v. State, 84 So.2d 314, 315 (Fla. 1955).

42. 123 N.E.2d 609, 615 (N.Y. 1954). See also dissent, id. at 618 et seq.

43. Statement of Dr. Guttmacher in ALI, Model Penal Code, Tent. Dr. No. 4, App. B to Commentary on § 4.01, p. 172 (1955); White, *The Abnormal Personality* 55, 514 (1956); Hall, *Criminal Law* 526 (1960); Hall, "Mental Disease and Criminal Responsibility," 33 *Ind. L. J.* 212, 213 (1958); *Report of Royal Commission on Capital Punishment* 73 (1953); Davidson, "Criminal Responsibility," in Hoch and Zubin, *Psychiatry and the Law* 65 (1955); Weihofen, *The Urge to Punish* 39 (1956). ("The psychiatrist will be inclined to act on the assumption that if the person is seriously disordered, his capacity to understand or to conform is equally disordered").

44. The quotations are from: Howard v. United States, Trial Tr. 98, aff'd 229 F.2d 602 (5 Cir. 1962); State v. Goza, 317 S.W.2d 609, 612 (Mo. 1958); People v. Roche, Trial Tr. 497, 506, 508, aff'd w/o opin. 128 N.E.2d 323 (N.Y. 1955); State v. Lucas, Trial Tr. 1349, aff'd 152 A.2d 50 (N.J. 1959); Johnson v. State, 76 So.2d 841, 843 (Miss. 1955); Thomas v. State, Trial Tr. 307, aff'd 112 A.2d 913 (Md. 1955); Mitchell v. State, Trial Tr. 119–20, 159–61, aff'd 104 So.2d 84 (Fla. 1958).

45. Thomas v. State, Trial Tr. 307, aff'd 112 A.2d 913 (Md. 1955).

46. Trial Tr. 1349, aff'd 152 A.2d 50, 64 (N.J. 1959).

47. 115 S.E.2d 547, 549–50 (Ga. 1960); see also Early v. State, 352 P.2d 112, 114 (Colo. 1960).

48. See Leavy, *Civil Commitment to Mental Hospitals in Connecticut* 48 et seq. (1959) (unpublished; on file in Yale Law Library). See infra p. 165; Davidson, *Forensic Psychiatry* 21 (1952) ("the law has repeatedly made it clear that psychopathic personality is to be classed, for forensic

purposes, as a character defect and not as a disease of the mind," citing no cases).

49. Group for the Advancement of Psychiatry, *Criminal Responsibility and Psychiatric Expert Testimony* 5 (1954); Diamond, "Criminal Responsibility of the Mentally Ill," 14 *Stan. L. Rev.* 59, 60–62 (1961) (conceding that "know" can be construed broadly, he says, "I don't like having to take refuge in such semantic devices"). Not all psychiatrists take the GAP view of M'Naghten as unconscionably narrow. See, e.g., Davidson, "Criminal Responsibility," in Hoch and Zubin, *Psychiatry and the Law* 67–70 (1955). And see dissent in United States v. Kunak, 17 CMR 346, 374 (1955) (expressing opinion that psychiatrists were giving legal rather than medical opinions); State v. White, 374 P.2d 942, 957 (Wash. 1962) (Psychiatrist testifying for the state: "Basically . . . I feel he is a sociopathic individual who is responsible before the law."); State v. Behler, 146 P.2d 338, 342 (Idaho, 1944).

CHAPTER FIVE

The Misnamed "Irresistible Impulse" Rule

1. The rule is generally applied in the federal system. See, e.g., Davis v. United States, 165 U.S. 373 (1897); Andersen v. United States, 237 F.2d 118, 127 (9 Cir. 1956); Sauer v. United States, 241 F.2d 640 (9 Cir. 1957), cert. den. 354 U.S. 940; Carter v. United States, 325 F.2d 697, 707 (5 Cir. 1963); Dusky v. United States, 295 F.2d 743, 759 (8 Cir. 1961); United States v. Cain, 298 F.2d 934 (7 Cir. 1962); and in the following states: Parsons v. State, 2 So. 854 (Ala. 1887); Downs v. State, 330 S.W.2d 281, 283 (Ark. 1959); State v. Donahue, 109 A.2d 364, 367–68 (Conn. 1954); Castro v. People, 346 P.2d 1020, 1027 (Colo. 1959); People v. Carpenter, 142 N.E.2d 11, 13–14 (Ill. 1957) (recently adopted ALI rule); Flowers v. State, 139 N.E.2d 185, 193, 195 (Ind. 1956); Terry v. Comm., 371 S.W.2d 862, 865 (Ky. 1963); Comm. v. Chester, 150 N.E.2d 914, 919 (Mass. 1958) (recently replaced by ALI rule); People v. Sharac, 176 N.W. 431, 433–34 (Mich. 1920); State v. Noble, 384 P.2d 504, 508 (Mont. 1963); State v. White, 270 P.2d 727, 731 (N.M. 1954); State v. Robinson, 168 N.E.2d 328, 331 (Ohio, 1958); State v. Kirkham, 319 P.2d 859, 860 (Utah, 1958); State v. Goyet, 132 A.2d 623, 651 (Vt. 1957) (Vermont has recently adopted the ALI test); Thompson v. Comm., 70 S.E.2d 284, 291–92 (Va. 1952); State v. Riggle, 298 P.2d 349, 367 (Wyo. 1956), cert. den. 352 U.S. 981. It also exists in the military court system. United States v. Kunak, 17 CMR 346 (1954); United States v. Smith, 17 CMR 314 (1954). For references to states which have adopted the ALI rule, see Ch. 6.

There is some question about the current status of the rule in the following states: Longoria v. State, 168 A.2d 695, 700 (Del. 1961), cert. den.

368 U.S. 10 (after describing a rule combining M'Naghten and a "control" rule, court characterizes it as a "right and wrong" rule); Mullins v. State, 115 S.E.2d 547, 551 (Ga. 1960) (uses language blending M'Naghten, delusional insanity, and a control test); State v. Beckwith, 46 N.W.2d 20, 30 (Iowa, 1951); Johnson v. State, 76 So.2d 841, 844 (Miss. 1955), cert. den. 349 U.S. 946 ("The defense of irresistible or uncontrollable impulse . . . [is] unavailable, unless the uncontrollable impulse spring from a mental disease existing to such a high degree as to overwhelm the reason, judgment and conscience, in which case . . . the accused would be unable to distinguish the right and wrong of a matter"); Comm. v. Woodhouse, 164 A.2d 98 (Pa. 1960), discussed in Note, 34 *Temp. L. Q.* 168 (1961); State v. Jensen, 296 P.2d 618, 625 (Ore. 1956) (In a state which prescribes *M'Naghten* by statute, trial court instructed jury, in addition, to determine whether defendant had "the power to do or refrain from doing the act"); but cf. State v. Schleigh, 310 P.2d 341, 351 (Ore. 1957).

See generally cases collected in Weihofen, *Mental Disorder as a Criminal Defense* 81 et seq. (1954). Though there was a time when the rule may have existed in English law, it was decisively rejected in R. v. Holt, 15 Crim. App. Rep. 10, 12 (1920); R. v. Kopsch, 19 Crim. App. Rep. 50 (1925). More recently, however, there have been intimations that if medical evidence were offered to establish a link between the "impulse" and the power to know, it would be admissible. *Attorney General for South Australia v. Brown* (1960) A.C. 432, 439–40.

2. See, e.g., Comm. v. Rogers, 48 Mass. 500 (1844). For a brief history, see Glueck, *Mental Disorder and the Criminal Law,* Ch. 5 (1925). See generally Keedy, "Irresistible Impulse as a Defense in the Criminal Law," 100 *U. Pa. L. Rev.* 956 (1952) which points out, at 969 et. seq., the widespread acceptance in Europe of the view that lack of volition may negate criminal responsibility.

3. See generally Weihofen, *Mental Disorder as a Criminal Defense* 94 et seq. (1954); Hall, "Psychiatry and Criminal Responsibility," 65 *Yale L. J.* 761 (1956).

4. 2 So. 854, 866–67 (Ala. 1887). The word "solely" does not appear in the rule in most jurisdictions. Weihofen, *Mental Disorder as a Criminal Defense* 90–91 (1954).

5. 2 So. at 859.

6. 165 U.S. 373, 378 (1897) (*Davis* added to *M'Naghten* the proviso that the accused would be classed as insane if "though conscious of [the nature of the act] and able to distingush between right and wrong, . . . yet his will, by which I mean the governing power of his mind, has been otherwise than voluntarily so completely destroyed that his actions are not subject to it, but are beyond his control").

7. See, e.g., Lee v. State, 93 So.2d 757, 760 (Ala. 1957); Downs v. State, 330 S.W.2d 281, 283 (Ark. 1959); Castro v. People, 346 P.2d

15. Campbell v. United States, 307 F.2d 597, 598 (D.C. Cir. 1962); Blocker v. United States, 274 F.2d 572, 573 (D.C. Cir. 1959). As to narcotics addiction, compare Brown v. United States 331 F.2d 822, 823 (D.C. Cir. 1965) and Castle v. United States, 347 F.2d 492, 494 (D.C. Cir. 1965), cert. den. 381 U.S. 929, which say that a showing of narcotics addiction ordinarily suffices to raise the defense, with Heard v. United States, 348 F.2d 43, 44 (D.C. Cir. 1965), which says a "mere showing of narcotics addiction, without more" will not suffice. The court has not been so adventurous in cases involving "mental defect," see, e.g., Moore v. United States, 277 F.2d 684 (D.C. Cir. 1960), for reasons which have not been articulated but which may be surmised. Existing tests of mental retardation are so culture-bound that there would be a real risk of classing as insane persons who are merely uneducated. Moreover, mental hospitals are not ordinarily equipped to deal with the mentally retarded. In the early cases, the court had assented to the proposition that a non-psychotic mental illness would suffice but it had not required the trial judge to charge the jury to that effect. Arens et al., "Jurors, Jury Charges and Insanity," 14 Cath. U. L. Rev. 1, 5-6 (1965).

16. See Carter v. United States, 252 F.2d 608, 617 (D.C. Cir. 1957) ("Mental 'disease' means mental illness. Mental illnesses are of many sorts and have many characteristics. . . . They differ widely in origin, in characteristics, and in their effects on a person's mental processes, his abilities and his behavior. To make a reasonable inference concerning the relationship between a disease and a certain act, the trier of the facts must be informed with some particularity. Unexplained medical labels—schizophrenia, paranoia, psychosis, neurosis, psychopathy are not enough"); Wechsler, "The Criteria of Criminal Responsibility," 22 U. Chi. L. Rev. 367, 369 (1955); Kuh, "The Insanity Defense—An Effort to Combine Law and Reason," 110 U. Pa. L. Rev. 771, 791 (1962).

17. Compare Frigillana v. United States, 307 F.2d 665, 666 et seq. (D.C. Cir. 1962) with Campbell v. United States, 307 F.2d 597, 598 et seq. (D.C. Cir. 1962). See also Arens et al., "Jurors, Jury Charges and Insanity," 14 Cath. U. L. Rev. 1, 7 et seq. (1965); James, "Jurors' Assessment of Criminal Responsibility," 7 Soc. Prob. 58, 63-64, 67-68 (1959) (reporting results of mock jury trials administered by University of Chicago's jury project).

18. McDonald v. United States, 312 F.2d 847, 851 (D.C. Cir. 1962). See also Hightower v. United States, 325 F.2d 616, 619 (D.C. Cir. 1963), cert. den. 384 U.S. 994 (referring to "serious mental disease"); Acheson, "McDonald v. United States: The Durham Rule Redefined," 51 Geo. L. J. 580, 586-88 (1963).

19. ALI, Model Penal Code, Proposed Official Draft, § 4.01 (1962). The proposal was presented to the Institute for consideration at the May 1955 meeting.

1020, 1027 (Colo. 1959); State v. Robinson, 168 N.E.2d 328, 331 (Ohio, 1958).

8. Of the five allegedly "leading" American "irresistible impulse" cases cited by the British Royal Commission on Capital Punishment, Report, pp. 409-10 (1953), only Comm. v. Rogers, 48 Mass. 500, 502-03 (1844), uses the word "impulse." For other cases which also use the word but not always prominently, see Flowers v. State, 139 N.E.2d 185, 193 (Ind. 1956); Comm. v. Chester, 150 N.E.2d 914, 919 (Mass. 1958); State v. Goyet, 132 A.2d 623, 650 (Vt. 1957); Snider v. Smith, 187 F. Supp. 299, 302 (E.D. Va. 1960), aff'd 292 F.2d 683 (4 Cir. 1961); Phillips v. Comm., 59 S.W.2d 579, 583 (Ky. 1933).

9. See United States v. Pollard, 171 F. Supp. 474, 477 et seq. (E.D. Mich. 1959), rev'd o/g 282 F.2d 450 (6 Cir. 1960); State v. Kirkham, 319 P.2d 859, 860 (Utah, 1958); Comm. v. Chester, 150 N.E.2d 914, 919 (Mass. 1958); People v. Carpenter, 142 N.E.2d 11, 12 (Ill. 1957) (Illinois has since adopted ALI rule).

10. Report of Royal Commission on Capital Punishment 110, § 313 (1953). For an early reference to the "implication," which is described as an improper one, see Bucknill, Unsoundness of Mind in Relation to Criminal Acts 84 (1856).

11. Durham v. United States, 214 F.2d 862, 873-74 (D.C. Cir. 1954).

12. ALI, Model Penal Code, § 4.01, Comments, at 157 (Tent. Draft No. 4, 1955); Weihofen, The Urge to Punish 69 (1956); Calif. Spec. Comm. on Insanity and Criminal Offenders 25 (July 7, 1962); Glueck, Law and Psychiatry 57-58 (1962); United States v. Freeman, 357 F.2d 606, 620 (2 Cir. 1966); but compare Wechsler, "The Criteria of Criminal Responsibility," 22 U. Chi. L. Rev. 367, 370 n.14 (1955).

13. See, e.g., State v. Davies, 148 A.2d 25 (Conn. 1957); Comm. v. Harrison, 173 N.E.2d 87 (Mass. 1961); Carter v. United States, 325 F.2d 697, 704 (5 Cir. 1963).

14. 14 Atl. 550 (Del. 1888).

15. Id. at 552.

16. Id. at 551; see United States v. Smith, 17 CMR 314, 335-36 (1954); Hall, Studies in Jurisprudence and Criminal Theory 286 (1958).

17. Snider v. Smith, 187 F. Supp. 299, 302 (E.D. Va. 1960), aff'd 292 F.2d 683 (4 Cir. 1961).

18. See United States v. Kunak, 17 CMR 346, 357-58 (1954).

19. 75 Va. 867, 878 (1881), discussed in Thompson v. Commonwealth, 70 S.E.2d 284, 292 (Va. 1952).

20. See, e.g., State v. Stacy, 160 Atl. 257 (Vt. 1932) where defendant asked for an instruction "that an irresistible impulse might exist for a moment or for a long time" (Id. at 270). The court denied the request

but it did *not* instruct the jury that the impulse must be sudden and un-planned, even though the evidence supported a "brooding and reflection" theory.

21. *Report of Royal Commission on Capital Punishment* 409–10 (1953).

22. Wertham, *Show of Violence* 13 (1949). See also United States v. Smith, 5 USCMA 314, 334 n.27, 17 CMR 314, 334 n.27 (1954); Wootton, *Social Science and Social Pathology* 233–34 (1959); Cressey, "The Differential Association Theory and Compulsive Crimes," 45 *J. Crim. L. & Crimin.* 29, 35 (1954); Comm. v. Harrison, 173 N.E.2d 87, passim (Mass. 1961).

23. Guttmacher, in ALI, *Model Penal Code*, § 4.01, Appendix B, p. 174 (1955), referring, inter alia, to a survey by Dr. Philip Roche which is briefly described in Keedy, "Irresistible Impulse in Criminal Law," 100 *U. Pa. L. Rev.* 956, 989 (1952).

24. Sauer v. United States, 241 F.2d 640, 650 (9 Cir. 1957).

25. See, e.g., Hall, *Criminal Law* 486 et seq. (1960); Hall, "Psychiatry and Criminal Responsibility," 65 *Yale L. J.* 761 (1956).

26. Guttmacher, ALI, *Model Penal Code*, § 4.01, Appendix B, p. 175 (1955).

27. Weihofen, *Mental Disorder as a Criminal Defense* 85 (1954); Glueck, *Law and Psychiatry* 341 et seq. (1962).

28. See, e.g., Sollars v. State, 316 P.2d 917, 920 (Nev. 1957); Comm. v. Woodhouse, 164 A.2d 98, 106 (Pa. 1960); Sauer v. United States, 241 F.2d 640, 650 (9 Cir. 1957), cert. den. 354 U.S. 940; Waelder, "Psychiatry and the Problem of Criminal Responsibility," 101 *U. Pa. L. Rev.* 378, 383 (1952); *Calif. Spec. Comm. on Insanity and Criminal Offenders* 25 (July 7, 1962).

29. Weihofen, *Mental Disorder as a Criminal Defense* 82 (1954); Keedy, "Irresistible Impulse as a Defense in Criminal Law," 100 *U. Pa. L. Rev.* 956, 989 (1952).

30. Dusky v. United States, 295 F.2d 743, 759 (8 Cir. 1961). For other federal courts which have taken a similar position, see Ch. 6, note 31.

31. Compare McDonald v. United States, 312 F.2d 847, 851 (D.C. Cir. 1962).

CHAPTER SIX

The New Rules; Insanity as Legal Standard

1. Ray, *A Treatise on the Medical Jurisprudence of Insanity*, Ch. 1 (2d ed. 1844). See State v. Pike, 49 N.H. 399 (1869).

2. *Report of Royal Commission on Capital Punishment* 80 (1953).

3. Id. at 103–04 et seq.

4. Id. at 116.

5. Id. at 116 and 111.

6. Id. at 286, 287.

7. 214 F.2d 862, 869 et seq. (D.C. Cir. 1954).

8. Id. at 874–75 (Said the court, "We use 'disease' in the sense of a condition which is considered capable of either improving or deteriorating. We use 'defect' in the sense of a condition which is not considered capable of either improving or deteriorating and which may be either congenital, or the result of injury, or the residual effect of a physical or mental disease").

9. Id. at 876. For illustrations of the applause with which the opinion was greeted, see Roche, "Criminality and Mental Illness—Two Faces of the Same Coin," 22 *U. Chi. L. Rev.* 320 (1955); Guttmacher, "The Psychiatrist as Expert Witness," 22 *U. Chi. L. Rev.* 325 (1955); Weihofen, "The Flowering of New Hampshire," 22 *U. Chi. L. Rev.* 356, 359 (1955).

10. Me. Rev. Stat. Ann. 15–§ 102 (1965) (but note the exclusion of repeated criminality, drug addiction, and alcoholism as bases for "mental disease"); V. I. Code Ann. Tit. 14–§ 14 (1957) (using "mentally ill" rather than "mental disease or mental defect"). The Maine statute is discussed in State v. Hathaway, 211 A.2d 558 (Me. 1965). See note 1 supra.

11. See generally Krash, "The Durham Rule and Judicial Administration of the Insanity Defense in the District of Columbia," 70 *Yale L. J.* 905 (1961). The rise in insanity acquittals is discussed in Acheson, "McDonald v. United States: The Durham Rule Redefined," 51 *Geo. L. J.* 580, 589 (1963). The possibility that it traces to a redirection from the cases of incompetency to stand trial is discussed in Judicial Conference of D.C., *Report of Committee on Problems Connected with Mental Examination of the Accused in Criminal Cases* 44 et seq. (1965).

12. See e.g., Hall, "Psychiatry and Criminal Responsibility," 65 *Yale L. J.* 761, 779–80 (1956); Hall, *Criminal Law* 500 et seq. (1960); Krash, supra note 11, at 928 et seq. and his citation of cases rejecting *Durham*, at 906 n.8; United States v. Currens, 290 F.2d 751, 773–74 (3 Cir. 1961); Blocker v. United States, 288 F.2d 853, 857 et seq. (Burger J. concurring).

13. Durham v. United States, 241 F.2d 862, 872–74 (D.C. Cir. 1954), especially its frequent references to the *Report of the Royal Commission on Capital Punishment* (1953). The Royal Commission treated "mental disease" as roughly corresponding to "major diseases of the mind, or psychoses," Id. at 73.

14. 214 F.2d at 872, 876.

20. Kuh, "The Insanity Defense—An Effort to Combine Law and Reason," 110 *U. Pa. L. Rev.* 771, 797 et seq. (1962); Hall, "Psychiatry and Criminal Responsibility," 65 *Yale L. J.* 761, 777 (1956); Weihofen, *The Urge to Punish* 77, 85, 99–100 (1956).

21. Compare Weihofen, "The Definition of Mental Illness," 21 *Ohio St. L. J.* 1, 6–7 (1960) and Diamond, "From M'Naghten to Currens, and Beyond," 50 *Calif. L. Rev.* 189, 193–94 (1962) with Wechsler, "The Criteria of Criminal Responsibility," 22 *U. Chi. L. Rev.* 367, 374 (1955).

22. Kuh, "A Prosecutor Considers the Model Penal Code," 63 *Col. L. Rev.* 608, 626 (1963). See also United States v. Currens, 290 F.2d 751, 762 (3 Cir. 1961); United States v. Freeman, 357 F.2d 606, 625 (2 Cir. 1966).

23. Ill. Ann. Stat., Ch. 38, § 6–2 (Smith-Hurd, 1964); Vt. Stat. Ann., Tit. 13 § 4801 (1958); Mo. Stat. Ann. § 552.030 (Vernon, 1966) (with slight changes); Comm. v. McHoul, N.E.2d   (Mass. 1967); Md. Stat., Ch. 709, approved May 4, 1967, 1 *Crim. L. Rep.* 1017 (May 17, 1967). Cf. State v. Shoffner, 143 N.W.2d 458, 464 (Wis. 1966) (see note 31 infra); United States v. Freeman, 357 F.2d 606 (2 Cir. 1966); Wion v. United States, 325 F.2d 420, 427 (10 Cir. 1963). Several states have been considering adoption of the ALI test or a variant thereof. See, e.g., Calif., *Report on Insanity and Criminal Offenders* 26 (1962). One of the inhibiting factors in "broadening" the rule in the federal courts has been the uncertainty as to whether federal courts outside the District of Columbia had the power to commit persons acquitted by reason of insanity. See Sauer v. United States, 241 F.2d 640, 650–52 (9 Cir. 1957); Pollard v. United States, 282 F.2d 450, 464 (6 Cir. 1961); United States v. Freeman, supra at 625–26.

24. N.Y. Rev. Penal Law § 30.05 (McKinney, 1965).

25. United States v. Currens, 290 F.2d 751, 774 (1961) ("The jury must be satisfied that at the time of committing the prohibited act the defendant, as a result of mental disease or defect, lacked substantial capacity to conform his conduct to the requirements of the law which he is alleged to have violated"). See Diamond, "From M'Naghten to Currens, and Beyond," 50 *Calif. L. Rev.* 189, 191 (1962).

26. Weihofen, *The Urge to Punish* 85 (1956).

27. Carter v. United States, 252 F.2d 608, 617 (D.C. Cir. 1957). See Fingarette, "The Concept of Mental Disease in Criminal Law Insanity Tests," 33 *U. Chi. L. Rev.* 229, 240 (1966); Swartz, "Mental Disease," 111 *U. Pa. L. Rev.* 389 (1963).

28. Waelder, "Psychiatry and The Problem of Criminal Responsibility," 101 *U. Pa. L. Rev.* 378, 384 (1952).

29. See discussion supra pp. 34–36. See also Szasz, *Law, Liberty and Psychiatry* 11–38, 91–108 (1964); J. Goldstein and Katz, "Abolish The Insanity Defense . . . Why Not?" 72 *Yale L. J.* 873 (1963).

30. For a collection of cases rejecting *Durham,* see Krash, "The Durham Rule and Judicial Administration of the Insanity Defense in the District of Columbia," 70 *Yale L. J.* 905, 906 n.8 (1961). Many of the more recent cases cited in Chs. 4 and 5, supra, also contain discussions, and rejections, of *Durham.* See, e.g., State v. Schantz, 403 P.2d 521 (Ariz. 1965); State v. Noble, 384 P.2d 504 (Mont. 1963); Chase v. State, 369 P.2d 997 (Alaska, 1962). For expressions of particular concern about extending the insanity defense to psychopathy, neuroses, etc., see State v. Lucas, 152 A.2d 50, 68 (N.J. 1959); Sauer v. United States, 241 F.2d 640, 646 (9 Cir. 1957); United States v. Smith, 17 CMR 314, 325 (1954).

31. Dusky v. United States, 295 F.2d 743, 759 (8 Cir. 1961); Carter v. United States, 325 F.2d 697, 707 (5 Cir. 1963), cert. den. 377 U.S. 946; United States v. Cain, 298 F.2d 934 (7 Cir. 1962); Wion v. United States, 325 F.2d 420, 427 (10 Cir. 1963); cf. State v. Shoffner, 143 N.W.2d 458, 464 (Wis. 1966) (offering defendant the option of a broad *M'Naghten* or the ALI rule, with different rules of burden of proof attaching to each); Glueck, *Law and Psychiatry* 105–06 (1962). As to the frequently held view that the insanity defense should be changed only by the legislature, see State v. Schantz, 403 P.2d 521 (Ariz. 1965) (indicating approval of ALI rule); State v. Finn, 100 N.W.2d 508, 511 (Minn. 1959); for the opposing view, see Durham v. United States, 214 F.2d 862, 874 (D.C. Cir. 1954).

32. Blocker v. United States, 288 F.2d 1099, 858, 862 et seq. (D.C. Cir. 1961). See also Blocker v. United States, 320 F.2d 800, 801 (D.C. Cir. 1963).

CHAPTER SEVEN

A Note on Expert Opinion and the Test Questions

1. Weihofen, *Mental Disorder as a Criminal Defense* 284, 311 (1954); 7 Wigmore, *Evidence,* § 1958 (2) (1940); Bryant v. State, 13 S.E.2d 820, 840 (Ga. 1941); State v. Wade, 113 Atl. 458, 463 (Conn. 1921); State v. McGruder, 101 N.W.646, 648 (Iowa, 1904); People v. Tuczkewitz, 43 N.E. 548, 552 (N.Y. 1896). For an interesting opinion on lay testimony, see Carter v. United States, 252 F.2d 608, 618 (D.C. Cir. 1964); and see generally Pederson, "The Opinion Evidence Rule in Oregon," 33 *Ore. L. Rev.* 243 (1954).

2. 10 Clark & Fin. 200, 211–12 (1843).

3. Archbold, *Criminal Pleading, Evidence and Practice* § 39 (1959); see note 1 supra. But cf. King and Pillinger, *Opinion Evidence in Illinois* 230–31 (1942) (taking the position that the right-wrong question is not addressed to the ultimate issue, that it is merely one of several questions which, taken together, raise the ultimate issue). In some of the cases, the court eventually concluded that it was only lay witnesses who would not

be permitted to invade the province of the jury by testifying on the ultimate issue. See, e.g., State v. Evans, 133 S.W.2d 389, 393 (Mo. 1939).

4. 12 D.C. 498, 546 (D.C. Sup. Ct. 1882).

5. 109 Pac. 865, 867 (Ore. 1910); State v. Leland, 227 P.2d 785, 800 (1951), aff'd 343 U.S. 790 (1952); R. v. Holmes, [1953] 2 All Eng. Rep. 324, 325.

6. 7 Wigmore, *Evidence*, § 1958 (2) (1940); Weihofen, *Mental Disorder as a Criminal Defense* 286 (1954). Wigmore's position probably derives from a very deep hostility to the "opinion rule" and the impossible task it seemed to set witnesses of separating facts from inferences. Id. at §§ 1917 et seq.

7. The quotation is from 7 Wigmore, *Evidence*, § 1958 (1940). See State v. Cochran, 203 S.W.2d 707, 713 (Mo. 1947); R. v. Layton, 4 Cox 149, 156–57 (1849); cf. State v. White, 374 P.2d 942, 958 (Wash. 1962).

8. Guttmacher and Weihofen, "The Psychiatrist on the Witness Stand," 32 *B. U. L. Rev.* 287, 294–95 (1952); but cf. Weihofen, *Mental Disorder as a Criminal Defense* 286 (1954). For a fuller statement and an effort at reconciliation, see Weihofen, "The Definition of Mental Illness," 21 *Ohio St. L. J.* 1, 12–14 (1960).

9. Group for Advancement of Psychiatry, *Criminal Responsibility and Psychiatric Expert Testimony* 5 (1954); see also Roche, *The Criminal Mind* 173 (1958); Waelder, "Psychiatry and the Problem of Criminal Responsibility," 101 *U. Pa. L. Rev.* 378, 380–81, 385 (1952); Dession, "Psychiatry and the Conditioning of Criminal Justice," 47 *Yale L. J.* 319, 337–38 (1938); Glueck, *Mental Disorder and the Criminal Law* 33–34, 309 n. (1925); People v. Monroe, 154 N.E.2d 225, 229 (Ill. 1958).

10. Guttmacher, "Principal Difficulties with the Present Criteria of Responsibility and Possible Alternatives," in ALI, Model Penal Code, Tent. Dr. No. 4, p. 171 et seq. (1955) (Appendix B to Commentary on § 4.01).

11. Hall, "Psychiatry and Criminal Responsibility," 65 *Yale L. J.* 761, 770, 782 et seq. (1956); cf. Guttmacher, supra note 10, at 173 ("It is maintained that knowledge of right and wrong is a problem for the theologian and not for the physician. Furthermore it is charged that such discernments necessitate value judgments that must be taboo to scientists. . . . This has never had much meaning for me. We are not being asked whether a defendant acted according to our accepted standards of morality or whether his own theoretical standards were the generally accepted ones. What we are asked is whether the defendant had sufficient intellect or a sufficiently clear mind at the time of the crime to know what these generally accepted standards were. We are balking at this, it seems to me, primarily because of our inability to measure this with any degree of accuracy").

12. Group for the Advancement of Psychiatry, supra note 9, at 5–6.

13. Briscoe v. United States, 248 F.2d 640, 644 (D.C. Cir. 1957); cf. Hawkins v. United States, 310 F.2d 849, 851 (D.C. Cir. 1962).

14. ALI, Model Penal Code, Proposed Official Draft, § 4.05 (3) (1962) and Commentary, Tent. Dr. No. 4, pp. 196–97 (1955).

15. The quoted assertion, which is commonly made, is from Glueck, *Law and Psychiatry* 66 (1962). For persuasive evidence challenging the assertion, see Simon, "Jurors' Assessment of Criminal Responsibility," 7 *Social Problems* 58 (1959).

16. See discussion in Hawkins v. United States, 310 F.2d 849, 851–52 (D.C. Cir. 1962); Blocker v. United States, 288 F.2d 858, 862 (D.C. Cir. 1961) (concurring opinion); Carter v. United States, 252 F.2d 608, 617 (D.C. Cir. 1957); United States v. Currens, 290 F.2d 751, 772 (3 Cir. 1961); People v. Wolff, 394 P.2d 959, 969 (Calif. 1964).

CHAPTER EIGHT

Pleading, Proof, and Presumptions

1. See generally A. Goldstein, "The State and the Accused: Balance of Advantage in Criminal Procedure," 69 *Yale L. J.* 1149, 1172 et seq. (1960); Packer, "Two Models of the Criminal Process," 113 *U. Pa. L. Rev.* 1 (1964). As to the question of competency to stand trial and "plea bargaining," see pages 184–86.

2. The quotation is from Orfield, *Criminal Procedure from Arrest to Appeal* 309 (1947). Illustrative cases are State v. James, 128 So.2d 21, 23–24 (La. 1961); State v. Gunter, 23 So.2d 305, 307 (La. 1945); State v. Fitzgibbon, 203 P.2d 1016 (Wash. 1949); People v. Egan, 23 P.2d 755 (Calif. 1933). The failure to plead specially will not bar the insanity issue if the state introduces evidence sufficient to raise it. State v. Wallace, 131 P.2d 222, 227 (Ore. 1942). See generally Weihofen, *Mental Disorder as a Criminal Defense* 357–59 (1954); Dean, "Advance Specifications of Defense in Criminal Cases," 20 *A.B.A.J.* 435 (1934); ALI, Code of Criminal Procedure, § 235 and Commentary at p. 679 (1931).

3. See discussion infra pages 186–88.

4. This may occur when a defendant, having put in no case of his own, requests an instruction on insanity; or when he argues on appeal that it was "plain error" for the trial judge to have failed to instruct the jury on the insanity issue. See, e.g., Tatum v. United States, 190 F.2d 612, 615 (D.C. Cir. 1950); State v. Wallace, 131 P.2d 222, 227 (Ore. 1942); Territory v. Adiarte, 37 Haw. 463, 470–71 (1947).

5. The cases are collected in Weihofen, *Mental Disorder as a Criminal Defense* 214 et seq. (1954).

6. See James, *Civil Procedure* 248 et seq. (1965).

7. See discussion in Douglas v. United States, 239 F.2d 52 (D.C. Cir. 1956); Fielding v. United States, 251 F.2d 878, 880 (D.C. Cir. 1957); Pollard v. United States, 282 F.2d 450, 460 (6 Cir. 1960); McKenzie v. United States, 266 F.2d 524, 527 (10 Cir. 1959); Mitchell v. State, 104 So.2d 84, 86 (Fla. 1958); Gambrell v. State, 120 So.2d 758, 762–63 (Miss. 1960). But cf. Dusky v. United States, 295 F.2d 743, 757–58 (8 Cir. 1961); Bowker v. United States, 373 P.2d 500, 501–02 (Alaska, 1962).

8. The cases are collected and classified by Weihofen, *Mental Disorder as a Criminal Defense* 219–28, 241 et seq. (1954). See, in addition, Bradford v. State, 200 A.2d 150 (Md. 1964); Thomas v. State, 112 A.2d 913, 918–19 (Md. 1955); State v. Barton, 236 S.W.2d 596 (Mo. 1951); Territory v. Adiarte, 37 Haw. 463, 469 et seq. (1947); ALI, Model Penal Code, Proposed Official Draft, § 4.03 (1962) and Commentary, Tent. Dr. No. 4, at 193–94 (1955).

9. For illustrations of cases along the continuum, see Davis v. United States, 160 U.S. 469, 485 et seq. (1895); Carter v. United States, 325 F.2d 697, 704 (5 Cir. 1963); Hall v. United States, 295 F.2d 26, 27–29 (4 Cir. 1961) (reviewing the federal cases); Smith v. United States, 353 F.2d 838 (D.C. Cir. 1965); McDonald v. United States, 312 F.2d 847, 849–50 (D.C. Cir. 1962); Wilson v. United States, 288 F.2d 121 (D.C. Cir. 1960); Ragsdale v. Overholser, 281 F.2d 943, 947 (D.C. Cir. 1960); Tatum v. United States, 190 F.2d 612, 615–17 (D.C. Cir. 1951); Thompson v. State, 68 N.W.2d 267, 271 (Neb. 1955).

10. Fitts v. United States, 284 F.2d 108, 112 (10 Cir. 1960).

11. McDonald v. United States, 312 F.2d 847, 850 (D.C. Cir. 1962).

12. See discussion in Acheson, "McDonald v. United States: The Durham Rule Redefined," 51 *Geo. L. J.* 580, 586 (1963). Illustrations are to be found in the cases cited in note 9 supra; and see State v. Trantino, 209 A.2d 117, 123 (N.J. 1965). On the admissibility of lay testimony, see Wigmore, *Evidence* §§ 568, 689, 1933 et seq. (1940).

13. See note 8 supra. Some states say the defense must be proved "to the satisfaction of the jury" or to its "reasonable satisfaction" or "clearly proved to the reasonable satisfaction of the jury," or "to the satisfaction of the jury by a preponderance of the evidence." Until recently, Oregon required proof of insanity "beyond a reasonable doubt." Though this was held to be constitutionally permissible, Leland v. Oregon, 343 U.S. 790 (1952), the legislature subsequently adopted the lesser burden of "preponderance of the evidence." Ore. Rev. Stat., § 136–390 (1963).

14. McGee v. State, 238 S.W.2d 707, 710–11 (Tex. 1951). See, in addition, People v. Samman, 97 N.E.2d 778, 780–81 (Ill. 1951); State v. Garver, 225 P.2d 771, 777–78 (Ore. 1950); Orange v. State, 47 S.E.2d 756, 759 (Ga. 1948); Kizer v. State, 92 S.W.2d 439, 440 (Tex. 1936); Anno., 27 A.L.R.2d 105 (1953).

15. In addition to the cases cited in note 14 supra, see State v. Elsea, 251 S.W.2d 650, 651 (Mo. 1952); Comm. v. Smith, 40 A.2d 701, 703–04 (Pa. 1945); Corbin v. State, 176 So. 435 (Fla. 1937); Kizer v. State, 92 S.W.2d 439, 440 (Tex. 1936); Murray v. State, 182 S.W.2d 475, 477 (Tex. 1944); cf. People v. Jensen, 275 P.2d 25, 29 (Calif. 1954).

16. As to epilepsy and the presumption of insanity, see People v. Baker, 268 P.2d 705, 714 (Calif. 1954). On the general point as to the need for "permanent" insanity, see People v. Wolff, 394 P.2d 959, 973 (Calif. 1964); Comm. v. Ashe, 71 A.2d 107, 114–15 (Pa. 1950); State v. Linders, 224 S.W.2d 386, 391 (Mo. 1949); Grammer v. State, 196 So. 268, 271 (Ala. 1940); Glover v. State, 69 S.W.2d 136, 138–39 (Tex. 1934).

17. Trahan v. State, 35 S.W.2d 169, 170 (Tex. 1931); McKenny v. State, 288 S.W. 465, 467 (Tex. 1926); Clark v. State, 145 S.E. 647, 650 (Ga. 1928); People v. Keyes, 175 Pac. 6, 9 (Calif. 1918); Russell v. State, 78 So. 916 (Ala. 1918); State v. Austin, 73 N.E. 218 (Ohio, 1905); Ford v. State, 19 Miss. 665 (1896).

18. State v. Elsea, 251 S.W.2d 650, 651 (Mo. 1952); State v. Paulsgrove, 101 S.W. 27, 30 (Mo. 1907); Kizer v. State, 92 S.W.2d 439, 441 (Tex. 1936) (but note that the prior insanity had been adjudicated by a court); cf. Farrell v. State, 101 So.2d 130, 133 (Fla. 1958).

19. Illustrative cases are Williams v. United States, 104 A.2d 827, 828 (Mun. App. D.C. 1954); State v. Stricker, 180 S.W.2d 719, 722 (Mo. 1944); Smith v. Roach, 106 P.2d 536, 537–38 (Wyo. 1940); Cannon v. Comm., 47 S.W.2d 1075, 1078 (Ky. 1932).

20. State v. Shoffner, 143 N.W.2d 458, 465 (Wis. 1966).

CHAPTER NINE

Epert Witnesses and an Effective Defense;
The Special Problem of the Indigent Accused

1. Gideon v. Wainwright, 372 U.S. 335 (1963); White v. Maryland, 373 U.S. 59 (1963); Miranda v. Arizona, 384 U.S. 437, 467 et seq. (1966). See generally Special Committee to Study Defender Systems, *Equal Justice For the Accused* 64, 81 (1959). The right to appointed counsel is coming to be recognized in civil commitment processes as well. See People v. Breese, 213 N.E.2d 500 (Ill. 1966); State ex rel. Rogers v. Stanley, 270 N.Y.S.2d 573 (Ct. App. 1966); In re Spencer, 406 P.2d 33, 40 et seq. (Calif. 1965) (holding that defendant is entitled to appointed counsel to help him determine whether to submit to examination by court-appointed psychiatrist).

2. See generally Silverstein, *Defense of the Poor in Criminal Cases in American State Courts* (1965); Attorney General's Committee, *Report on Poverty and the Administration of Criminal Justice* (1964).

3. See address by Shirley Star, "The Public's Ideas About Mental Illness," National Opinion Research Center, University of Chicago, 1955.

4. The defense of insanity may occasionally be made by a person found later to be incompetent. This occurs in the ten or eleven states following the common-law position which gave the trial judge discretion to submit both issues—competency to stand trial and insanity at the time of the crime—to the jury simultaneously. Weihofen, *Mental Disorder as a Criminal Defense* 456 (1954).

5. For a useful discussion of the manner in which the lawyer should use the psychiatrist as a witness, see Flannery, "Meeting the Insanity Defense," 51 *J. Crim. L. & Crimin.* 309 (1960). See also Carter v. United States, 252 F.2d 608, 617 (D.C. Cir. 1957).

6. See Winn v. United States, 270 F.2d 326, 328 (D.C. Cir. 1959), cert. den. 365 U.S. 848 (1961); Blunt v. United States, 244 F.2d 355, 364 n.23 (D.C. Cir. 1957); English and Finch, *Introduction to Psychiatry* 70–100 (2d ed. 1957); Noyes and Kolb, *Modern Clinical Psychiatry* 130–69 (5th ed. 1958); Menninger, Satten, and Fruyser, "The Development of a Psychiatric Criminology," 25 *Bull. Menninger Clinic* 164, 168 et seq. (1961).

7. See generally Hollingshead and Redlich, *Social Class and Mental Illness* 28–29, 155–65 (1958); Jahoda, *Current Concepts of Positive Mental Health* (1958); Szasz, *The Myth of Mental Illness* (1961); Wootton, *Social Science and Social Pathology* 203–67 (1959); Bowman & Rose, "A Criticism of the Terms 'Psychosis,' 'Psychoneurosis' and 'Neurosis,'" 108 *Am. J. Psychiatry* 161 (1951); Friedman, "Conformity and Nonconformity," in Hoch and Zubin, *Psychiatry and the Law* 41 (1955); Hartmann, "Psychoanalysis and the Concept of Health," 20 *Int'l J. of Psychoanalysis* 308 (1939); Stouffer, "Indices of Psychological Illness," in Lazarsfeld, *The Language of Social Research* 63 (1955). For an unusually perceptive discussion, see Rollerson v. United States, 343 F.2d 269 (D.C. Cir. 1964). For an illustration of what may be lost to the defendant who is indigent, see Adams v. United States, 337 F.2d 548, 549 (D.C. Cir. 1964).

8. Though the text discussion refers almost entirely to the psychiatrist as principal witness on the insanity issue, there is authority for the proposition that a psychologist may also be qualified to perform that function. See Jenkins v. United States, 307 F.2d 637, 642 et seq. (D.C. Cir. 1962); State v. Padilla, 347 P.2d 312, 318–19 (N.M. 1959).

9. A tabulation of the states, and the provisions for expert assistance in each, are to be found in an earlier version of this chapter, Goldstein and Fine, "The Indigent Accused, the Psychiatrist and the Insanity Defense," 110 *U. Pa. L. Rev.* 1061, 1091–92 (1962).

10. See cases collected in Anno., "Compelling Expert to Testify," 77 A.L.R.2d 1182, 1186 n.12 (1961). For states without specialized pro-

cedures, see Appendix to Goldstein and Fine, supra note 9. At that time the states were Alaska, Arizona, Georgia, Idaho, Kansas, Mississippi, Montana, New Mexico, New Jersey, and Washington.

11. Id. at 1187–88.

12. Id. at 1188 n.3; Anno. "Right of physician to give expert testimony based on hypothetical question," 64 A.L.R.2d 1056 (1959); State v. Bell, 111 S.W. 24, 28 (Mo. 1908); Philler v. Waukesha County, 120 N.W. 829, 830–31 (Wis. 1909); Barnes v. Boatmen's Nat'l Bank, 156 S.W.2d 597, 600–01 (Mo. 1941); Burnett v. Freeman, 103 S.W. 121, 122 (Mo. 1907).

13. In addition to the cases cited in note 12 supra, see Blair v. United States, 250 U.S. 273, 281–82 (1919), describing the duty to testify in court or before a grand jury as one "which every person within the jurisdiction . . . is bound to perform upon being properly summoned, and for performance of which he is entitled to no further compensation than that which the statutes provide. The personal sacrifice involved is a part of the necessary contribution of the individual to the welfare of the public."

14. See, e.g., Board of Comm'rs v. Lee, 32 Pac. 841, 842 (Colo. 1893); Dixon v. People, 48 N.E. 108, 110–11 (Ill. 1897).

15. The New York cases are reviewed in People v. Marx, 168 N.Y.S.2d 562 (Queens County Ct. 1957). Although the constitutionality of such procedures has been challenged, County of Dane v. Smith, 13 Wis. 585, 588–89 (1861), the courts have generally upheld them.

16. People ex rel. Whedon v. Board of Supervisors, 183 N.Y. Supp. 438 (App. Div. 1920); People v. Marx, 168 N.Y.S.2d 562, 566 (Queens County Ct. 1957); Presby v. Klickitat County, 31 Pac. 876, 877 (Wash. 1892).

17. Thiel v. Southern Pac. Co., 328 U.S. 217, 224 (1946).

18. See Albee, *Mental Health Manpower Trends* 59, tables 28–30, 32, 37, 48 (1959).

19. Ala. Code, tit. 7, § 366 (1960); Ind. Ann. Stat. § 2–1722 (Supp. 1966); cf. Mont. Rev. Codes Ann. § 25–414 (1947).

20. Ala. Code tit. 15, § 425 (1959) (limited to capital cases); Ark. Stat. Ann. §§ 43–1301, 1302 (1964); Calif. Penal Code Ann. § 1027 (Supp. 1966); Colo. Rev. Stat. Ann. § 39–8–2 (1963); Conn. Gen. Stat. Ann. § 54–50 (1958); Del. Code Ann. tit. 16, § 5142(c) (1953) (authorizes state mental hygiene clinic to "observe, examine, study, and treat any person charged with any offense . . . when requested to do so by a judge or judges thereof"); Fla. Stat. Ann. §§ 917.01–.03 (1944); Hawaii Rev. Laws § 258–36 (Supp. 1965); Ind. Stat. Ann. 39–1706a (Burns Supp. 1966); La. Rev. Stat. Ann., Code Crim. Proc. Art. 643 et seq. (West, 1966); Me. Rev. Stat. Ann. 15– § 101 (1965); Md. Ann. Code Art. 59,

§§ 7, 11 (1957); Mass. Ann. Laws, Ch. 123, §§ 99, 100A (1965); Mich. Stat. Ann. § 28.967 (Supp. 1965); N.H. Rev. Stat. Ann. § 122–91 (1964); N.D. Rev. Code §§ 29–20–21 et seq. (1960); Ohio Rev. Code Ann. § 2945.40 (Page, 1954); Ore. Rev. Stat. § 136–150 (1965); Pa. Stat. Ann. tit. 50, §§ 1222, 1225 (1954); R.I. Gen. Laws Ann. §§ 9–17–19 to –20 (1956); S.C. Code § 32–969 (Supp. 1966); Tenn. Code Ann. § 33–513 (5) (1955); Utah Code Ann. § 77–24–17 (1953); Vt. Stat. Ann. tit. 13, § 4803 (1959); Va. Code Ann. § 19.1–228 (Supp. 1966); W. Va. Code Ann. § 27–6–7 (1966); Wis. Stat. Ann. § 957.27 (West, 1958); Wyo. Stat. Ann. §§ 7–241 to –242 (1957); D.C. Code Ann. § 24–301 (1961). In the notes that follow, I shall refer to these sections without repeating the citations. A similar provision is applicable to federal criminal trials, 18 U.S.C. § 4244 (1958).

21. See articles cited note 27 infra. For cases suggesting that court appointment of an expert violated the principle of separation of powers, see People v. Dickerson, 129 N.W. 199, 200–01 (Mich. 1910); People v. Scott, 157 N.E. 247, 255–56 (Ill. 1927); see People v. Pugh, 100 N.E.2d 909, 911 (Ill. 1951). But the overwhelming current of authority has found court appointment of an expert to be "a most appropriate" judicial function, ancient in origin, and offering great advantage in the search for truth. See, e.g., Jessner v. State, 231 N.W. 634, 636–39 (Wis. 1930); Hunt v. State, 20 So.2d 186, 190–93 (Ala. 1946); People v. Strong, 300 Pac. 84 (Calif. 1931); Commonwealth v. Butler, 173 A.2d 468, 472–73 (Pa. 1961).

22. Where the issue is competency to stand trial, the defendant cannot always be expected to demand an examination for himself. But where insanity at the time of the crime is in issue, most states require that the defendant plead insanity before the procedure can be invoked. In California, Colorado, and Indiana, the court is required to invoke the procedure whenever the insanity defense is raised. In Tennessee, either defense counsel or prosecution may apply. Under the statutes of Arkansas, Florida, New York, South Carolina, Virginia, and West Virginia, the judge has explicit statutory authority to invoke the procedure without a request from the defendant. See statutes cited note 20 supra. As a practical matter, this authority in the court may depend upon the prosecutor's "suggestion" that the statutes be used. The problem of judicial assertion of the insanity defense, over the defendant's objection, has recently become a much controverted one. See infra pp. 186–88.

23. In fourteen states, these are staff members of the state mental hospital or mental health department. In others, a government psychiatrist must be a member of an examining commission appointed by the court. In twelve states, in the federal courts, and under the ALI, Model Penal Code, Proposed Official Draft § 4.05 (1962), any competent, disinterested expert may be appointed, including a government-employed psychiatrist. Where psychiatrists are scarce, courts are com-

pelled to draw on government employees if they are to comply with the manadatory provisions of laws requiring psychiatric examinations.

24. In California, the examiner is supplied with a form including, inter alia, the following items: "Kindly make an examination of this defendant and report your findings to the court as to the defendant's_____; was the defendant sane at the time of commission of offense? Is he sane at the present time?" Communication from Mark Brandler, Judge, Superior Court, Los Angeles, California.

The term "communication" is used in the notes throughout this chapter to designate research material collected in October and November 1961, unless otherwise indicated. Fuller notes are to be found in an earlier version of this chapter—the article by Goldstein and Fine, supra note 9.

25. A typical statute provides only that the hospital staff member is "to conduct observations and investigations of the mental condition of the defendant, and to prepare a written report thereof." Ark. Stat. Ann. § 43-1301 (1964). Information is occasionally furnished about patient's life history, present condition, and history of mental disorder. The fees paid for these examinations varied widely, in obvious relationship to the time and care devoted to the tasks. Questionnaire responses in 1962 indicate that the fees ranged from $35 in Oregon and California to as much as $250 in Ohio.

26. It seems clear that defense counsel may at least call the expert as a fact witness, and cross-examine him if he is called by the court or prosecutor. The most that is expressly provided with respect to his aid in the preparation of the defense is that names and addresses of such experts be furnished to defense counsel (Louisiana and Ohio), that the written report be made available to him (Alabama, Louisiana, Massachusetts, and Hawaii), and that he may call the expert as his own witness (California, Colorado, Rhode Island, and Utah). See note 20 supra. Occasional consultation between the examiner and the prosecutor or defense counsel is reported, mainly to prepare the expert for testifying and to aid in cross-examination of opposing witnesses.

27. In Wisconsin, the designation is explicitly required. Accord, Model Expert Testimony Act § 8. Elsewhere, as in Indiana, the designation follows implicitly from the fact that the expert's evidence follows that of both prosecution and accused. Ind. Ann. Stat. § 9–1702 (1956). In still other jurisdictions, such as Louisiana and Ohio, the designation is brought home to the jury by the fact that the expert is examined by the court. La. Rev. Stat. Ann. § 15:268 (1951); Ohio Rev. Code Ann. § 2945.40 (Page, 1954). In Alabama, it appears to be discretionary with the trial court whether it will permit the expert to testify that he was appointed by the court. Hunt v. State, 27 So.2d 186, 189, 194 (Ala. 1946). See generally McGarty v. O'Brien, 188 F.2d 151, 156 (1st Cir. 1951) (dictum), cert. den. 341 U.S. 928; Application of Perkins, 331 P.2d 712,

717 (Calif. 1958); Glueck, "Psychiatric Examination of Persons Accused of Crime," 36 *Yale L. J.* 632, 636 (1927); Guttmacher, "The Psychiatrist as an Expert Witness," 22 *U. Chi. L. Rev.* 325, 330 (1955); Lefler, "The Criminal Procedure Reforms of 1936—Twenty Years After," 11 *Ark. L. Rev.* 117, 125 (1957); Overholser, "The Briggs Law of Massachusetts: A Review and an Appraisal," 25 *J. Crim. L. & Crimin.* 859, 874 (1935); Weihofen, "Eliminating the Battle of Experts in Criminal Insanity Cases," 48 *Mich. L. Rev.* 961, 967–68, 972 (1950). The system employed on the continent is similar but it operates against the backdrop of an inquisitorial system, in which the trial judge or magistrate has the primary responsibility for investigating the facts. When he deems it necessary, he appoints experts from official lists or from medico-legal institutes. Because of the supposed impartiality of the court's expert, his opinion is usually decisive. See generally Harder, "Forensic Psychiatry in Switzerland," 9 *Clev-Mar. L. Rev.* 467 (1960); Ploscowe, "The Expert Witness in Criminal Cases in France, Germany and Italy," 2 *Law & Contemp. Prob.* 504 (1935); Schroeder, "Problems Faced by the Impartial Expert Witness in Court: The Continental View," 34 *Temp. L. Q.* 378 (1961).

28. See Diamond, "The Fallacy of the Impartial Expert," *Arch. Crim. Psychodyn.* 221 (1959). See also Zeisel, "The New York Expert Testimony Project: Some Reflections on Legal Experiments," 8 *Stan. L. Rev.* 730, 738 (1956); Albee, *Mental Health Manpower Trends* 228, Table 18 (1959).

29. Diamond, supra note 28, at 221, 228; but see Bush v. McCallum, 231 F. Supp. 560, 563 (D. Tex. 1964), aff'd 344 F.2d 672 (5 Cir. 1965) (note 48 infra).

30. See references in note 7 supra; and see Hunt et al., "A Theoretical and Practical Analysis of the Diagnostic Process," in Hoch and Zubin, *Current Problems in Psychiatric Diagnosis* 53 (1953).

31. The terminology is drawn from Hollingshead and Redlich, *Social Class and Mental Illness* 66–135 (1958).

32. Of 17 responses to a questionnaire on the subject to superintendents of state hospitals, 13 indicated that minority views, which may exist, are never recorded in the report.

33. Communication from Ralph Robinson, Psychiatric Clinic, Crim. Ct., Cleveland, Ohio. This occurred in five or six of the 115 cases referred to the clinic during 1959 and 1960. Such experts were paid fees ranging from $100 to $250. Communication from John M. Murphy, Public Defender for New Haven County, New Haven, Conn.

34. See United States ex rel. Smith v. Baldi, 192 F.2d 540, 547 (3 Cir. 1951), aff'd 344 U.S. 561 (1953); McGarty v. O'Brien, 188 F.2d 151, 157 (1st Cir. 1951), cert. den. 341 U.S. 928.

35. See State v. Weeks, 101 Atl. 35, 36 (N.H. 1917); Commonwealth v. Green, 29 A.2d 491, 493 (Pa. 1943); Philler v. Waukesha County, 120

N.W. 829, 831 (Wis. 1909). For the "inherent power" view, see Commonwealth ex rel. Smith v. Ashe, 71 A.2d 107, 113 (Pa. 1950), cert. den. 340 U.S. 812. Some of the answers to questionnaires indicate that "inherent power" may be invoked more frequently than is usually assumed and that psychiatric assistance is furnished without regard to the statutes. Communications from Jacob A. Latona, County Judge, Erie County Ct., Buffalo, N.Y.; Aram A. Arabian, Att'y, Providence, R.I. Nor is reliance on "inherent power" without precedent in a closely related area. In Wisconsin, for example, the courts are said to have power, apart from statute—and even in the face of a statute to the contrary—to order payment of counsel for an indigent accused out of public funds. Carpenter v. Dane County, 9 Wis. 274, 276–77 (1859); County of Dane v. Smith, 13 Wis. 585, 588 (1861).

36. Colo. Rev. Stat. Ann. § 39–7–29 (1964); Del. Super. Ct. Crim. R. 17(b); Fla. Stat. Ann. §§ 932.36–.37 (1944); Hawaii Rev. Laws § 222–11 (1955); Mich. Stat. Ann. § 28.1252 (1954); Minn. Stat. Ann. § 357.32 (1966); Neb. Rev. Stat. § 29–1903 (1956); N.D. Cent. Code § 31–01–19 (1960); N.H. Rev. Stat. Ann. §§ 604:1–2 (1955); Okla. Stat. Ann. tit. 22, § 718 (1937); R.I. Gen. Laws Ann. § 12–17–8 (1956); Utah Code Ann. § 21–5–14 (1953); Wis. Stat. Ann. § 325.10 (1958); Wyo. Stat. Ann. § 7–245 (1957). See also D.C. Code Ann. § 23–109 (1961); Fed. R. Crim. P. 17(b). In several other states provision exists for payment of defense witnesses whether or not defendant is indigent. Calif. Penal Code § 1329 (1966); Conn. Gen. Stat. Ann. § 54–153 (1960); Iowa Code Ann. § 781.2 (1950); Mass. Ann. Laws, Ch. 277, § 66 (1956) (limited to capital and life-imprisonment cases); Nev. Rev. Stat. § 48.300 (1961); N.Y. Code Crim. Proc. § 617 (McKinney, 1958). These are ordinarily invoked by the filing of an affidavit alleging the necessity for such testimony. Where the procedure is for the defendant to make a request before trial, decision is within the court's discretion. Goldsby v. United States, 160 U.S. 70, 73 (1895); Murdock v. United States, 283 F.2d 585, 587 (10th Cir. 1960), cert. den. 366 U.S. 953; Dupuis v. United States, 5 F.2d 231 (9th Cir. 1925). Along with the provision authorizing payment of witness fees for the indigent, a few states have another one authorizing the court to set reasonable fees for expert witnesses. Del. Code Ann. tit. 10, § 8906 (1953); Minn. Stat. Ann. § 357.25 (1957). In these states a construction applying the witness statutes to expert fees seems more likely than where there is no judicial control over fees.

37. To ascertain the practice under these statutes, I wrote to the trial court clerks in the largest cities in ten states having such legislation. Eight responded. One said that such fees were authorized only if the "state jointly uses" the expert. None had an accurate count of the number of times the statute had been invoked for this purpose. Where estimates were made, they ranged from three authorizations in several years in Milwaukee, Wis., to four a year in Concord, N.H. The fees authorized also

varied greatly, ranging from $50 per day to $500 maximum for all services rendered. Only two appellate cases have been found, both of which intimate "expert" fees are not contemplated. Osborn v. People, 262 Pac. 892, 895 (Colo. 1927); State v. Weeks 101 Atl. 33, 36 (N.H. 1917).

38. In a few states the judge is authorized to fix fees for experts which will compensate them reasonably for their time. They say nothing as to whether the state will pay the fee if the defendant is unable to, but they do protect him against the possibility of being charged an unreasonably high fee. Iowa has gone even further by legislating a fixed fee ($4 per day) for experts, but inflation has made the statute obsolete.

39. Reilly v. Berry, 166 N.E. 165, 167 (N.Y. 1929) (Cardozo, C.J.).

40. R.I. Gen. Laws Ann. § 9–17–19 (1956). What is not clear is whether this practice, which is reported by a former public defender, occurs under this statute, under an inherent power of the court, or as part of the general public defender apparatus. Communication from Aram A. Arabian, Att'y, Providence, R.I.

41. *California:* Calif. Code Civ. Proc. § 1871 (Supp. 1966); cf. People v. Gorg, 291 P.2d 469, 471 (Calif. 1955); People v. Rickson, 246 P.2d 700, 703 (Calif. Dist. Ct. App. 1952); People v. Spraic, 262 Pac. 795, 797 (Calif. Dist. Ct. App. 1927). *New York:* N.Y. Code Crim. Proc. § 308 (McKinney, 1966); see People v. Marx, 168 N.Y.S.2d 562, 564 (Queens County Ct. 1957); People v. Fernandez, 109 N.Y.S.2d 561, 565 (Sup. Ct. 1951). Under this statute, defense counsel is ordinarily permitted to choose his own psychiatrist. The compensation paid the expert will vary but no more than $1,500 is made available. See also Tex. Code Crim. Proc. Art. 26.05 (Vernon, 1966) (authorizing "not more than $250.00"). The federal statute is 18 U.S.C. § 3006 A. For the origins of the statute, see Attorney General's Committee, *Poverty and the Administration of Criminal Justice* (1964).

42. See, e.g., Calif. Penal Code § 987a (Supp. 1966); Ind. Ann. Stat. § 13–1404 (1956); Mass. Gen. Laws Ann., Ch. 277, § 56 (1956); N.H. Rev. Stat. Ann. § 604:3 (Supp. 1961); N.Y. Code Crim. Proc. § 308 (McKinney, 1966); Pa. Stat. Ann. tit. 19, § 784 (Supp. 1961).

43. In Los Angeles, Oakland, San Francisco, Memphis, and Chicago the staff includes a full-time investigator. Bliss, "Defense Detective," 47 *J. Crim. L. & Crimin.* 264, 265 (1956). In the District of Columbia, the Legal Aid Agency has four full-time investigators. It has sometimes employed psychiatrists on its own initiative but, as a general matter, it uses the federal statute providing witness fees for indigent defendants. Communication from Charles B. Murray, Director, April 16, 1962. Only six of fifty defenders responding to a questionnaire indicated the existence of a fund for extraordinary expenses such as those for expert witnesses. See Institute of Judicial Administration, *Public Defenders* 15 (1956). See also Greenwell v. United States, 317 F.2d 108 (D.C. Cir. 1963) (discussing

requirement that indigent defendant justify his request to summon witnesses).

44. McGarty v. O'Brien, 188 F.2d 151, 154 (1st Cir. 1951), cert. den. 341 U.S. 928; United States ex rel. Smith v. Baldi, 192 F.2d 540, 546 (3 Cir. 1951), aff'd 344 U.S. 561, 568.

45. 192 F.2d at 547, 559.

46. 188 F.2d at 155, 157. See also Perry v. United States, 347 P.2d 813, 816 (D.C. Cir. 1964); State v. Superior Court, 409 P.2d 742 (Ariz. 1966).

47. 351 U.S. 12, 19 (1956). See Allen, "Griffin v. Illinois: Antecedents and Aftermath," 25 U. Chi. L. Rev. 151, 156–57 (1957); Wilcox and Bloustein, "The Griffin Case—Poverty and the Fourteenth Amendment," 43 Cornell L. Q. 1, 23 (1957).

48. In the three cases decided since Griffin in which the issue of the "right to an expert" has been raised, the decisions have been based principally upon non-Griffin grounds. Their tenor, however, is generally resistant to a literal extension of Griffin, but the matter is deliberately left ambiguous. See United States v. Brodson, 241 F.2d 107 (7 Cir. 1957), cert. den. 354 U.S. 911 (court noted in dicta that there was no requirement of expert aid "invariably and as a matter of law." Id. at 110); State v. Crose, 357 P.2d 136, 137 (Ariz. 1960) (right to an expert cannot be derived from the right to counsel. A fair trial, noted the court, might well be conducted without experts, although it conceded that, "as a practical matter, . . . [the right to] the assistance of experts in advance of trial often lies at the very heart of a successful defense." Id. at 138); Willis v. United States, 285 F.2d 663, 665 (D.C. Cir. 1960), cert. den. 366 U.S. 953 (Due process may be satisfied by virtually any psychiatric testimony bearing on insanity and available to the accused. In the particular case, the defense of insanity could have been raised by summoning existing fact witnesses, among whom were psychiatrists). The equal protection issue was raised and rejected in United States v. Naples, 307 F.2d 618, 624 (D.C. Cir. 1962); but compare Brown v. United States, 331 F.2d 822, 823 (D.C. Cir. 1964); Bush v. McCallum, 231 F. Supp. 560, 563 (D. Tex. 1964), aff'd 344 F.2d 672 (5 Cir. 1965) (holding insufficient an examination by County Medical Officer who was not a psychiatrist) and see People v. Watson, 35 Law Week 2331 (Ill., Dec. 20, 1966) (holding that defendant has right to summon a questioned document examiner at state expense).

CHAPTER TEN

Acquittal as Preventive Detention: The Problem of Release

1. See the statutory summary in Lynch v. Overholser, 369 U.S. 705, 724 et seq. (1962) (concurring opinion by Clark, J.); and see generally

Weihofen, "Institutional Treatment of Prisoner Acquitted by Reason of Insanity," 38 *Tex. L. Rev.* 849 (1960); Note, "Releasing Defendants Acquitted and Committed Because of Insanity," 68 *Yale L. J.* 293 (1958) and statutory Appendix; Note, "Compulsory Commitment Following a Successful Insanity Defense," 56 *N.W. U. L. Rev.* 409 (1961); ALI, *Model Penal Code,* Proposed Official Draft, § 4.08 (1962); Anno., 95 A.L.R.2d 54 (1964). As to the place of confinement, see Rubin, *Law of Criminal Correction* 277-79, 517-19 (1963).

2. The District of Columbia requires that the jury be told, in a summary way, of the consequences of an acquittal by reason of insanity. Lyles v. United States, 254 F.2d 725 (D.C. Cir. 1957), cert. den. 356 U.S. 961. The Florida court has suggested that it is for the trial judge to decide whether such an instruction should be given, McClure v. State, 104 So.2d 601, 604 (Fla. 1958), while the Wisconsin court recommends it. State v. Shoffner, 143 N.W.2d 458, 465-66 (Wis. 1966). But the more common view is that it is improper to give the instruction because it would distract the jury from the insanity issue and would invite compromise verdicts. See, e.g., Pope v. United States, 298 F.2d 507 (5 Cir. 1962); State v. Wade, 113 Atl. 458, 460 (Conn. 1921); State v. Rideau, 137 So.2d 283, 297 (La. 1962); State v. Hood, 187 A.2d 499, 500-01 (Vt. 1963); Gambrell v. State, 120 So.2d 758, 762 (Miss. 1960); Anno., 11 A.L.R. 3d 737 (1967). The issue may ordinarily not be argued to the jury by counsel but it sometimes slips in. Ewalt v. United States, 359 F.2d 534, 544 (9 Cir. 1966) Anno., 44 A.L.R. 2d 978 (1954).

3. But note that the District of Columbia courts have held that an acquittal by reason of insanity carries with it the implicit findng that, the question of insanity apart, the defendant was guilty as charged. Ragsdale v. Overholser, 281 F.2d 943, 948 (D.C. Cir. 1960); see also People v. Morgan, 50 P.2d 1061, 1062 (Calif. 1935).

4. In about half the states, the defendant must persuade the jury, by a preponderance of the evidence, that he was insane. In the remainder, the introduction of "some evidence" of insanity by the defendant shifts the burden to the prosecution to prove sanity beyond a reasonable doubt. See discussion supra pp. 111-14. As to presumptions, see supra pp. 115-20. In such jurisdictions, therefore, a verdict of not guilty by reason of insanity is not an adjudication of insanity. See Lynch v. Overholser, 369 U.S. 705, 713 (1962).

5. The usual provisions for release are described in Weihofen, *Mental Disorder as a Criminal Defense* 376 et seq. (1954); Lindman and McIntyre, *The Mentally Disabled and the Law* 353 et seq. and Table XI-A (1961); see also note 1 supra. In most states, some form of court approval must be obtained. This may be preceded by a certificate from the hospital authority, or by a patient's petition. In a handful of states, the issue of release must, or may, be tried by a jury. Provision is some-

times made for an independent examination of the patient's mental condition by a board of experts at the time of the application. There are, however, a goodly number of states which place the decision to release entirely in the hands of the hospital superintendent or an administrative board, treating the patient much the same as any other mental hospital patient.

6. See, e.g., Calif. Penal Code Ann. § 1026 (1956); Conn. Gen. Stat. § 54–37 (1958); Ind. Stat. Ann. § 9–1705 (Burns, Supp. 1966); Mich. Rev. Stat. § 28.967 (1965 Supp.); N.J. Stat. 2A:163–3 (1953); W. Va. Code § 27–6–8 (1966).

7. Md. Code Ann. Art. 59, § 8 (1957); Ky. Rev. Stat. § 202.350 (1960).

8. See, e.g., Del. Code 11– § 4702(c) (1966 Supp.); Me. Rev. Stat. Ann. 15– § 104 (1964); N.Y. Code Crim. Proc. § 454(2)(3) (1966 Supp.); N.C. Gen. Stat. Ann. § 122: 86 (1950); Note, 68 *Yale L. J.* 293, 306 (1958).

9. J. Goldstein and Katz, "Dangerousness and Mental Illness," 70 *Yale L. J.* 225, 235 (1960).

10. ALI, Model Penal Code, Proposed Official Draft, § 4.08 (1962). For commentary, see Tent. Draft No. 4, p. 199 (1955).

11. Fahy, J., concurring in Ragsdale v. Overholser, 281 F.2d 943, 950–51 (D.C. Cir. 1960).

12. 283 F.2d 195, 198 (D.C. Cir. 1960); Overholser v. O'Beirne, 302 F.2d 852, 857 et seq. (D.C. Cir. 1962). For statements supporting the Fahy view, supra note 11, see Bazelon, J., concurring in *Russell,* 283 F.2d at 199, and Edgerton, J., dissenting in *O'Beirne,* 302 F.2d at 862 et seq.

13. See, e.g., Wis. Stat. § 957.11(4) (1957); R.I. Gen. Stat. § 26–4–7 (1956).

14. See, e.g., Kans. § 62–1532 (1949); Minn. Stat. § 631.19 (1957); Vt. Stat. Ann. 13– § 4812 (1959); Wash. Rev. Code § 10.76.070 (1966 Cum. Supp.).

15. Conditional release may also be called conditional discharge, parole, furlough, leave of absence, probation, or convalescent leave. Some states have provisions which explicitly make such release available to patients committed after an acquittal by reason of insanity, e.g., Calif. Welf. & Inst. Code § 6761b (1966); Ohio Rev. Code Ann. § 2945.39 (1953). But most merely extend to such patients the provisions applicable to all mental patients, e.g., Kans. Gen. Stat. Ann. § 62–1532 (1949); Tex. Code Crim. P. Art. 46.02 (1966). A small number of states seem to leave the matter to the discretion of the trial judge, e.g., Fla. Stat. Ann. § 919.11 (1960). In some states, the criminally insane are specifically

barred from conditional release, e.g., Conn. Gen. Stat. § 17–198 (Supp. 1966); Ky. Rev. Stat. § 202.370 (1960).

Illustrative of the several standards are the following: (1) Public safety —Ala. Code § 45.219 (1959); Calif. Welf. & Inst. Code § 6761b (1954); (2) Improved—Ariz. Rev. Stat. Ann. § 36–524(A) (Supp. 1966); (3) Best interest—Geo. Code Ann. 88–1612a (1963); (4) No standard— Colo. Rev. Stat. Ann. § 39–8–4(3) (1953). See generally Lindman and McIntyre, *The Mentally Disabled and the Law* 124–25, 362 (1961); Hough v. United States, 271 F.2d 458 (D.C. Cir. 1959).

16. Rosen, "Management of the Patient," in Whitaker, *Psychotherapy of Chronic Schizophrenic Patients* 184 et seq. (1958); see generally Joint Commission on Mental Illness and Health, *Action for Mental Health* (1961).

17. Eissler, "Objective (behavioristic) Criteria of Recovery from Neuropsychiatric Disorders," 106 *J. Nerv. and Ment. Dis.* 550, 556 (1947); State ex rel. Rogers v. Stanley, 270 N.Y.S.2d 573, 575–76 (Ct. App. 1966) (dissenting opinion, citing statistics).

18. For a dramatic illustration, see Comm. ex rel. Ross v. Dye, 102 *Pitts. L. J.* 485 (Pa. 1954); see also Note, 68 *Yale L. J.* 293, 303 (1958); and compare Boslow et al., "The Maryland Defective Delinquency Law," 10 *Br. J. Delinq.* 5, 10 (1959).

19. See Note, "Hospitalization of Mentally Ill Criminals in Pennsylvania and New Jersey," 110 *U. Pa. L. Rev.* 78, 91–98 (1961); Salinger v. Superintendent, 112 A.2d 907, 910 (Md. 1955); Comm. ex rel. Ross v. Dye, 102 *Pitts. L. J.* 485 (Pa. 1954); Madsen v. Obermann, 22 N.W.2d 350, 357 (Iowa, 1946); State v. District Court of Hennepin County, 241 N.W. 39, 40–41 (Minn. 1932).

20. In re Rosenfield, 157 F. Supp. 18, 19 (D.D.C. 1957).

21. Trial judge, quoted in Application of Perkins, 331 P.2d 712, 715 (Calif. 1958); see also references to lower court in Hough v. United States, 271 F.2d 458, 462 (D.C. Cir. 1959); Ex parte Dubina, 18 N.W.2d 902, 904 (Mich. 1945); Ex parte Remus, 162 N.E. 740, 742 (Ohio, 1928); Ex parte Rath, 254 Pac. 466 (Wash. 1927); Ex parte Palmer, 59 Atl. 746, 752 (R.I. 1904).

22. Ragsdale v. Overholser, 281 F.2d 943, 947 (D.C. Cir. 1960); Overholser v. Leach, 257 F.2d 667, 669–70 (D.C. Cir. 1958).

23. Barry v. White, 64 F.2d 707, 709 (D.C. Cir. 1933); Orencia v. Overholser, 163 F.2d 763, 765 (D.C. Cir. 1947); see also State v. Behan, 124 N.W.2d 179, 181 (S.D. 1963), 131 N.W.2d 81, 84 (S.D. 1964). As to burden of proof, see pages 111–14.

24. See Rouse v. Cameron, 373 F.2d 451 (D.C. Cir. 1966); Birnbaum, "The Right to Treatment," 46 *A.B.A.J.* 499 (1960); Wolff, *Contemporary Psychotherapists Examine Themselves* 15, 21, 30, 95 (1956); Obern-

dorf, "Unsatisfactory Results of Psychoanalytic Therapy," 19 *Psychoanalytic Q.* 393 (1950); Oberndorf et al., "Symposium on the Evaluation of Therapeutic Results," 29 *Int'l J. of Psychoanalysis* 7 (1948).

25. See Note, "A Logical Analysis of Criminal Responsibility and Mandatory Commitment," 70 *Yale L. J.* 1354, 1364 (1961); A. Goldstein, "The Psychiatrist and The Legal Process," 33 *Am. J. Orthopsych.* 123, 130 (1963); Morris, "Impediments to Penal Reform," 33 *U. Chi. L. Rev.* 627, 638 et seq. (1966).

26. See generally Kittrie, "Compulsory Mental Treatment and the Requirements of 'Due Process,' " 21 *Ohio St. L. J.* 28 (1960); Ross, "Commitment of the Mentally Ill," 57 *Mich. L. Rev.* 945 (1959); Comment, "Analysis of Legal and Medical Considerations in Commitment of the Mentally Ill," 56 *Yale L. J.* 1178 (1947).

27. The statutes are described in detail in Lindman and McIntyre, *The Mentally Disabled and the Law* 17 et seq., 44 et seq. (1961). Compare the provisions for commitment and detention of sexual psychopaths, defective delinquents, etc., id. at 298–329.

28. See, e.g., In re Johnson, 36 *Erie L. J.* 187 (Pa. 1953); Gahwiller v. Gahwiller, 25 N.W.2d 485, 486–87 (Iowa, 1946); Soderquist v. Keller, 149 P.2d 528, 530 (Wash. 1944); In re Wright, 15 Pa. Dist. Rep. 179, 100 (1906); Brush's Case, 5 Abb. N.C. 005, 006 (N.Y. 1877).

29. 79 N.E.2d 459, 463 (N.Y. 1948) (see dissent at 464, 466). Cases illustrating shadings along the continuum are Schutte v. Schutte, 104 S.E. 108, 109–10 (W.Va. 1920); Ex parte Harcourt, 150 Pac. 1001, 1003 (Calif. 1915); In re Wright, 15 Pa. Dist. Rep. 179, 499 (1906); In re King, 30 D.L.R. 599, 601–02 (Manitoba, 1916); cf. In re Williams, 157 F. Supp. 871 (D.D.C. 1958), aff'd 252 F.2d 629; Dittrich v. Brown County, 9 N.W.2d 510, 512 (Minn. 1943) (involving commitment of a sexual psychopath).

30. Brock v. Southern Pac. Co., 195 P.2d 66, 76–77 (Calif. 1958).

31. See, e.g., In re Heukelekian, 94 A.2d 501, 503 (N.J. 1953); Ex parte R.R., 54 A.2d 814 (N.J. 1947); Ex parte Perry, 43 A.2d 885, 886 (N.J. 1945); Comm. ex. rel. Baird v. Noyes, 83 D. & C. 311 (Pa. 1952).

32. See Application of Anonymous No. 13, 159 N.Y.S.2d 842 (Sup. Ct. 1957); Certification of Anonymous No. 1 to 12, 138 N.Y.S.2d 30 (Sup. Ct. 1954); Board of Commissioners v. Ristine, 24 N.E. 990, 991 (Ind. 1890).

33. Ex parte Bowyer, 54 Can. C.C. 392, 398 (1930).

34. Paul v. Longino, 28 S.E.2d 286 (Ga. 1943) (quoted passage at 289); Marx v. State, 141 N.E.2d 126, 131 (Ind. 1957) (dissenting opinion); but see In re Pickle's Petition, 170 So.2d 603, 613 (Fla. 1965).

35. See discussion by Edgerton, J., dissenting in Overholser v. O'Beirne, 302 F.2d 852, 864 (D.C. Cir. 1962).

36. 157 F. Supp. 871 (D.D.C. 1958), aff'd 252 F.2d 629 (1958).

37. See generally Lindman and McIntyre, *The Mentally Disabled and the Law,* Ch. 10 (1961).

38. Rouse v. Cameron, 373 F.2d 451 (D.C. Cir. 1966); cf. Darnell v. Cameron, 348 F.2d 64, 67 (D.C. Cir. 1965) (suggests that confinement without treatment for four years, following acquittal of a minor charge by reason of insanity, may be unlawful); Sas v. Maryland, 334 F.2d 506, 509, 516–17 (4 Cir. 1964); Daniels v. Director of Patuxent Institution, 206 A.2d 726 (Md. 1965); and see Birnbaum, "The Right to Treatment," 46 *A.B.A.J.* 499 (1960).

39. In addition to references in note 25 supra, see Special Committee to Study Commitment Procedures, *Mental Illness and Due Process* 19–39 (1962); N.Y. Stat. Ann. 34A: §§ 73, 74, 84 (McKinney, Supp. 1966); English Mental Health Act, 1959, 7 & 8 Eliz. 2. Ch. 72, § 43. Compare the provisions of the Model Sentencing Act and of the Model Penal Code dealing with the dangerous, mentally abnormal offender, discussed in Rubin, *Psychiatry and Criminal Law* 179–80, 191 et seq. (1965).

CHAPTER ELEVEN

Competing Processes and Attrition Before Trial

1. The police are usually authorized to exercise "common law" powers of arrest to enforce public welfare laws and to guard the public health. See Anno., 92 A.L.R.2d 570 (1963); People v. Pershaec, 15 N.Y.S.2d 215, 235 (Gen. Sess. 1939); Forsythe v. Ivey, 139 So. 615, 617–18 (Miss. 1932); Christiansen v. Weston, 284 Pac. 149, 152–53 (Ariz. 1930). They also perform specific duties with regard to the various civil commitment procedures. Some of these involve "emergency" situations which raise the need for immediate detention—e.g. the "person who is fighting, or doing mischief, or disturbing a congregation, or has fallen in a fit, or is so sick as to be helpless, or is unconsciously going into great danger, or is drunk." Look v. Dean, 108 Mass. 116, 120 (1871). Others involve invoking the regular commitment processes. See generally Lindman and McIntyre, *The Mentally Disabled and the Law,* Chs. 2, 10 and tables incident thereto (1961).

2. See, e.g., Matthews and Rowland, *How to Recognize and Handle Abnormal People* (Nat'l Ass'n of Mental Health); Weihofen, "Institutional Treatment of Persons Acquitted by Reason of Insanity," 38 *Tex. L. Rev.* 849, 852 (1960); Special Comm. to Study Commitment Procedures, *Mental Illness and Due Process* 220–21 (1965) (describing use of the minor offense charge as a way of accomplishing emergency detention of the mentally ill).

3. J. Goldstein, "Police Discretion Not to Invoke the Criminal Process," 69 *Yale L. J.* 543, 559 et seq. (1960); La Fave, *Arrest* 63 et seq.

(1965). In some states, the policeman is also under a conflicting "duty" to initiate civil proceedings.

4. See generally Lindman and McIntyre, supra note 1. But compare the English Mental Health Act which provides for relatively easy movement, at various stages, from the criminal to the civil process. Walker, *Crime and Punishment in Britain,* Ch. 13 (1965). For statement that statutory civil commitment procedures are generally held to be unavailable to persons under a criminal charge, see Rubin, *Law of Criminal Correction* 498 (1963).

5. Leavy, "Civil Commitment to Mental Hospitals in Connecticut" 62-70 (1960) (unpublished manuscript on file in Yale Law Library); see Foote, "Vagrancy-Type Law and Its Administration," 104 *U. Pa. L. Rev.* 603, 633 et seq. (1956); Hollingshead and Redlich, *Social Class and Mental Illness* 175, 184 (1958).

6. See Lindman and McIntyre, supra note 1. The prosecutor can initiate emergency measures under provisions authorizing a "public official" or "any person" to do so. The first of the two states is Utah, Utah Code § 77-48-2 (1959 Supp.). The second is New Hampshire, N.H. Rev. Stat. Ann. § 607:2, 3 (1955).

7. See, e.g., Powell v. Katzenbach, 359 F.2d 234 (D.C. Cir. 1966); United States v. Cox, 342 F.2d 167 (5 Cir. 1965), Hassan v. Magistrates' Court, 191 N.Y.S.2d 238 (Sup. Ct. 1959); State v. Langley, 323 P.2d 301 (Ore. 1958); State v. Winne, 96 A.2d 63 (N.J. 1953); Howell v. Brown, 85 F. Supp. 537, 539-40 (D. Neb. 1949); United States v. Brokaw, 60 F. Supp. 100, 103 (D. Ill. 1945); State v. Wallach, 182 S.W.2d 313, 318 et seq. (Mo. 1944); cf. State v. Hicks, 325 P.2d 794, 802 et seq. (Ore. 1958), cert. den. 359 U.S. 917. And see generally Ploscowe, *Manual for Prosecuting Attorneys* 315 et seq. (1956); Note, "Prosecutors' Discretion," 103 *U. Pa. L. Rev.* 1057 (1955).

8. See the proposal contained in President's Commission on Law Enforcement, *The Challenge of Crime in a Free Society* 133-34 (1967). And see Becker, *The Outsiders* 31 (1963) ("One of the most crucial steps in the process of building a stable pattern of deviant behavior is likely to be the experience of being caught and publicly labeled as a deviant").

9. Acheson, "McDonald v. United States: The Durham Rule Redefined," 51 *Geo. L. J.* 580 (1963); Flannery, "Meeting the Insanity Defense," 51 *J. Crim. L. & Crimin.* 309 (1960).

10. Foote, "Vagrancy-Type Law and its Administration," 104 *U. Pa. L. Rev.* 603, 647 (1956).

11. See A. Goldstein, "The State and the Accused: Balance of Advantage in Criminal Procedure," 69 *Yale L. J.* 1149, 1166 et seq. (1960); ALI, Code of Criminal Procedure, Commentary at 311-16 (1930). The magistrate may also be authorized to try minor crimes. The discussion in the text is not addressed to that part of his function.

12. N.Y. Code Crim. Proc. § 870 (McKinney, Supp. 1966); Miss. Code § 2573 (1958); see People v. McDermitt, 37 N.Y.S.2d 64 (Mag. Ct. 1942).

13. The only Supreme Court pronouncement suggests he does not. Charlton v. Kelly, 229 U.S. 447, 462 (1913); see also the lower court decision at 185 Fed. 880 (C. Ct. 1911). And see Slough and Wilson, "Mental Capacity to Stand Trial," 21 *U. Pitt. L. Rev.* 593, 603 (1960); Weihofen, *Mental Disorder as a Criminal Defense* 436 (1954); Anno., 142 A.L.R. 961 (1943). Present codifications of the common-law rule as to the power of the trial court include: Ariz. Rev. Stat. § 13–1621 (1956); Ark. Stat. Ann. § 41–110 (1947); Calif. Penal Code Ann. § 1367 (1956); Colo. Rev. Stat. Ann. § 39–8–6 (1) (1963); Ga. Code Ann. § 27–1504 (1953); Okla. Stat. t. 22, § 1161 (1951); Idaho Code, § 19–1301 (1948); Minn. Stat. § 638.18 (1957); Nev. Rev. Stat. § 178–400 (1957); N.M. Stat. Ann. § 41–13–3 (1953) (at trial or arraignment); Ore. Rev. Stat. 150 (1957); Tenn. Code Ann. 33.513 (5) (1956); Montana Rev. Code Ann. § 94–9301 (1947); N.C. Gen. Stat. Ann. § 122–83 (1950); 18 U.S.C.A. § 4244 (1951). Unless the word "trial" is to be construed to include the preliminary hearing, which is an unlikely prospect, these statutes cannot be used by the magistrates, especially where a jury trial on the issue is required and the magistrate's court does not have the power to empanel a jury.

14. See, e.g., Pa. Stat. Ann. t. 50 § 1222 (Purdon, 1954); N.H. Rev. Stat. Ann. § 135.17 (1955); Mass. Ann. Law, c. 123, § 99 (1957); D.C. Code § 24–301(a) (1961); R.I. Gen. Laws § 26–4–3 to 5 (1957).

15. See People v. Pershaec, 15 N.Y.S.2d 215, 234 (Gen. Sess. 1939); People v. Bieber, 100 N.Y.S.2d 821, 824 (Mag. Ct. 1950); ALI, Code of Criminal Procedure, §§ 45, 47, 49 and Commentary at pp. 293–97 (1930); Note, "Metropolitan Criminal Courts of First Instance," 70 *Harv. L. Rev.* 320, 327 (1956); Note, "The Preliminary Hearing," 51 *Iowa L. Rev.* 164 (1966).

16. See note 11 supra.

17. See discussion supra p. 123.

18. Jurisdiction over civil commitment is ordinarily given to probate courts or to the courts of general civil jurisdiction. Magistrates sit in minor criminal courts. As noted earlier, the magistrate may be authorized to initiate civil commitment proceedings under statutes which authorize a "public official" or "any person" to do so. See Lindman and McIntyre, *The Mentally Disabled and the Law* 49–52, 94–99 (1961). But that is quite different from having the judicial power to commit, which is ordinarily denied him. But see Special Comm. to Study Commitment Procedures, *Mental Illness and Due Process* 221 (1965). He may, however, be able to continue the criminal case before him while others seek civil

commitment. This, too, meets with problems. It has been held, on occasion, that once the jurisdiction of the criminal courts has attached,
civil commitment proceedings must await the outcome of the criminal
case. It is, of course, arguable if not persuasive that the criminal jurisdiction takes hold only after an indictment has been returned—which is a
point following the magistrate stage. See generally Weihofen, *Mental
Disorder as a Criminal Defense* 450–51 (1954); Rubin, *Law of Criminal
Correction* 498 (1963); State v. England, 328 S.W.2d 732, 735 (Mo.
1959); Bonner v. Phay, 359 P.2d 157 (Wash. 1961).

19. ·The quotaton is from United States v. Kilpatrick, 16 Fed. 765,
772–73 (D. N.C. 1883). Other illustrative cases are McFarland v. Superior
Court, 198 P.2d 318, 322 (Calif. 1948); State v. Lane, 263 N.W. 608
(Minn. 1935); Comm. v. McNary, 140 N.E. 255, 256–57 (Mass. 1923);
People v. Bailey, 171 N.Y. Supp. 394 (Sup. Ct. 1918); United States v.
Lawrence, 26 Fed. Cas. 886 (No. 15,576; 1835). The Georgia and New
York experience is reflected in Cadle v. State, 113 S.E.2d 180, 186–87
(Ga. 1960); People v. Blair, 33 N.Y.S.2d 183 (Gen. Sess. 1942). See
generally Orfield, *Criminal Procedure from Arrest to Appeal*, Ch. 4
(1947); A. Goldstein, "The State and the Accused: Balance of Ad-
vantage in Criminal Procedure," 69 *Yale L. J.* 1149, 1169 et seq. (1960).

20. See Weihofen, *Mental Disorder as a Criminal Defense* 354–55,
437–38 (1954). In addition to the eleven statutes referred to by Weihofen,
see Ohio Rev. Code Ann. § 2945.37 (Page, 1954). If any of these statutes
should be construed to mean that an accused must be committed to a
mental hospital as the result of a grand jury proceeding in which he did
not participate, they would raise the most serious constitutional questions.
If, however, they are construed to mean only that commitment will follow
upon a showing of present mental condition in a proceeding in which the
defendant may participate, they would be little different from the usual
civil commitment proceeding.

21. See generally Slough and Wilson, "Mental Capacity to Stand
Trial," 21 *U. Pitt. L. Rev.* 593 (1960); Foote, "A Comment on Pre-trial
Commitment of Criminal Defendants," 108 *U. Pa. L. Rev.* 832 (1960);
Rubin, *Psychiatry and the Criminal Law* 45 et seq. (1965); Special Comm.
to Study Commitment Procedures, *Mental Illness and Due Process* 228–37
(1965); Szasz, *Psychiatric Justice* (1965); Note, 59 *Mich. L. Rev.* 1078
(1961). In several states, the issue of incompetency to stand trial may be
submitted to the jury together with the issue of guilt. As a result, a person
who is in fact incompetent may be required to stand trial. See Weihofen,
Mental Disorder as a Criminal Defense 456 (1954).

22. Matthews, *Mental Illness and the Criminal Law*, p. 3 (American
Bar Foundation, 1967). One study reports that 40 per cent of the persons
returned to court as competent, after a finding of incompetency to stand
trial, are acquitted by reason of insanity. Smith et al., "Mental Com-

petency Proceedings in Federal Criminal Cases," 75 *Public Health Rep.* 595 (1960).

23. See generally Newman, *Conviction* (1966). The defendant who pleads guilty "voluntarily" will not later be able to set aside his conviction on the ground of insanity at the time of the crime. He will be held to have waived the defense, unless he was mentally incompetent at the time he entered his plea. See Poole v. United States, 250 F.2d 396, 400–01 (D.C. Cir. 1957); Bishop v. United States, 223 F.2d 582, 584 et seq. (D.C. Cir. 1955), vacated and remanded 350 U.S. 961; Hahn v. United States, 178 F.2d 11, 12 (10 Cir. 1949); United States v. Baldi, 192 F.2d 540, 544 et seq. (3 Cir. 1951), aff'd 344 U.S. 561; People v. Robinson, 89 N.E.2d 32 (Ill. 1949); People v. Lang, 83 N.E.2d 688 (Ill. 1949); Comm. v. Smith, 40 A.2d 701 (Pa. 1945); People v. Morgan, 50 P.2d 1061, 1062–63 (Calif. 1935). He may, however, be able to get a new trial if he can make a persuasive showing of "newly discovered evidence." People v. Oxnam, 149 Pac. 165, 167–68 (Calif. 1915); People v. Johnson, 131 N.E. 149, 152–53 (Ill. 1921); cf. State v. Virgi, 81 N.E.2d 295 (Ohio, 1948). In Pennsylvania, a defendant who has pleaded guilty may petition for admission to a mental hospital pursuant to the state's Mental Health Act of 1951. See Comm. v. Moon, 117 A.2d 96 (Pa. 1955).

24. See generally, as to mental hospitals and related facilities, the discussion at pp. 20–21 supra, the notes thereto and Rubin, *Psychiatry and the Criminal Law* 29–32 (1965). As to probation, parole, and correctional systems, see Brancale, "Diagnostic Techniques in Aid of Sentencing," 23 *Law and Contemp. Prob.* 442 (1958); Rubin, *Law of Criminal Correction* (1963); American Correctional Ass'n, *Manual of Correctional Standards* (1966).

25. The opinion of the Court of Appeals is at 288 F.2d 388 (D.C. Cir. 1961). The Supreme Court opinion is at 369 U.S. 705 (1962) (if a defendant is acquitted by reason of insanity after refusing to raise the defense, the automatic commitment procedures are inapplicable and civil commitment would have to be sought). See Carter v. United States, 283 F.2d 200, 203 (D.C. Cir. 1960); Halleck, "The Insanity Defense in the District of Columbia—A Legal Lorelei," 49 *Geo. L. J.* 294 (1960); J. Goldstein and Katz, "Dangerousness and Mental Illness," 70 *Yale L. J.* 225, 230 (1960).

26. People v. Merkouris, 297 P.2d 999, 1008–09 (Calif. 1956). See also State v. Hall, 125 N.W.2d 918, 925–26 (Neb. 1964) (court instructed jury on insanity defense despite fact that defendant offered evidence of mental disorder only to reduce grade of offense); State v. Hermann, 283 S.W.2d 617 (Mo. 1955); Boyd v. People, 116 P.2d, 193, 195 (Colo. 1941). Introduction of the insanity "defense" by someone other than the defendant seems to be authorized by statute in some states. See,

e.g., Ark. Stat. Ann. § 43–1301 (1947); S.C. Code § 32–927 (1952); W. Va. Code Ann. § 6198 (1955). And see discussion in Ch. 12, pp. 206–07 infra.

27. 190 F.2d 612 (D.C. Cir. 1951). It should be noted that the D.C. Court, in a post-*Lynch* case, has said a defendant may refuse to raise the insanity defense but he may not "prevent the court from injecting it." Whalem v. United States, 346 F.2d 812, 818 (D.C. Cir. 1965).

28. English Mental Health Act, 1959, 7 & 8 Eliz. 2. Ch. 72, § 60(2). See the discussion of alternatives to criminal prosecution in Report of President's Commission on Law Enforcement, *The Challenge of Crime in a Free Society* 133–34 (1964).

29. Under the English Mental Health Act, supra note 28, § 60, a person who is convicted and who suffers from mental illness, psychopathic disorder, or mental subnormality may be made the subject of a hospital order by the sentencing court. See Walker, *Crime and Punishment in Britain* 268–72 (1965); Wootton, *Crime and the Criminal Law* 60–62 (1963). The California correction system has developed a wide variety of facilities for the mentally disordered offender, as have other states to a lesser degree.

CHAPTER TWELVE

Competing Defenses; The Trend Toward Subjective Liability

1. The quotations are from Dean v. State, 17 So. 28, 29 (Ala. 1895); Fitzpatrick v. Comm., 81 Ky. 357, 361 (1883); see also Comm. v. Trippi, 167 N.E. 354, 355–56 (Mass. 1929); Rogers v. State, 57 S.E. 227, 228 (Ga. 1907); Comm. v. Szachewicz, 154 Atl. 483, 484 (Pa. 1931). See generally Holmes, *The Common Law* 41 et seq. (Howe ed. 1963); Lowe, "Murder and the Reasonable Man," [1958] *Crim. L. Rev.* 289, 374, 453; Hall, *Criminal Law,* Ch. 5 (1960); Wechsler and Michael, "A Rationale of the Law of Homicide," 37 *Col. L. Rev.* 701 (1937); cf. Comm. v. Pierce, 138 Mass. 165, 176 et seq. (1884).

2. State v. Johnson, 261 P.2d 638, 641 (Idaho, 1953). Compare cases holding intoxication irrelevant in a crime of general intent, Note, "Intoxication as a Criminal Defense," 55 *Col. L. Rev.* 1210 (1955), and mistake of fact a sufficient defense only when it is reasonable, Williams, *Criminal Law* 52–74 (1961). On mens rea generally, see Morrisette v. United States, 342 U.S. 246, 251 (1952) and discussion in Packer, "Mens Rea and the Supreme Court," 1962 *Supreme Court Review* 107; Hall, *Criminal Law* 72 (1960); H. L. A. Hart, "Legal Responsibility and Excuses," in Hook, *Determinism and Freedom* 95 (1961).

3. See Handler, "Background Evidence in Murder Cases," 51 *J. Crim. L. & Crimin.* 317 (1960).

4. Weihofen, *Mental Disorder as a Criminal Defense* 176 et seq. (1954); Fisher v. United States, 328 U.S. 463 (1946), discussed in Weihofen and Overholser, "Mental Disorder Affecting the Degree of a Crime," 56 *Yale L. J.* 959 (1947). To get a sense of the trend, see Glueck, *Mental Disorder and the Criminal Law* 203 et seq. (1925); Weihofen, *Insanity as a Defense in Criminal Law* 101 et seq. (1933); State v. Padilla, 347 P.2d 312, 314 et seq. (N.M. 1959); Anno., 8 A.L.R.2d 1236 (1949); but see State v. Sikora, 210 A.2d 193, 202-03 (N.J. 1964). The English provisions are set out in Prevezer, "The English Homicide Act," 57 *Col. L. Rev.* 624, 636-37 (1957). The statutory definition is "such abnormality of mind (whether arising from a condition of arrested or retarded development of mind or any inherent causes or induced by disease or injury) as substantially impairs his mental responsibility." See R. v. Byrne, 2 Q.B. 396 (1960).

5. See Sparks, " 'Diminished Responsibility' in Theory and Practice," 27 *Mod. L. Rev.* 9, 31-32 (1964). Under the English practice, a successful plea of diminished responsibility may lead either to a reduced sentence or to an order sending the offender to a hospital. See Walker, *Crime and Punishment in Britain*, Ch. 13 (1965).

6. Note, "Manslaughter and the Adequacy of Provocation," 106 *U. Pa. L. Rev.* 1021 (1958); Prevezer, "The English Homicide Act," 57 *Col. L. Rev.* 624, 642 et seq. (1957); Williams, "Provocation and the Reasonable Man," [1954] *Crim. L. Rev.* 740; People v. Danielly, 202 P.2d 18, 27 (Calif. 1954); Bishop v. United States, 107 F.2d 297, 302 (D.C. Cir. 1939); Jacobs v. Commonwealth, 15 Atl. 465 (Pa. 1888); Regina v. McCarthy, [1954] 2 All Eng. Rep. 262, 265.

7. Bedder v. Director of Public Prosecutions, [1954] 2 All Eng. Rep. 801.

8. State v. Green, 6 P.2d 177, 186 (1931); Davis v. State, 28 S.W.2d 993, 996 (Tenn. 1930); cf. State v. Thomas, 114 S.E. 834 (N.C. 1922); Allison v. State, 86 S.W. 409, 413 (Ark. 1904).

9. See, e.g., People v. Bridgehouse, 303 P.2d 1018, 1022 (Calif. 1956); State v. Hazlett, 113 N.W. 374, 379-80 (N.D. 1907); Maher v. People, 10 Mich. 212, 221 et seq. (1862). Compare 2 Harper and James, *Torts,* § 16.7 (1956).

10. ALI, Model Penal Code, § 201.3, Tent. Draft No. 9 (1959). The pertinent comments are at pages 41 and 48. See also Tent. Draft No. 4, p. 126 (1955); Tent. Draft No. 10, pp. 2 et seq. (1960) (dealing with duress).

11. Hart v. United States, 130 F.2d 456, 458 (D.C. Cir. 1942).

12. 202 P.2d 53, 62-63 (Calif. 1949), cert. den. 337 U.S. 919. See Diamond, "With Malice Aforethought," 2 *Arch. Crim. Psychodyn.* 1 (1957).

13. 336 P.2d 492, 503 (Calif. 1959). See also People v. Conley, 411 P.2d 911, 916 (Calif. 1966). But see dissent in People v. LeTourneau, 211 P.2d 865, 877 et seq. (Calif. 1949) (complaining of majority's grudging application of the *Wells* rule).

14. 15 CMR 143, 148 (1954).

15. United States v. Storey, 25 CMR 424, 429 (1958).

16. Colo. Rev. Stat. 39-8-1. See Battalino v. People, 199 P.2d 897 (Colo. 1948).

17. Rhodes v. United States, 282 F.2d 59, 60–61 (4 Cir. 1960); but see United States v. Cain, 298 F.2d 934 (7 Cir. 1962) (evidence of mental disorder admitted on issue of willfulness of tax evasion but trial judge, sitting without jury, took position that defendant was "responsible" if he satisfied the insanity standard).

18. ALI, Model Penal Code, Proposed Official Draft § 4.02 (1) (1962). For commentary, see Tent. Draft No. 4, p. 193 (1955). See also Weihofen, *The Urge to Punish* 73–74 (1956).

19. See Fox v. State, 316 P.2d 924, 926 (Nev. 1957).

20. ALI, Model Penal Code, Proposed Offical Draft § 2.01 (1962). For commentary, see Tent. Draft No. 4, p. 119 (1955).

21. 78 Ky 181 (1873). See also People v. Gibson, 206 P.2d 375 (Calif. 1949).

22. See generally Fox, "Physical Disorder, Consciousness and Criminal Liability," 63 *Col. L. Rev.* 645 (1963); Prevezer, "Automatism and Involuntary Conduct," [1958] *Crim. L. Rev.* 361, 440; People v. Conley, 411 P.2d 911, 919 (Calif. 1966); People v. Freeman, 142 P.2d 435, 438 (Calif. 1943); State v. Gooze, 81 A.2d 811 (N.J. 1951); R. v. Kemp, [1956] 3 All Eng. Rep. 249. But see People v. Codarre, 245 N.Y.S.2d 81 (App. Div. 1963) (epilepsy gives rise to insanity defense if the crime occurs during an epileptic disturbance).

23. See, e.g., State v. Francis, 112 S.E.2d 756, 758 (N.C. 1960); People v. Johnson, 117 N.E.2d 95 (Ill. 1954); Robidoux v. State, 34 S.W.2d 863, 865 (Tex. 1931); People v. Giacolone, 217 N.W. 758, 760 (Ariz. 1928); State v. Padula, 138 Atl. 456, 457 (Conn. 1927); cf. Viliborghi v. State, 43 P.2d 210, 214 (Ariz. 1935).

24. 181 N.E. 448, 449 (Ohio, 1932); State v. McLeod, 80 N.E.2d 697, 700 (Ohio, 1948); see Grainger v. State, 13 Tenn. 459, 462 (1830); People v. Sonier, 248 P.2d 155, 156 (Calif. 1952).

25. ALI, Model Penal Code, Proposed Official Draft § 304. For commentary, see Tent. Draft No. 8, p. 14 (1958).

26. The British cases are: Bratty v. Attorney General, [1963] A.C. 386, 26 *J. Crim. L.* 45; H. M. Adv. v. Cunningham, [1963] J. C. 80, 28 *J. Crim. L.* 80 (1964); see Prevezer, "Automatism and Involuntary

Conduct," [1958] *Crim. L. Rev.* 361, 440; Macaulay, "Insanity and the Prosecution," [1963] *Crim. L. Rev.* 817. The American cases are cited in Ch. 11, note 26. And see Williams, *The Mental Element in Crime* 111–15 (1965).

CHAPTER THIRTEEN

Reflections on the Insanity Defense

1. Robinson v. California, 370 U.S. 660 (1962) (It is cruel and unusual punishment to make the condition of narcotics addiction a crime); Easter v. District of Columbia, 361 F.2d 50 (D.C. Cir. 1966); Driver v. Hinnant, 356 F.2d 761 (4 Cir. 1966) (same re alcoholism and the offense of public intoxication).

2. See, e.g., Roche, *The Criminal Mind* 273–74 (1958); McCord and McCord, *Psychopathy and Delinquency* 186–87 (1956); Glueck, *Crime and Correction* 94 (1952); Mannheim, *Criminal Justice and Social Reconstruction* 223–37 (1946); Comm. v. Woodhouse, 164 A.2d 98, 109 (Pa. 1960) (dissent by Bok, J.); Knight, "The Meaning of Punishment," in Lindner et al., *Handbook of Correctional Psychology* 675 (1947); cf. Burger, "Psychiatrists, Lawyers and the Courts," *Fed. Prob.*, p. 9 (June 1964); Weintraub, "Criminal Responsibility," 49 *A.B.A.J.* 1075 (1963); but see Dession, "Psychiatry and the Conditioning of Criminal Justice," 47 *Yale L. J.* 319, 329 et seq. (1938); Szasz, "Psychiatry, Ethics and the Criminal Law," 58 *Col. L. Rev.* 183, 188–89 (1958); Hakeem, "A Critique of the Psychiatric Approach to Crime and Correction," 23 *Law and Contemp. Prob.* 650 (1958). See generally J. Goldstein and Katz, "Abolish the Insanity Defense—Why Not?" 72 *Yale L. J.* 873 (1963).

3. Louisell and Hazard, "Insanity as a Defense: The Bifurcated Trial," 49 *Calif. L. Rev.* 805 (1961). Wisconsin has recently adopted the "split-trial." 1 *Crim. L. Rep.* 1017 (May 17, 1967).

4. State v. Strasburg, 110 Pac. 1020 (Wash. 1910).

5. Sinclair v. State, 132 So. 581, 583 et seq. (Miss. 1931).

Index